Java: the first semester

Quentin Charatan and Aaron Kans
East London Business School
University of East London

THE McGRAW-HILL COMPANIES

London · Chicago · New York · St Louis · San Francisco · Auckland
Bogotá · Caracas · Lisbon · Madrid · Mexico · Milan
Montreal · New Delhi · Panama · Paris · San Juan · São Paulo
Singapore · Sydney · Tokyo · Toronto

Published by
McGraw-Hill Publishing Company
SHOPPENHANGERS ROAD, MAIDENHEAD, BERKSHIRE, SL6 2QL, ENGLAND
Telephone +44 (0) 1628 502500
Fax: +44 (0) 1628 770224
Web site: http://www.mcgraw-hill.co.uk

British Library Cataloguing in Publication Data
A catalogue record for this book is available from the British Library

ISBN 0-07-709757-2

Library of Congress Cataloguing-in-Publication Data
The LOC data for this book has been applied for and may be obtained from the Library
of Congress, Washington, D.C.

Further information on this and other McGraw-Hill titles is to be found at
http://www.mcgraw-hill.co.uk

Authors' website address: http://www.mcgraw-hill.co.uk/textbooks/charatan

Publisher:	David Hatter
Editorial Assistant:	Sarah Douglas
Senior Marketing Manager:	Jacqueline Harbor
Production Editorial Manager:	Penelope Grose
Produced by:	Steven Gardiner Ltd
Cover by:	Hybert Design
Printed by:	Bell & Bain Ltd, Glasgow

To my mother and father (AK)

To my brother, Ivan (QC)

Contents

Preface   **ix**

1   **The first step**   **1**
1.1   Introduction   1
1.2   Software   2
1.3   Developing software   2
1.4   Conventional compilers   4
1.5   Interpreters   6
1.6   The Java development process   6
1.7   Your first program   9
             Tutorial exercises   16
             Practical work   16

2   **The building blocks**   **17**
2.1   Introduction   17
2.2   Simple data types in Java   18
2.3   Declaring variables in Java   19
2.4   Assignments in Java   21
2.5   Creating constants   24
2.6   Arithmetic operators   24
2.7   Expressions in Java   26
2.8   Output in Java   28
2.9   Input in Java: the *EasyIn* class   30
2.10   Program design   34
             Tutorial exercises   35
             Practical work   38

3   **Taking control**   **39**
3.1   Introduction   39
3.2   Selection   39
3.3   Iteration   53
             Tutorial exercises   67
             Practical work   69

4   **Classes and objects**   **71**
4.1   Introduction   71
4.2   What is object-orientation?   71
4.3   Attributes and methods   74
4.4   Encapsulation   75
4.5   Classes and objects in Java   76
4.6   Using the *String* class   83
4.7   The *BankAccount* class   87
4.8   The *SmileyFace* class   88
             Tutorial exercise   92
             Practical work   92

5   Implementing classes   93
5.1   Introduction   93
5.2   Implementing classes in Java   93
5.3   The *static* keyword   110
5.4   More on parameter passing   114
5.5   Wrapper classes   117
          Tutorial exercises   120
          Practical work   121

6   Arrays and collection classes   123
6.1   Introduction   123
6.2   Creating an array   125
6.3   Accessing array elements   127
6.4   Passing arrays as parameters   132
6.5   Collection classes   136
          Tutorial exercises   161
          Practical work   162

7   Extending classes with inheritance   163
7.1   Introduction   163
7.2   Defining inheritance   163
7.3   Implementing inheritance in Java   165
7.4   Overriding class methods   176
7.5   Abstract classes   178
7.6   The *final* modifier   184
7.7   Generic collection classes   185
7.8   Pros and cons of generic collections   192
          Tutorial exercises   193
          Practical work   193

8   Software quality   195
8.1   Introduction   195
8.2   Maintainability   196
8.3   Reliability   200
8.4   Robustness   213
8.5   Usability   219
          Tutorial exercises   231
          Practical work   232

9   Graphics and event-driven programs   233
9.1   Introduction   233
9.2   The Abstract Window Toolkit   233
9.3   The *SmileyFace* class revisited   235
9.4   The *EasyFrame* class   237

9.5	The *ChangingFace* class	237
9.6	Event-handling in Java	240
9.7	An interactive graphics class	245
9.8	A graphical user interface (GUI) for the *Oblong* class	248
9.9	A metric converter	252
9.10	Layout policies	257
9.11	Compound containers	260
9.12	GUIs for collections of objects	260
	Tutorial exercises	262
	Practical work	264

10	**Case study – part 1**	**265**
10.1	Introduction	265
10.2	The requirements	265
10.3	The specification	266
10.4	The design	266
10.5	Implementing the *Payment* class	268
10.6	Implementing the *Tenant* class	274
10.7	Implementing the *TenantList* class	276
	Tutorial exercises	289
	Practical work	290

11	**Case study – part 2**	**291**
11.1	Introduction	291
11.2	Keeping permanent records	291
11.3	Design of the GUI	292
11.4	Designing the event-handlers	294
11.5	Implementation	300
11.6	Testing the system	308
	Tutorial exercises	312
	Practical work	312

12	**Programming for the World Wide Web**	**313**
12.1	Introduction	313
12.2	Running an applet in a browser	314
12.3	Guidelines for creating applets	317
12.4	Passing parameters from an HTML file	317
12.5	Special applet methods	322
12.6	The *RedCircle* applet	322
12.7	What next?	330
	Tutorial exercises	332
	Practical work	332

Appendix 1: Selected AWT component methods	**333**
Appendix 2: Utility classes	**337**
Index	**346**

Preface

This book is designed for university students taking a first module in software development or programming. The book uses Java as the vehicle for the teaching of programming concepts; design concepts are explained using the UML notation. The topic is taught from first principles and assumes no prior knowledge of the subject. It is thus intended to prepare students for the more advanced programming modules that they may take in the future.

The project was conceived in response to an overwhelming need for a book that provides a gentle introduction to software development and programming; in particular, it aims at the type of student entering university with no background in the subject matter, often coming from pre-degree courses in other disciplines, or perhaps returning to study after long periods away from formal education. It is the authors' experience that such students have enormous difficulties in grasping the fundamental programming concepts the first time round, and therefore require a simpler and gentler introduction to the subject than is presented in most standard texts.

This book therefore spends considerable time concentrating on the fundamental programming concepts such as declarations of variables and basic control structures, prior to introducing students to the concepts of classes and objects, arrays and collection classes, inheritance, software quality, graphics and event-driven programming, applets and programming for the World Wide Web. Prior to students learning how to create graphical interfaces, they use a text console with input being made straightforward by the provision of a simple utility class, `EasyIn.java`, that can be downloaded from the web, or copied from the appendix.

The book takes an integrated approach to software development by covering such topics as basic design principles and standards, testing methodologies and HCI.

The book is organized so as to support a twelve-week, one-semester module, which might typically comprise a two-hour lecture, a one-hour tutorial and a two-hour laboratory session. The tutorial exercises at the end of each chapter provide the foundation for the practical tasks that follow. In addition to these exercises and questions, a case study is developed towards the end of the book to illustrate the use of the techniques covered in the text to develop a non-trivial application. Lecturers who teach a ten-week as opposed to a twelve-week module could easily treat this case study as a self-directed student learning experience rather than as a taught topic.

In addition to the utility classes needed for the practical work, much supporting material is available on the website (**http://www.mcgraw-hill.co.uk/textbooks/charatan**); this includes the sample programs used in the text as well as additional questions and answers for tutors, which are password-protected.

We would like to thank our publisher, David Hatter of McGraw-Hill, for his encouragement and guidance throughout the production of this book. We would also like to thank especially the computing students of the University of East London for their thoughtful comments and feedback. For support and inspiration, special thanks are due to our families and friends.

Quentin Charatan (q.h.charatan@uel.ac.uk)
Aaron Kans (a.kans@uel.ac.uk)
London, UK, February 2001

1 The first step

1.1   Introduction

Like any student starting out on a first programming module, you will be itching to do just one thing – get started on your first program. We can well understand that, and you won't be disappointed, because you will be writing programs in this very first chapter. Designing and writing computer programs can be one of the most enjoyable and satisfying things you can do, although sometimes it can seem a little daunting at first because it is like nothing else you have ever done. But with a bit of perseverance you will not only start to get a real taste for it but you may well find yourself sitting up till two o'clock in the morning trying to solve a problem. And just when you have given up and you are dropping off to sleep the answer pops into your head and you are at the computer again until you notice it is getting light outside! So if this is happening to you, then don't worry – it's normal!

However, before you start writing programs you need some background; so the first part of this chapter is devoted to some fundamental issues that you need to get to grips with before you can understand what programming itself is all about. This chapter therefore starts off with an explanation of some of the terms you will come across, particularly the notion of *software*. It goes on to give a little bit of background as to how software is produced in industry, and the way in which this has changed in recent times. This is followed by a general look at programming languages and the way that programs are written and developed. After this we discuss the Java language and the way in which developing Java programs differs from that of conventional programming languages. Once we have done all this, we will show you how to write and adapt your first program.

1.2   Software

A computer is not very useful unless we give it some instructions that tell it what to do. This set of instructions is called a **program**. The word **software** is the name given to a single program or a set of programs.

   There are two main kinds of software. **Application software** is the name given to useful programs that a user might need; for example, word-processors, spreadsheets, accounts programs and so on. **System software** is the name given to special programs that help the computer to do its job; for example, operating systems such as UNIX or Windows98 (which help us to use the computer) and network software (which helps computers to communicate with each other).

1.3   Developing software

We will now take a brief look at how software is developed in industry. This has begun to change over the past decade or so – until quite recently the method was for software developers to go through a number of phases and complete each of these before moving on to the next. It was then necessary to go back one, two or more phases to make corrections. The first phase consisted of **analysis and specification**, the process of determining what the system was required to do (analysis) and writing it down in a clear and unambiguous manner (specification). The next phase was **design**; this phase consisted of making decisions about how the system would be built in order to meet the specification. After this came **implementation**, at which point the design was turned into an actual program. This was followed by the **testing** phase. When testing was complete the system would be **installed** and a period of **operation and maintenance** followed, whereby the system was improved, and if necessary changed to meet changing requirements. This approach to software development (often called the **waterfall model**) is summarized in figure 1.1.

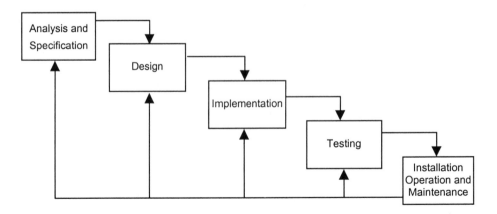

Fig 1.1   The traditional approach to software development (the waterfall model)

One problem with this approach was that it often meant that customers had to wait a very long time before they actually saw the product. Another problem was that in practice software produced in this way was actually very difficult to adapt to changing needs (consider, for example, the Y2K problem).

Nowadays it is therefore common to use a RAD approach; this stands for **rapid application development**. The RAD approach involves doing the activities described above a "little bit at a time"; in this way we build **prototypes** of the product and the potential user can be actively involved in testing them out and rebuilding until we eventually end up with the best possible product in the most satisfactory time period. Several programming tools such as *Visual Basic* and *JBuilder* exist to facilitate this process. The RAD process is summarized in figure 1.2.

Crucial to the RAD approach has been the advent of **object-oriented** methods of developing software. This term, *object-oriented*, is going to play a very important role in this book; however, we are not going to explore its meaning just yet as there are a few other concepts that we need to understand first. Nonetheless, we will start to get an idea of its meaning later in this chapter, and we will really start to get to grips with it from chapter 4 onwards. But right now it is time to start exploring the way in which programs are actually written.

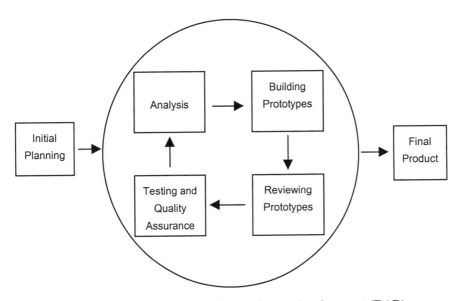

Fig 1.2   The modern approach to software development (RAD)

1.3.1   Programming languages

A program is written by a developer in a special computer language; these include C++, Java, BASIC, Pascal and many more. It is then translated by a special program (a **compiler**) into something called **machine code**, or, in the case of Java, to **Java byte code**. Machine code and Java byte code consist of binary numbers (0s and 1s) which the computer can understand. For example, 01010011 might mean ADD whereas 01010100 could mean SUBTRACT.

It is of course very difficult to write even the shortest of programs in machine code (although this is what had to be done in the early days of computing) and it is for this reason that programming languages such as Java have been developed. The first, and most basic, of these languages was known as **assembly language**. In assembly language each one of the separate instructions that the computer understands is represented by a word that is a bit like an English word; for example MOV (for "move"), JMP (for "jump"), SUB (for "subtract") and so on. A special piece of software (an **assembler**) is then used to turn what we have written into machine code. Assembly language is called a **low-level language**.

Most programs require fairly sophisticated instructions for control and data-manipulation, and writing such programs in assembly language is a very tedious business. It was for this reason that **high-level** languages – such as C, COBOL, Pascal and Basic – were created. Such languages (also known as **third generation languages** or **3GLs**) combine several basic computer instructions into a single statement or set of statements such as `if` .. `else`, or `do` .. `while`. So, when you write program instructions in these languages you write lines that are a bit like English. The set of instructions that you write in a programming language is called the **program code** or **source code**. In the case of high-level languages the translation of our source code into machine code is known as **compilation**, and the software that we use to perform this translation is called a **compiler**. The code that is produced by a compiler is often referred to as **object code**.

Java, the language that you will be studying, is an **object-oriented programming language**; object-oriented languages represent the most recent development in the history of programming languages. As we have pointed out earlier, it will not be long before the meaning of this term starts to become clear.

At this stage it is worth mentioning that Java programs are compiled and run in a rather different way to programs written in other programming languages such as C, Pascal or C++ (which is another object-oriented language). In order to appreciate the difference, you need to understand how conventional compilers work, so we will take a brief look at this before exploring the Java development process.

1.4   Conventional compilers

The program code that we write must obey the rules of the programming language. These rules are known as the **syntax** (the grammatical structure) of the language. It is very common to make **syntax errors** when we write programs; programs with errors (or **bugs**) in them cannot be compiled. Therefore most compiler programs, when they try to compile what we have written, also tell us about the errors we have made and where they are in the program. So we go through a process of typing the code, trying to compile, correcting the errors (**debugging**) and trying to compile again.

These days, compilers do much more than just compile your programs. They usually provide what is called an **integrated development environment (IDE)**. This means that the one piece of software allows us to write and edit our programs, compile them into object code, and make changes in response to error messages that are generated by the compiler during compilation. In any major project, different bits of the program are developed separately and need to be integrated; this process is called **linking**, and an IDE will also perform this process. This also includes linking any necessary pre-compiled pieces of code which most IDEs provide (collections of pre-written pieces of code are known as **libraries**).

Once the program is compiled and linked it is saved as an **executable** file – that is, a file that can be loaded into the computer's memory (by a special piece of system software called a **loader**) and run. Most IDEs will load and run the program for you without your having to exit from the IDE itself. The process of compiling and running programs in the conventional way is summarized in figure 1.3.

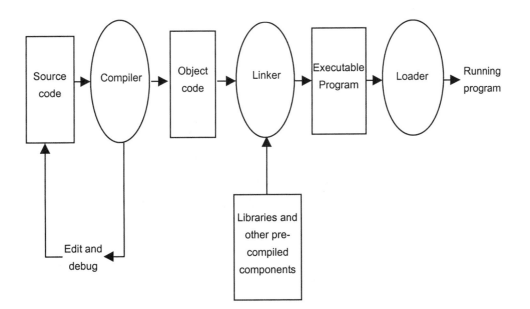

Fig 1.3   Compiling and running conventional programs

Compiling programs in this way is only one way of doing it – at one time it was more common to use another method of translating and running programs. This method is called **interpretation** and we will take a brief look at this now, because, as we shall see, it plays an important role in the Java development process.

1.5   Interpreters

At one time it was common to use an **interpreter** rather than a compiler. As we have seen, compilers operate on the entire program, providing a permanent binary file which may be **executed** (or **run**). An interpreter, on the other hand, translates and executes the program one line at a time. This of course is less efficient and execution is slower. It does have the advantage, however, of enabling a program to be changed frequently without going through the whole compilation process again. Until recently, interpreters were not used very much for real-life programs – but with the coming of Java the processes of compilation and interpretation have been cleverly combined to give us the best of both worlds.

1.6   The Java development process

As we have explained above, until recently all programs tended to be compiled and linked so that they formed a separate executable file. At first sight, this sounds like the ideal thing – compile a program so that you can take it away and run it on your computer or some other computer. But there is one major drawback with this process. A compiled program is suitable only for a particular type of computer. For example, a program that is compiled for a PC will not run on an Apple Mac or a UNIX machine. Again, until recently, this was not such a huge problem – but then along came the World Wide Web!

With the advent of the Web it became desirable for us to be able to download a program from a remote site and run it on our machine – and we want it to run in exactly the same way irrespective of whether our machine is a PC, an Apple Mac or any other machine. We need a language that is **platform-independent.**

Java is the language for this! It is designed to work within the World Wide Web of computers through special pieces of software called **browsers**, the most common of which are *Netscape* and *Internet Explorer*. Java programs that run on the Web are called **applets** (meaning little applications).

Inside a modern browser there is a special program, called a **Java Virtual Machine,** or **JVM** for short. This JVM is able to run a Java program for the particular computer on which it is running.

We saw earlier that conventional compilers translate our program code into machine code. This machine code would contain the particular instructions appropriate to the computer it was meant for. Java compilers do not translate the program into machine code –

they translate it into special instructions called **Java byte code.** These instructions are then *interpreted* by the JVM for that particular machine.

So the process consists of typing in the program (source code), compiling it into byte code, correcting errors (debugging) if necessary, and then, if there are no more errors, interpreting the byte code. At this final stage the JVM loads not only your program's byte code but also that contained in any libraries that are required.

Java IDEs such as *J++* or *JBuilder* are also able to compile programs that are not just applets, but **applications**; an application is a program designed to run on your machine just like any other program. Applications are interpreted by the compiler's built-in interpreter rather than the browser's JVM.

Until chapter 12 we will be creating applications only, and not worrying about applets designed for the World Wide Web. However, once you have grasped the programming principles in this book it will be an easy step to move on to writing applets; indeed in chapter 9, the graphical applications that we will write will be constructed in such a way that converting them to applets in the future will be an easy matter.

The process of compiling, interpreting and running Java programs is summarized in figure 1.4.

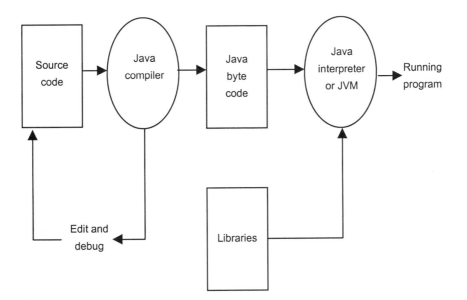

Fig 1.4   Compiling, interpreting and running Java programs

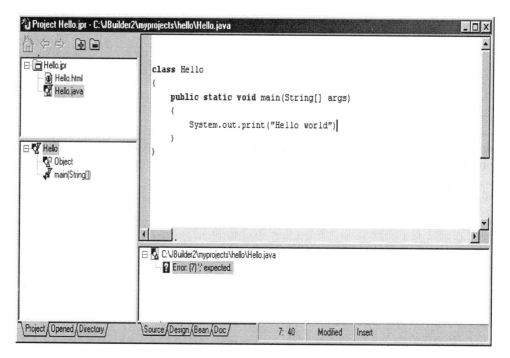

Fig 1.5   A typical Java IDE screen

If you are working in a Windows or Windows-type environment, your compiler program will provide you with an easy-to-use window into which you can type your code; other windows will provide information about the files you are using; and a separate window will be provided to tell you of your errors. Your screen will probably look something like that in figure 1.5.

The source code that you write will be saved in a file with an extension **.java** (for example myProgram.java) and once it is compiled into byte code it will be kept in a file with an extension **.class** (for example myProgram.class).

If you are working in a UNIX or UNIX-type environment you will be working from a command line interface. You will therefore be using a text editor to write your code, and – if you are writing a program called myProgram, for example – you will probably have to write something like:

```
vi myProgram.java
```

You will then need to invoke the compiler with a line like:

```
javac myProgram.java
```

And to run your program you will need to invoke the interpreter with a line like:

```
java myProgram
```

1.7 Your first program

At last it is time to write your first program. Anyone who knows anything about programming will tell you that the first program that you write in a new language has always got to be a program that displays the words "Hello world" on the screen; so we will stick with tradition, and your first program will do exactly that!

When your program runs you will get a black screen with the words "Hello world" displayed in white characters; if you are using a Windows-type environment there will probably be some additional stuff displayed before the "Hello world" line. The black screen will remain like this until you press the "Enter" key. Then the program will end and – in a Windows-type environment – the screen will disappear.

It sounds like a rather simple program, and so it is. However, before you type it in and compile and run it there is something we need to tell you about: Java wasn't really designed to write simple text messages on boring black screens! It is a language that can produce interesting and attractive graphical applications that run over the Web – but before you can begin to write such programs you need to learn the basics and you are going to be using this simple text screen right up till chapter 9; by that time you will have the fundamentals of programming firmly understood.

Now, because of the potential of the Java language, the people who developed it never really bothered to provide simple methods of getting text from the keyboard and displaying it on the screen, because it is usually done with attractive icons and mouse-clicks and so on. So getting input from the keyboard can involve lots of lines of program code that can look pretty complicated and get in the way of your learning the basic programming principles.

But don't worry! We have made it easy for you! We have created something called `EasyIn`. You will need to download the file called `EasyIn.java` from our website (or copy it from appendix 2). You should put this in the folder where your compiler automatically looks for files, so that `EasyIn.java` can be interpreted along with your program.

So now we can get on with our "Hello world" program, which is written out for you below as program 1.1.

Program 1.1

```
class Hello
{
    public static void main(String[] args)
    {
        System.out.print("Hello world");
        EasyIn.pause();
    }
}
```

As we have said, when you run the program, you should get a screen with the words "Hello world" written on it. If you are using a Windows-type environment the screen will remain like this until you press the *enter* key, at which point the program ends and the black screen disappears. In a UNIX-type environment you will simply be returned to your usual prompt when the program terminates.

Let's examine what is really going on here. The program we are writing is really incredibly simple. It displays the words "Hello world" on the screen, then it pauses and waits for you to press the *Enter* key. A simple sequence involving two actions: the program displays the message on the screen and then it pauses until the user presses *Enter*. If we didn't have the `pause` statement here, then, in a Windows environment, the screen would simply disappear before you had a chance to read what was on it.

1.7.1   Analysis of the "Hello world" program

We will consider the meaning of the program line by line. The first line looks like this:

```
class Hello
```

The first, and most important, thing to pay attention to is the word **class**. We noted earlier that Java is referred to as an **object-oriented programming language**. Now the true meaning of this will start to become clear in chapter 4 – but for the time being you just need to know that object-oriented languages require the program to be written in separate units called **classes**. There are two aspects to a class: the information that it holds and the things that it can do. The different bits of information (or **data**) that belong to a class are referred to as the **attributes** of the class; the operations that a class can perform are referred to as the **methods** of the class.

In forthcoming chapters we will be using the notation of the **Unified Modeling Language (UML)**[1] to specify and design our classes; UML is the standard method of specifying and designing object-oriented systems. In UML a class is represented diagrammatically by a rectangle divided into three sections as shown in figure 1.6:

---

[1] Simon Bennett, Steve McRobb and Ray Farmer, *Object-Oriented Systems Analysis and Design using UML*, McGraw-Hill UK, 1999

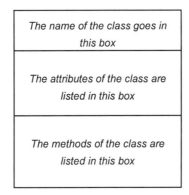

Fig 1.6 A UML class template

The simple programs that we are starting off with will contain only one class (although they will interact with other classes like `EasyIn`, and the "built-in" Java libraries) – in this case we have called our class `Hello`. The first line therefore tells the Java compiler that we are writing a class with the name `Hello`.

Notice that everything in the class has to be contained between two curly brackets that look like this { }; these tell the compiler where the class begins and ends.

There is one important thing that we should point out here. Java is *case-sensitive* – in other words it interprets upper case and lower case characters as two completely different things – it is very important therefore to type the statements exactly as you see them here, paying attention to the case of the letters.

The next line that we come across (after the opening curly bracket) is this:

```
public static void main(String[] args)
```

This looks rather strange if you are not used to programming – but you will see that every program we write in the first few weeks is going to follow on from this line. Now, we have already noted that the Java language requires that every program consists of at least one class and that a class will contain attributes and methods. Our `Hello` class in fact contains no attributes and just one method and this line introduces that method. In fact it is a very special method called a **main** method. Applications in Java (as opposed to applets, which run in a browser) must always contain a class with a method called **main**: this is where the program begins. A program starts with the first instruction of **main**, then obeys each instruction in sequence (unless the instruction itself tells it to jump to some other place in the program). The program terminates when it has finished obeying the final instruction of **main**.

So this line that we see above introduces the **main** method; the program instructions are now written in a second set of curly brackets that show us where this **main** method begins and ends. At the moment we will not worry about the words in front of **main** (**public static void**) and the bit in the brackets (String[] args) – we will just accept that they always have to be there; you will begin to understand their significance as you learn more about programming concepts.

Now, at last we are in a position to examine the important bits – the two lines of code that represent our instructions, *display "Hello world"* and *pause*.

The line that gets "Hello world" displayed on the screen is this one:

```
System.out.print("Hello world");
```

This is the way we are always going to get stuff printed on the screen; we use System.out.print (or sometimes System.out.println, as explained below) and put whatever we want to be displayed in the brackets. You won't understand at this stage why it has to be in this precise form (with each word separated by a full stop, and the actual phrase in double quotes), but do make sure that you type it exactly as you see it here, with an upper case *S* at the beginning and all the rest in lower case. Also, you should notice the semi-colon at the end of the statement. This is important; every Java instruction has to end with a semi-colon.

The next line is the *pause* line:

```
EasyIn.pause();
```

As you can see, we are already starting to make use of the EasyIn class; we will do this every time we want to get input from the keyboard. In this case we are simply waiting for the user to press the *Enter* key, and to do this we use the `pause` method of `EasyIn`. In the next chapter you will see how to use other `EasyIn` methods to get other types of input.

1.7.2   Some variations to the *Hello world* program

As we mentioned above, there is an alternative form of the `System.out.print` statement, which uses `System.out.println`. The `println` is short for "print line" and the effect of using this statement is to start a new line after displaying whatever is in the brackets. We can see the effect of this from program 1.2 – we have renamed our class `Hello2` to avoid confusion; the change to the code is in bold:

Program 1.2

```
class Hello2
{
   public static void main(String[] args)
   {
      System.out.println("Hello world");
      EasyIn.pause();
   }
}
```

At first glance the output from this program might not look very different – but notice that the cursor is now flashing at the start of the line following the "Hello world" line, instead of at the end of the "Hello world" line!

So now you could add extra lines if you wanted, as, for example, in program 1.3:

Program 1.3

```
class Hello3
{
   public static void main(String[] args)
   {
      System.out.println("Hello world");
      System.out.print("This is my third Java Program");
      EasyIn.pause();
   }
}
```

Finally, there is another way in which we can use the pause method of EasyIn. We can get a message printed on the screen by placing text in the brackets. This is demonstrated in program 1.4.

Program 1.4

```
class Hello4
{
    public static void main(String[] args)
    {
        System.out.println("Hello world");
        EasyIn.pause("Press <Enter> to quit");
    }
}
```

When you try this out you will see the words "Press <Enter> to quit" displayed beneath "Hello world". In future we are going to end all our text-based programs with a line like this.

Before we finish there is one more thing to tell you. When we write program code, we will often want to include some comments to help remind us what we were doing when we look at our code a few weeks later, or to help other people to understand what we have done.

Of course we want the compiler to ignore these comments when the code is being compiled. There are two ways of doing this. For short comments we place two slashes (//) at the beginning of the line – everything after these slashes, up to the end of the line, is then ignored by the compiler.

For longer comments (that is, ones that run over more than a single line) we usually use another method. The comment is enclosed between two special symbols; the opening symbol is a slash followed by a star (/*) and the closing symbol is a star followed by a slash (*/). Everything between these two symbols is ignored by the compiler. Program 1.5 below shows examples of both types of comment; when you compile and run this program you will see that the comments have no effect on the code, and the output is exactly the same as that of program 1.4.

Program 1.5

```
// this is a short comment, so we use the first method

class Hello5
{
   public static void main(String[] args)
   {
       System.out.println("Hello world");
       EasyIn.pause("Press <Enter> to quit");
   }
 /* this is the second method of including comments - it is more
   convenient to use this method here, because the comment is longer and
   goes over more than one line */
}
```

Tutorial exercises

1. Explain what is meant by each of the following terms:

    * machine code;
    * assembly language;
    * high-level (third generation) language;
    * source code;
    * Java byte code;
    * library.

2. Explain the difference between *compilation* and *interpretation* of programs.

3. Explain the difference between a Java compiler and a conventional compiler.

Practical work

1. Type, compile and run programs 1.1 to 1.5 from this chapter.

2. Write a program that displays your name, address and telephone number, each on separate lines.

3. Adapt the above program to include a blank line between your address and telephone number.

4. Write a program that displays your initials in big letters made of asterisks. For example:

```
* * * * * *    * * * * * *              *         *       *
*         *    *                      *   *       *     *
*   *  *       *              or     * * * * *     *   *
*     * *      *                    *       *      *     *
* * * * * *    * * * * * *          *         *    *       *
          *
        *
```

2 The building blocks

Learning objectives

By the end of this chapter you should be able to:

- distinguish between the eight built-in **scalar types** of Java;
- declare **variables**;
- **assign** values to variables;
- create **constant** values with the keyword **final**;
- join messages and values in output commands by using the **concatenation** (+) operator;
- use the input methods of the EasyIn class to get data from the keyboard;
- design the functionality of a method using **pseudocode**.

2.1   Introduction

You will have discovered that writing and running your first program is a very exciting moment. The idea that you can control a computer's actions by giving it a series of instructions is a very powerful one. Machines as tiny as calculators to systems as complex as those that launch space shuttles are controlled in this way – by computer programs.

Of course the first few programs that you wrote do not compare to the examples discussed above – but the programmers of these complex systems all took the same initial steps as you! Now it is time to move on from those first steps and start to look at some of the basic building blocks of a piece of software.

One way in which your first few programs were rather limited is that they had no *data* to work on (see figure 2.1). All interesting programs will have to store data in order to give interesting results; what use would a calculator be without the numbers the user types in to add and multiply? For this reason, one of the first questions you should ask when learning any programming language is "what types of data does this language allow me to store in my programs?"

A program controlling the space shuttle would not be very useful if it could not record the shuttle's coordinates!

Fig 2.1   **An illustration of a program without data**

We begin this chapter by taking a look at the basic types available in the Java language.

2.2   Simple data types in Java

The types of value used within a program are referred to as **data types**. If you wish to record the *price* of a cinema ticket in a program, for example, this value would probably need to be kept in the form of a **real number** (a number with a decimal point in it). Whereas if you wished to record *how many* tickets have been sold you would probably need to keep this in the form of an **integer** (whole number). It is necessary to know whether suitable types exist in the programming language to keep these bits of data.

In Java there are a few simple data types that programmers can use. These simple types are often referred to as the **scalar types** of Java as they relate to a single piece of information (a single real number, a single character etc.)

Table 2.1 lists the names of these types in the Java language, the kinds of value they represent, and the exact range of these values. As you can see, some kinds of data, namely integer and real numbers, can be kept as more than one Java type. For example, you can use both the **byte** type and the **short** type to keep integers in Java. However, while each numeric Java type allows for both positive and negative numbers, *the maximum size of numbers that can be stored varies from type to type*.

For example, the type **byte** can represent integers ranging only from −128 to 127, whereas the type **short** can represent integers ranging from −32768 to 32767. Unlike some programming languages, these ranges are *fixed* no matter which Java compiler or operating system you are using.

The character type, **char**, is used to represent characters from a standard set of characters known as the **Unicode** character set. This contains nearly all the characters from most known languages. For the sake of simplicity, you can think of this type as representing any character on your keyboard.

Table 2.1 The scalar types of Java		
Java type	**Allows for**	**Range of values**
`byte`	very small integers	−128 to 127
`short`	small integers	−32768 to 32767
`int`	big integers	−2147483648 to 2147483647
`long`	very big integers	−9223372036854775808 to 9223372036854775807
`float`	real numbers	+/− $1.4 * 10^{-45}$ to $3.4 * 10^{38}$
`double`	very big real numbers	+/− $4.9 * 10^{-324}$ to $1.8 * 10^{308}$
`char`	characters	Unicode character set
`boolean`	true or false	not applicable

Finally, the **boolean** type is used to keep only one of two possible values: **true** or **false**. This type can be useful when creating tests in programs. For example, the answer to the question "have I passed my exam?" will be either *yes* or *no*. In Java a **boolean** type could be used to keep the answer to this question, with the value **true** being used to represent *yes* and the value **false** to represent *no*.

2.3   Declaring variables in Java

The data types listed in table 2.1 are used in programs to create named locations in the computer's memory that will contain values while a program is running. This process is known as **declaring**. These named locations are called **variables** because their values are allowed to *vary* over the life of the program.

For example, a program written to develop a computer game might need a piece of data to record the player's score as secret keys are found in a haunted house. The value held in this piece of data will vary as more keys are found. This piece of data would be referred to as a variable. To create a variable in your program you must:

- give that variable a name (of your choice);
- decide which data type in the language best reflects the kind of values you wish to store in the variable.

What name might you choose to record the score of the player in our computer game?

Although you can choose almost any name, such as *x*, it is best to pick a name that describes the purpose of the item of data; an ideal name would be *score*. You can choose any name for variables as long as:

- the name is not already a word in the Java language (such as **class**, **void**);
- the name has no spaces in it;
- the name does not include mathematical symbols such as + and –;
- the name starts either with a letter, an underscore (_), or a dollar sign ($).

Although the name of a variable can begin with *any* letter, the convention in Java programs is to begin the name of a variable with a *lower case* letter.

Which data type in table 2.1 should you use if you wish to record a player's score? Well, since the score would always be a whole number, an integer type would be appropriate. There are four Java data types that can be used to hold integers (**byte**, **short**, **int** and **long**). As we said before, the only difference among these types is the range of values that they can keep. Unless there is specific reason to do otherwise, however, the **int** type is very often chosen to store integer values in Java programs. We don't want to be unconventional so we will stick to the **int** type as well! For a similar reason, when it comes to storing real numbers we will choose the **double** type rather than the **float** type.

Once the name and the type have been decided upon, the variable is declared as follows:

```
dataType variableName;
```

where `dataType` is the chosen scalar type and `variableName` is the chosen name of the variable. So, in the case of a player's score, the variable would be declared as follows:

```
int score;
```

Figure 2.2 illustrates the effect of this instruction on the computer's memory. As you can see, a small part of the computer's memory is set aside for use in your program. You can think of this reserved space in memory as being a small box, big enough to hold an integer. The name of the box will be `score`.

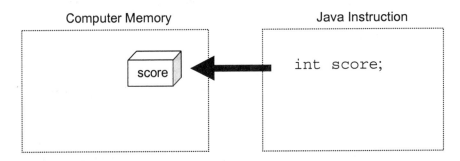

Fig 2.2   The effect of declaring a variable in Java

In this way, many variables can be declared in your programs. Let's assume that the player of a game can choose a difficulty level (A, B or C); another variable could be declared in a similar way.

What name might you give this variable? An obvious choice would be *difficulty level* but remember names cannot have spaces in them. You could use an underscore to remove the space (*difficulty_level*) or start the second word with a capital letter to distinguish the two words (*difficultyLevel*). Both are well-established naming conventions in Java. Alternatively you could just shorten the name to, say, *level*. Let us adopt this last approach.

Now, what data type in table 2.1 best represents the difficulty level? Since the levels are given as characters (A, B and C) the **char** type would be the obvious choice. At this point we have two variables declared: one to record the score and one to record the difficulty level.

```
int score;
char level;
```

Finally, several variables can be declared on a *single line* if they are *all of the same type*. For example, let's assume that there are ghosts in the house that hit out at the player; the number of times a player gets hit by a ghost can also be recorded. We can call this variable *hits*. Since the type of this variable is also an integer it can be declared along with `score` in a single line as follows:

```
int score, hits;     // two variables declared at once
char level;  // this has to be declared separately
```

Figure 2.3 illustrates the effect of these three declarations on the computer's memory.

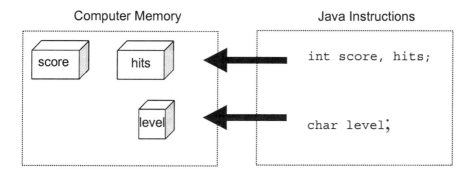

Fig 2.3   The effect of declaring many variables in Java

Notice that the character box, `level`, is half the size of the integer boxes `score` and `hits`. That is because in Java the **char** type requires half the space of the **int** type. You should also be aware that the **double** type in Java requires twice the space of the **int** type.

You're probably wondering: if declaring a variable is like creating a box in memory, how do I put values into this box? The answer is with assignments.

2.4   Assignments in Java

Assignments allow values to be put into variables. They are written in Java with the use of the equality symbol (=). In Java this symbol is known as **the assignment operator**. Simple assignments take the following form:

```
variableName = value;
```

For example, to put the value zero into the variable `score`, the following assignment statement could be used:

```
score = 0;
```

This is to be read as "*set* the value of `score` *to* zero". Effectively, this puts the number zero into the box in memory we called `score`. If you wish, you may combine the assignment statement with a variable declaration to put an initial value into a variable as follows:

```
int score = 0;
```

This is equivalent to the two statements below:

```
int score;
score = 0;
```

Although in some circumstances Java will automatically put initial values into variables when they are declared, this is not always the case and it is better explicitly to initialize variables that require an initial value. Notice that the following declaration will not compile in Java:

```
int score = 2.5;
```

Can you think why?

The reason is that, as we mentioned before, the space required to store a value of type **int** is half that required to store a value of type **double** (see figure 2.4), and the real number 2.5 is considered to be of type **double** in Java. The bigger box just won't fit into the smaller box!

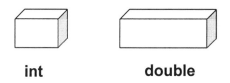

int   **double**

Fig 2.4   Java types take up different amounts of memory

You may be wondering if it is possible to fit the smaller box into the bigger box? The answer is yes. The following is perfectly legal:

```
double someNumber = 1000;
```

Although the value on the right-hand side (1000) appears to be an integer, it can be placed into a variable of type **double** because it takes up less space in memory. Once this number is put into the variable of type **double**, it will be treated as the real number 1000.0.

Clearly, you need to think carefully about the best data type to choose for a particular variable. For instance, if a variable is going to be used to hold whole numbers *or* real numbers, use the **double** type as it can cope with both. If the variable is only ever going to be used to hold whole numbers, however, then although the **double** type might be adequate, use the **int** type as it is specifically designed to hold whole numbers.

When assigning a value to a character variable, you must enclose the value in single quotes. For example, to set the initial difficulty level to A, the following assignment statement could be used:

```
char level = 'A';
```

Remember: you need to declare a variable only once. You can then assign to it as many times as you like. For example, later on in the program the difficulty level might be changed to a different value as follows:

```
char level = 'A';    // initial difficulty level
// other Java instructions
level = 'B';         // difficulty level changed
```

2.5   Creating constants

There will be occasions where data items in a program have values *that do not change*. The following are examples of such items:

- the maximum score in an exam (100);
- the number of hours in a day (24);
- the mathematical value of π (3.1417).

In these cases the values of the items do not vary. Values that remain constant throughout a program (as opposed to variable) should be named and declared as **constants**.

Constants are declared much like variables in Java except that they are preceded by the keyword **final**, and are always initialized to their fixed value. For example:

```
final int HOURS = 24;
```

Notice that the standard Java convention has been used here of naming constants in UPPERCASE. Any attempt to change this value later in the program will result in a compiler error. For example:

```
final int HOURS = 24;        // create constant
HOURS = 12;                  // will not compile!
```

2.6   Arithmetic operators

Rather than just assign simple values (such as 24 and 2.5) to variables, it is often useful to carry out some kind of arithmetic in assignment statements. Java has the four familiar arithmetic operators, plus a remainder operator for this purpose. These operators are listed in table 2.2.

Table 2.2 The arithmetic operators of Java	
Operation	**Java operator**
addition	+
subtraction	−
multiplication	*
division	/
remainder	%

You can use these operators in assignment statements, much like you might use a calculator. For example, consider the following instructions:

```
int x;
x = 10 + 25;
```

After these instructions the variable x would contain the value 35: the result of adding 10 to 25. Terms on the right-hand side of assignment operators (like 10 + 25) that have to be *worked out* before they are assigned are referred to as **expressions**. These expressions can involve more than one operator.

Let's consider a calculation to work out the price of a product after a sales tax has been added. If the initial price of the product is 500 and the rate of sales tax is 17.5%, the following calculation could be used to calculate the total cost of the product:

```
double cost;
cost = 500 * (1 + 17.5/100);
```

After this calculation the final cost of the product would be 575.50.

By the way, in case you are wondering, the order in which expressions such as these are evaluated is the same as in most programming languages: with terms in brackets being calculated before division and multiplication, which in turn are calculated before subtraction and addition. This means that the term in the bracket

```
(1 + 17.5/100)
```

evaluates to 1.175, not 0.185, as the division is calculated before the addition. The final operator (%) in table 2.2 returns the remainder after *integer division* (often referred to as the **modulus**). Table 2.3 illustrates some examples of the use of this operator together with the values returned.

Table 2.3 Examples of the modulus operator in Java	
Expression	**Value**
29 % 9	2
6 % 8	6
40 % 40	0
10 % 2	0

As an illustration of the use of both the division operator and the modulus operator, consider the following example:

A large party of 30 people go to visit the roller-coaster rides at a local theme park. When they get to the ultimate ride, "Big Betty", they are told that only groups of four can get on!

To calculate how many groups in the party can get on the ride and how many people in the party will have to miss the ride, the division and modulus operators could be used as follows:

```
int catchRide, missRide;
catchRide = 30/4;          // number of groups on ride
missRide = 30%4;           // number who missed ride
```

After these instructions the value of `catchRide` will be 7 (the result of dividing 30 by 4) and the value of `missRide` will be 2 (the remainder after dividing 30 by 4). You may be wondering why the calculation for `catchRide`

```
30 / 4
```

did not yield 7.5 but 7. The reason for this is that there are, in fact, two different in-built division routines in Java, one to calculate an integer answer and another to calculate the answer as a real number.

Rather than having two division operators, however, Java has a single division symbol (/) to represent *both* types of division. The division operator is said to be **overloaded**. This means that the same operator (in this case the division symbol) can behave in different ways. This makes life much easier for programmers as the decision about which routine to call is left to the Java language.

How does the Java compiler know which division routine we mean? Well, it looks at the values that are being divided. If *at least one value* is a real number (as in the computer cost example), it assumes we mean the division routine that calculates an answer as a real number, otherwise it assumes we mean the division routine that calculates an answer as a whole number (as in the roller-coaster example).[1]

2.7   Expressions in Java

So far, variable names have appeared only on the left-hand side of assignment statements. However, the expression on the right-hand side of an assignment statement can itself contain variable names. If this is the case then the name does not refer to *the location*, but

---

[1] To force the use of one division routine over another, a technique known as **type casting** can be used. We will return to this technique later on in the book.

to *the contents of the location.* For example, the assignment to calculate the cost of the product could have been rewritten as follows:

```
double price, tax, cost; // declare three variables
price = 500; // set price
tax = 17.5; // set tax rate
cost = price * (1 + tax/100); // calculate cost
```

Here, the variables `price` and `tax` that appear in the expression

```
price * (1 + tax/100)
```

are taken to mean *the values contained in* `price` and `tax` respectively. This expression evaluates to 575.5 as before. Notice that although this price happens to be a whole number, it has been declared to be a **double** as generally prices are expressed as real numbers.

There is actually nothing to stop you using the name of the variable you are assigning to in the expression itself. This would just mean that the old value of the variable is being used to calculate its new value. Rather than creating a new variable, `cost`, to store the final cost of the product, the calculation could, for example, have updated *the original price* as follows:

```
price = price * (1 + tax/100);
```

Now, only two variables are required, `price` and `tax`. Let's look at this assignment a bit more closely.

When reading this instruction, the `price` in the right-hand expression is to be read as the *old value* of `price`, whereas the `price` on the left-hand side is to be read as *the new value* of `price`.

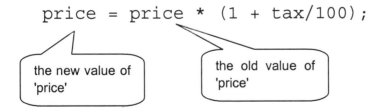

Of course, the code fragments we have been writing so far in this chapter are not complete programs. As you already know, to create a program in Java you must write one or more classes. In program 2.1, we write a class, `FindCost`, where the `main` method calculates the price of the product.

Program 2.1

```
/* a program to calculate the cost of a product after a sales tax has been
   added */

class FindCost
{
 public static void main(String[] args)
 {
   double price, tax;
   price = 500;
   tax = 17.5;
   price = price * (1 + tax/100);
 }
}
```

What would you see when you run this program? The answer is nothing! There is no instruction to display the result on to the screen. You have already seen how to display messages on to the screen. It is now time to take a closer look at the output command to see how you can also display results on to the screen.

2.8   Output in Java

As you have already seen when writing your first few programs, to output a message on to the screen in Java we use the following command:

```
System.out.println(message to be printed on screen);
```

which prints the given message on to the screen and then moves the cursor to a new line. For example, we have already seen:

```
System.out.println("Hello world");
```

This prints the message "Hello world" on to the screen and then moves the cursor to a new line. You have also seen the `print` command that displays a message but keeps the cursor on the same line. These messages are in fact what we call **strings** (collections of characters). In Java, literal strings like "Hello world" are always enclosed in speech marks. We shall look at strings in more detail in chapter 4. However, it is necessary to know how several strings can be printed on the screen using a single output command.

In Java, the two strings can be joined together with the plus symbol (+). When using this symbol for this purpose it is known as the **concatenation operator**. For example, instead of printing the single string "Hello world", we could have joined two strings, "Hello" and "world", for output using the following command:

```
System.out.println("Hello " + "world");
```

Note that spaces are printed by including them within the speech marks ("Hello "), not by adding spaces around the concatenation operator (which has no effect at all).

Java also allows any values or expressions of the simple types we showed you in table 2.1 to be printed on the screen using these output commands. It does this by implicitly converting each value/expression to a string before displaying it on the screen. In this way numbers, the value of variables, or the value of expressions can be displayed on the screen. For example, the square of 10 can be displayed on the screen as follows:

```
System.out.println(10*10);
```

This instruction prints the number 100 on the screen. Since these values are converted into strings by Java they can be joined on to literal strings for output.

For example, let's return to the party of 30 people visiting the roller-coaster rides we discussed in section 2.6. If each person is charged an entrance fee of 7.50, the total cost of tickets could be displayed as follows:

```
System.out.println("cost = " + (30*7.5) );
```

Here the concatenation operator (+) is being used to join the string, "cost = ", on to the value of the expression, (30*7.5). Notice that when expressions like 30*7.5 are used in output statements it is best to enclose them in brackets. This would result in the following output:

```
cost = 225.0
```

Bear these ideas in mind and look at program 2.2, where we have rewritten program 2.1 so that the output is visible.

Program 2.2

```
/* a program to calculate and display the cost of a product
 after sales tax has been added */

class FindCost2
{
  public static void main(String[] args)
  {
    double price, tax;
    price = 500;
    tax = 17.5;
    price = price * (1 + tax/100); // calculate cost
    // display results and pause before closing
    System.out.println("*** Product Price Check ***");
    System.out.println("Cost after tax = " + price);
    EasyIn.pause("Press <Enter> to quit");
  }
}
```

This program produces the following output:

```
*** Product Price Check ***
Cost after tax = 587.5
Press <Enter> to quit
```

When the user presses the *Enter* key the program will terminate.

Although being able to see the result of the calculation is a definite improvement, this program is still very limited. The formatting of the output can certainly be improved, but we shall not deal with such issues until later on in the book. What does concern us now is that this program can only calculate the cost of computers when the sales tax rate is 17.5% and the initial price is 500!

What is required is not to fix the rate of sales tax or the price of the computer but, instead, to get the *user of your program* to *input* these values as the program runs.

2.9   Input in Java: the *EasyIn* class

As we have already mentioned, Java was not really developed for use with simple text screens and to get around this we have provided you with the EasyIn class.

As long as the `EasyIn` class is accessible, you can use all the input methods that we have defined in this class. The `EasyIn` class has several input methods: *one for each type of data you may wish to input* (see table 2.4). Notice that the **boolean** type has no `EasyIn` method as such values are not directly input into programs from the keyboard.

Table 2.4 The input methods of the *EasyIn* class	
Java type	**EasyIn method**
byte	getByte()
short	getShort()
int	getInt()
long	getLong()
float	getFloat()
double	getDouble()
char	getChar()
boolean	n/a

A value can be input from the keyboard by accessing the appropriate method as follows:

```
someVariable = EasyIn.methodName();
```

Let's return to the haunted house game to illustrate this. Rather than *assigning* a difficulty level as follows:

```
char level;
level = 'A';
```

you could take a more flexible approach by asking the user of your program to *input* a difficulty level while the program runs. Since `level` is declared to be a character variable, you would have to use the specific input method for characters (called `getChar`) as follows:

```
level = EasyIn.getChar();
```

Notice that to access a method of a class you need to join the name of the method (`getChar`) on to the name of the class (`EasyIn`) by using the full-stop symbol '`.`'. Also you must remember the brackets after the name of the method.

In addition to these methods there are the two pause functions you have already met as well as an input method for strings. We shall return to this method when we look at the String class in chapter 4.

Each input method of EasyIn has error checking built in so that only values of the appropriate type are entered. If incorrect values are entered, an error message such as the following appears for character input:

```
Make sure you enter a single character
```

The user can then re-enter the value. This process continues until a value of the correct type has been entered. All this without any extra programming effort by you!

Let's rewrite program 2.2 so that the price of the product and the rate of sales tax are not fixed in the program, but are input from the keyboard. Since the type used to store the price and the tax is a **double**, the appropriate input method is getDouble.

Program 2.3

```
/* a program to input the initial price of a product and then
   calculate and display its cost after tax has been added */

class FindCost3
{
 public static void main(String[] args )
 {
    double price, tax;
    System.out.println("*** Product Price Check ***");
    System.out.print("Enter initial price: "); // prompt for input
    price = EasyIn.getDouble(); // input method called
    System.out.print("Enter tax rate: "); // prompt for input
    tax = EasyIn.getDouble(); // input method called
    price = price * (1 + tax/100);
    System.out.println("Cost after tax = " + price);
    EasyIn.pause("Press <Enter> to quit");
 }
}
```

Note that, by looking at this program code alone, there is no way to determine what the final price of the product will be, as the initial price and the tax rate will be determined *only when the program is run*.

Let's assume that we run the program and the user interacts with it as follows[2]:

```
*** Product Price Check ***
Enter initial price: 1000
Enter tax rate: 12.5%
Make sure you enter a double
12.5
Cost after tax = 1125.0
Press <Enter> to quit
```

When the user presses the *Enter* key, the program terminates. You should notice the following points from this test run:

- whatever the price of the computer and the rate of tax, this program could have evaluated the final price;

- entering numeric values with additional formatting information, such as currency symbols or the percentage symbol , is not permitted;

- `EasyIn`'s input methods allow for re-input with an appropriate error message if values of an incorrect type are entered.

The programs we are looking at now involve input commands, output commands and assignments. Clearly, the order in which you write these instructions affects the results of your programs. For example, if the instructions to calculate the final price and then display the results were reversed as follows:

```
System.out.println("Cost after tax = " + price);
price = price * (1 + tax/100);
```

the price that would be displayed would not be the price *after* tax but the price *before* tax! In order to avoid such mistakes it makes sense *to design your code* by sketching out your instructions before you type them in.

---

[2] We have used **bold italic** font to represent user input.

2.10 Program design

As we explained in chapter 1, d*esigning* a program is the task of considering exactly *how to build* the software, whereas writing the code (the task of *actually building* the software) is referred to as *implementation*. As programs get more complex, it is important to spend time on program design, before launching into program implementation.

As we have already said, Java programs consist of one or more classes, each with one or more methods. In chapter 1 we introduced you to the use of diagrams to help design such classes – your overall program design will be expressed using such diagrams. The programs we have considered so far, however, have only a single class and a single method (main). A class diagram would not be very useful here! So we will return to this design technique as we develop larger programs involving many classes.

At a lower level, the instructions that make up a method may also need to be designed if the method is complex. When you sketch out the code for your methods, you don't want to have to worry about the finer details of the Java compiler such as declaring variables, adding semi-colons and using the right brackets. Very often a general purpose "coding language" can be used for this purpose that conveys the meaning of each instruction without worrying too much about a specific language syntax.

Code expressed in this way is often referred to as **pseudocode**. The following is an example of pseudocode that could have been developed for the *main* method of program 2.3:

```
BEGIN
     DISPLAY program title
     DISPLAY prompt for price
     ENTER price
     DISPLAY prompt for tax
     ENTER tax
     SET price TO price * (1 + tax/100)
     DISPLAY new price
     PAUSE with message
END
```

Note that these pseudocode instructions are not intended to be typed in and compiled as they do not meet the syntax rules of any particular programming language. So, exactly how you write these instructions is up to you: there is no fixed syntax for them. However, each instruction conveys a well-understood programming concept and can easily be translated into a given programming language. Reading these instructions you should be able to see how each line would be coded in Java.

Wouldn't it be much easier to write your main method if you have pseudocode like this to follow! In future, when we present complex methods to you we will do so by presenting their logic using pseudocode.

Tutorial exercises

1. Why are the *scalar types* of Java so called?

2. Which of the following are valid variable names in Java?

    a) page one
    b) Page+ONE
    c) 1stPage
    d) pageOne
    e) page1
    f) Page1

3. A warehouse receives orders for goods from one of its 10 outlets (each outlet is identified by a letter). The warehouse needs to know the item number ordered, the price of each item, the number of items required, and the outlet to which the item is to be sent. A covering slip is then prepared as follows:

    ```
    *** ORDER SLIP***

    item code          2145
    item price         20.5
    quantity in stock  10


    TOTAL COST         205.0


    send to base        B
    ```

    Declare variables for each of the five items listed above.

4. Which of the following items of data should be declared as a constant?

    - the temperature in a room;
    - the number of months in a year;
    - the distance of the Earth from the Sun;
    - the average distance of the Earth from the Sun;
    - the winning jackpot in a lottery;
    - the population of Asia.

5. Identify and correct the errors in program 2.4 below, which prompts for the user's age and then attempts to work out the year in which the user was born.

Program 2.4

```
class SomeProg
{
   public static void main ()
   {
       final int CURRENT;
       int age;
       System.out.print("How old are you this year ? ");
       Age = EasyIn.getDouble();
       System.out.println("I think you were born in " + CURRENT-age);
       EasyIn.pause("Press <Enter> to quit);
   }
}
```

---

6. What would be the final output from program 2.5 if the user entered the number 7?

Program 2.5

```
class Calculate
{
    public static void main(String[] args )
    {
        int num1, num2;
        num2 = 4;
        System.out.print("Enter value ");
        num1 = EasyIn.getInt();
        num1 = num1 + 3;
        num2 = num1 / num2;
        System.out.println("result = " + num2);
        EasyIn.pause();
    }
}
```

---

7. A group of students has been told to get into teams of a specific size for their coursework. Use pseudocode to design a program that prompts for the number of students in the class and the size of the teams to be formed, and displays how many teams can be formed and how many students are left without a team.

Practical work

1. Write a program to display the order slip as given in tutorial question 3. The values to be printed on the slip should be entered by the user, and the total price calculated.

2. Write and run the corrected version of program 2.4.

3. Recently, the European Union has decreed that all traders in the UK sell their goods by the Kilo and not by the Pound (1 Kilo = 2.2 pounds). The following pseudocode has been arrived at in order to carry out this conversion:

```
BEGIN
    DISPLAY prompt for value in pounds
    ENTER value in pounds
    convert value in pounds to value in kilos
    DISPLAY value in kilos
    PAUSE
END
```

Implement this program, remembering to declare any variables that are necessary.

4.   Implement the program you designed in tutorial question 7.

3 Taking control

Learning objectives

By the end of this chapter you should be able to:

- explain the difference between **sequence, selection** and **iteration**;
- use **if** statements, **if...else** statements and **switch** statements to make choices in a program;
- repeat a section of code with a **for** loop, a **while** loop, and **do...while** loop;
- select the most appropriate construct for selection and iteration in a particular program;
- explain the term **input validation** and write simple validation routines.

3.1 Introduction

One of the most rewarding aspects of writing and running a program is knowing that it is *you* who have control over the computer. But looking back at the programs you have already written, just how much control do you actually have? Certainly, it was you who decided upon which instructions to include in your programs but *the order in which these instructions were executed* was *not* under your control. These instructions were always executed in **sequence**, that is one after the other, from top to bottom.

At first sight this might not seem a problem. After all, why would you need to execute your instructions in any other order? You will soon find that there are numerous instances when this order of execution is too restrictive and you will want to have much more control over the order in which instructions are executed.

3.2 Selection

Very often you will want your programs to make *choices among* different courses of action. For example, a program processing requests for airline tickets could have the following choices to make:

- display the price of the seats requested;
- display a list of alternative flights;
- display a message saying that no flights are available to that destination.

A program that can make choices can behave *differently* each time it is run, whereas programs in which instructions are just executed in sequence behave the *same* each time they are run.

As we have already mentioned, unless you indicate otherwise, program instructions are always executed in sequence. **Selection**, however, is a method of program control in which a choice can be made among which instructions to execute.   In Java there are three main forms of selection you may use:

- an **if** statement;
- an **if...else** statement;
- a **switch** statement.

3.2.1   The 'if' statement

During program execution it is not always appropriate to execute *every* instruction. For example, consider the following simple code fragment that welcomes customers queuing up for a roller-coaster ride:

```
System.out.println("How old are you?");
age = EasyIn.getInt();
System.out.println("Hello Junior!");
System.out.println("Enjoy your ride");
```

As you can see, there are four instructions in this code fragment. Remember that at the moment these instructions will be executed in sequence, from top to bottom. Consider the following interaction with this program:

```
How old are you?
10
Hello Junior!
Enjoy your ride
```

This looks fine but the message "*Hello Junior!*" is only meant for children. Now let's assume that someone older comes along and interacts with this program as follows:

```
How old are you?
45
Hello Junior!
Enjoy your ride
```

The message *"Hello Junior!"*, while flattering, might not be appropriate in this case! In other words, it is not always appropriate to execute the instruction:

```
System.out.println("Hello Junior!");
```

What is required is a way of *deciding* (while the program is running) whether or not to execute this instruction. In effect this instruction needs to be *protected* so that it is *only executed when appropriate*. What would be ideal would be if we could say something like the following:

```
System.out.println("How old are you?");
age = EasyIn.getInt();
IF age is that of a child
BEGIN
      System.out.println("Hello Junior!");
END
System.out.println("Enjoy your ride");
```

In the above, we have emboldened the lines that have been added to protect the *"Hello Junior!"* instruction. Actually these emboldened lines are not quite valid Java syntax; they are therefore to be read as lines of *pseudocode*. We will replace these pseudocode lines with appropriate Java syntax in a while, but for now let's look at the code fragment above in a bit more detail.

It is important to understand that in this code fragment *there are still only the same four instructions*. The emboldened lines that have been added are not to be read as additional *instructions*, they are simply a means *to control the flow* of the *existing* instructions. The emboldened lines say, in effect, that the instruction to display the message *"Hello Junior!"* should only be executed if the age entered is that of a child.

This then is an example of the form of control known as *selection*. At the moment we have used pseudocode lines to implement this selection. Let's now look at how to code these lines in Java.

This form of selection in Java involves the use of a **boolean condition**. A boolean condition is one that always evaluates to **true** or **false**. Examples of boolean conditions in everyday language are:

- this password is valid;
- there is an empty seat on the plane;
- all students in this group have passed their exams.

When the boolean condition evaluates to **true** the conditional instruction is executed, otherwise the conditional instruction is skipped. This boolean condition is combined with the reserved Java keyword **if** to implement selection as follows:

```
if ( /* boolean condition goes here */ )
{
      // conditional instruction(s) go here
}
```

Notice that the boolean condition must *always* be enclosed in round brackets. Notice also that more than one conditional instruction can be protected by the **if** and that all these instructions should be enclosed in curly brackets.[1]

One way to think of a boolean condition is as a *test*. In our example we are testing whether or not the age entered is that of a child.

If we assume that a child is someone less than 13 years of age, we can rewrite the initial set of instructions to include an **if** statement around the *"Hello Junior!"* message with the test (**age < 13**) as follows:

```
System.out.println("How old are you?");
age = EasyIn.getInt();
if (age < 13)// test
{
        System.out.print("Hello Junior!");
}
System.out.println("Enjoy your ride");
```

Now the message *"Hello Junior!"* will only be executed if the test is **true**, otherwise it will be skipped (see figure 3.1).

For example, let's assume we run this program again with the same values entered as before.

---

[1] Strictly speaking, if there is only a single instruction then it does not need to be surrounded by curly brackets.

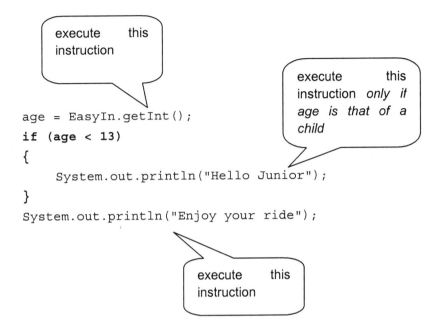

Fig 3.1   The 'if' statement allows a choice to be made in programs

First, the child approaches the ride:

```
How old are you?
10
Hello Junior!
Enjoy your ride
```

In this case, the condition has allowed the "*Hello Junior!*" message to be displayed as the age entered is less than 13. Now the adult approaches the ride:

```
How old are you?
45
Enjoy your ride
```

In this case the condition has not allowed the given instruction to be executed as the associated test was not **true**. The message is skipped and the program continues with the following instruction to display *"Enjoy your ride"*. As we have already mentioned, more than one instruction can be covered by an **if** statement.

For example, program 3.1 not only displays a welcoming message to customers waiting for a ride but also displays the price of a ticket (6.25 for adults, 2.75 for children under the age of 13).

Program 3.1

```
class RollerCoaster
{
  public static void main(String[] args)
  {
    int age;
    double price = 6.75; // set standard price of ticket
    System.out.println("How old are you?");
    age = EasyIn.getInt();
    if (age < 13) // condition
    { // conditional instructions
      System.out.print("Hello Junior!");
      price = 2.75; // overwrite standard price with child price
    }
    // remaining instructions
    System.out.println("Ticket price is "+ price);
    System.out.println("Enjoy your ride");
    EasyIn.pause();
  }
}
```

Here is a sample program run when the condition is **true**:

```
How old are you?
12
Hello Junior!
Ticket price is 2.75
Enjoy your ride
```

Here is another sample run when the condition is **false**:

```
How old are you?
25
Ticket price is 6.75
Enjoy your ride
```

3.2.2   The 'if...else' statement

Using the `if` statement in the way that we have done so far has allowed us to build the idea of a choice into our programs. In fact, the `if` statement made one of two choices before continuing with the remaining instructions in the program:

- execute the conditional instructions, or
- do not execute the conditional instructions.

The second option amounts to "do nothing". Rather than do nothing if the condition is `false`, an extended version of an `if` statement exists in Java to state an alternative course of action. This extended form of selection is the `if...else` statement. As the name implies, the instructions to be executed if the condition is `false` are preceded by the Java keyword `else` as follows:

```
if ( /* test goes here */ )
{
     // instruction(s) if test is true go here
}
else
{
     // instruction(s) if test is false go here
}
```

This is often referred to as a **double-branched** selection as there are strictly two alternative groups of instructions, whereas a single `if` statement is often referred to as a **single-branched** selection. Program 3.2 illustrates the use of a double-branched selection.

Program 3.2

```
class DisplayResult
{
    public static void main(String[] args)
    {
      int mark;
      System.out.println("What exam mark did you get?");
      mark = EasyIn.getInt();
      if (mark > 39)
      { // executed when test is true
        System.out.println("Congratulations, you passed");
      }
      else
      { // executed when test is false
```

```
        System.out.println("I'm sorry, but you failed");
    }
    System.out.println("Good luck with your other exams");
    EasyIn.pause();
    }
}
```

Program 3.2 checks a student's exam mark and tells the student whether or not he or she has passed (gained a mark over 39), before displaying a good luck message on the screen. Let's examine this program a bit more closely.

Prior to the **if...else** statement the following lines are executed in sequence:

```
int mark;
System.out.println("What exam mark did you get?");
mark = EasyIn.getInt();
```

Then the following condition is tested as part of the **if...else** statement:

```
(mark > 39)
```

When this condition is **true** the following line is executed:

```
System.out.print("Congratulations, you passed");
```

When the condition is **false**, however, the following line is executed *instead*:

```
System.out.println("I'm sorry, but you failed");
```

Finally, whichever path was chosen the program continues by executing the remaining lines in sequence:

```
System.out.println("Good luck with your other exams" );
EasyIn.pause();
```

The **if...else** form of control has allowed us to choose from *two* alternative courses of action. Here is a sample program run:

```
What exam mark did you get?
52
Congratulations, you passed
Good luck with your other exams
```

Here is another sample run where a different course of action is chosen.

```
What exam mark did you get?
35
I'm sorry, but you failed
Good luck with your other exams
```

Before we move on we should make clear that the instructions within **if** and **if...else** statements can themselves be *any* legal Java instructions. In particular they could contain other **if** or **if...else** statements. This form of control is referred to as **nesting**.

As an example, consider program 3.3, which is a variation on program 3.2 that not only determines whether or not a student has passed an exam, but also whether or not that student has earned a distinction by getting a mark of 70 or over.

Program 3.3

```java
class DisplayResult2
{
  public static void main(String[] args)
  {
    int mark;
    System.out.println("What exam mark did you get?");
    mark = EasyIn.getInt();
    if (mark > 69) // first test
    {
      System.out.println("Congratulations, you have a distinction");
    }
    else
    {
      if (mark > 39) // second test
      {
        System.out.println("You have passed");
      }
      else // when both tests are false
      {
        System.out.println("I'm sorry, you failed");
      }
```

```
        }
        System.out.println("Good luck with your other exams" );
        EasyIn.pause();
     }
   }
```

Once again this program uses an **if...else** statement to control program flow:

```
if (mark >69)
{
   System.out.println("Congratulations, you have a distinction");
}
else
{
     // second group of instructions go here
}
```

Now when the boolean condition (**mark>69**) is tested and found to be **true** the message "*Congratulations, you have a distinction*" is displayed. But when this condition is **false** and the mark is not a distinction, the **else** branch is reached. Look closely at the instructions inside this **else** branch.

```
else
{
    if (mark > 39)
    {
        System.out.println("You have passed");
    }
    else
    {
        System.out.println("I'm sorry, you failed");
    }
}
```

The instructions associated with this **else** branch are themselves another **if...else** selection! This is perfectly legal as we can write any Java instructions here. All we are doing is saying that we would like to make *another* choice in our program at this stage.

Having already decided that the mark cannot be a distinction we are left to decide whether or not the mark is in fact a pass or a fail. With two choices to make, obviously we would use another **if...else** statement!

Once the correct choice has been made the program continues with the remaining instructions:

```
System.out.println("Good luck with your other exams" );
EasyIn.pause();
```

Here is one sample run:

```
What exam mark did you get?
32
I'm sorry, you failed
Good luck with your other exams
```

Can you follow the program instructions to see how these results were arrived at? Run through the program instructions again and assume that the user types in 69. What results would you see on the screen then?

Just before we move on to look at another form of selection in Java, you might be wondering why we used the tests (mark > 39) and (mark > 69) rather than (mark ≥ 40) and (mark ≥ 60). The reason is that the symbol '≥' (greater than or equal to) cannot be used in a Java program as you cannot find it on a keyboard and we haven't yet shown you what the correct Java symbol is!

The alternative symbol in Java to represent this comparison operator is '>='; table 3.1 shows all the Java comparison operator symbols.

Table 3.1 The comparison operators of Java		
Comparison operator	**Meaning**	**Java operator**
=	equal to	==
≠	not equal to	!=
<	less than	<
>	greater than	>
≥	greater than or equal to	>=
≤	less than or equal to	<=

Since comparison operators give an answer of **true** or **false** they are often used in tests such as those we have been discussing. Note that a double equals (==) is used to check for equality in Java and not the single equals (=) which as you know is used for assignment.

For example, to check whether or not an angle is a right angle the following test could be used:

```
if (angle == 90)// note the use of the double equals
{
      System.out.println("This is a right angle");
}
```

3.2.3   The 'switch' statement

Although nested **if** statements can be used to make several choices, they can begin to make your code look a bit messy. Just look at program 3.3 for example! When they are needed they can be laid out so that the code is a bit more readable. Rather than indent each nested **if** they are often written as follows:

```
if (mark > 69)
{
   System.out.println("Great, you have a distinction");
}
else if (mark > 39) // nested selection on same line
{
    System.out.println("You have passed");
}
else
{
    System.out.println("I'm sorry, you failed");
}
```

While this style is preferred, there may be times when you can do away with the need for a nested **if** statement altogether, as shown in the following example.

Students are always forgetting when their classes are. To help them, consider program 3.4 which asks a student to enter his or her tutorial group (A, B or C) and then displays on the screen the time of the software lab.

Program 3.4

```
class Timetable
{
  public static void main(String[] args)
  {
      char group; // to store the tutorial group
      System.out.println("***Lab Times***"); // display header
      System.out.println("Enter your group (A,B,C)");
      group = EasyIn.getChar();
      // check tutorial group and display appropriate time
      if (group == 'A')
      {
        System.out.print("10.00 a.m"); // lab time for group A
      }
      else if (group == 'B')
      {
         System.out.print("1.00 p.m"); // lab time for group B
      }
      else if (group == 'C')
      {
         System.out.print("11.00 a.m"); // lab time for group C
      }
      else
      {
         System.out.print("No such group"); //invalid group entered
      }
      EasyIn.pause();
  }
}
```

This program is a little bit different from the ones before because it includes some basic **error checking**. That is, it does not *assume* that the user of this program will always type the *expected* values. If the wrong group (not A, B or C) is entered, an error message is displayed saying "*No such group*".

```
// valid groups checked here
else // if this 'else' is reached, group entered must be invalid
{
      System.out.print("No such group"); // error message
}
```

Error checking like this is a good habit to get into.

This use of nested selections is okay up to a point, but when the number of options becomes large the program can again look very untidy. Fortunately, this type of selection can also be implemented in Java with another form of control: a **switch** statement. This is demonstrated in program 3.5.

Program 3.5

```
class TimetableWithSwitch
{
  public static void main(String[] args)
  {
    char group;
    System.out.println("***Lab Times***");
    System.out.println("Enter your group (A,B,C)");
    group = EasyIn.getChar();
    switch(group) // beginning of switch
    {
      case 'A': System.out.print("10.00 a.m ");break;
      case 'B': System.out.print("1.00 p.m ");break;
      case 'C': System.out.print("11.00 a.m ");break;
      default:  System.out.print("No such group");
    } //end of switch
    EasyIn.pause();
  }
}
```

As you can see, this looks a lot neater. The **switch** statement works in exactly the same way as a set of nested **if** statements, but is more compact and readable. A **switch** statement may be used when

- only one variable is being checked in each condition (in this case every condition involves checking the variable group);
- the check involves specific values of that variable (e.g. 'A', 'B') and not ranges (for example >39).

As can be seen from the example above, the keyword **case** is used to precede a possible value of the variable that is being checked. There may be many **case** statements in a single **switch** statement. The general form of a **switch** statement in Java is given as follows:

```
switch(someVariable)
{
    case value1:  // instructions(s) to be executed
                  break;
    case value2:  // instructions(s) to be executed
                  break;
    // more  values to be tested can be added
    default: // instruction(s) for default case
}
```

where

- `someVariable` is the name of the variable being tested (this variable is usually of type `int` or `char` but it may also be of type `byte` or `short`);
- `value1, value2`...etc. are the possible values of that variable;
- **break** is an optional command that forces the program to skip the rest of the **switch** statement;
- **default** is an optional (last) case which allows you to code instructions that deal with the possibility of none of the cases above being **true**.

The **break** statement is important because it means that once a matching case is found, the program can skip the rest of the cases below. If it is not added, not only will the instructions associated with the matching case be executed but, also, all the instructions associated with all the cases below it. Notice that the last set of instructions does not need a **break** statement as they have no other cases to skip.

3.3   Iteration

So far we have considered sequence and selection as forms of program control. One of the advantages of using computers rather than humans to carry out tasks is that they can repeat those tasks over and over again without ever getting tired. With a computer we do not have to worry about mistakes creeping in because of fatigue, whereas humans would need a break to stop their becoming sloppy or careless when carrying out repetitive tasks over a long period of time. Neither sequence nor selection allows us to carry out this kind of control in our programs.

Iteration is the form of program control that allows us to instruct the computer to carry out a task over and over again by repeating a section of code. For this reason this form of control is often also referred to as **repetition**. The programming structure that is used to control this repetition is often called a **loop**. There are three types of loops in Java:

- **for** loop;
- **while** loop;
- **do...while** loop.

3.3.1   The 'for' loop

Consider a program that needs to display a square of stars (five by five) on the screen as follows:

```
*  *  *  *  *
*  *  *  *  *
*  *  *  *  *
*  *  *  *  *
*  *  *  *  *
```

This could be achieved with five output statements executed in sequence:

```
System.out.println("*****");
System.out.println("*****");
System.out.println("*****");
System.out.println("*****");
System.out.println("*****");
```

While this would work, all the program is really doing is executing the same instruction five times. Writing out the same line many times is somewhat wasteful of our precious time as programmers. Imagine what would happen if we wanted a square 40 by 40!

Rather than write out this instruction five times we would prefer to write it out once and get the program to *repeat that same line* five times. What we would require is some form of control as follows:

```
REPEAT 5 times // try this?
{
        System.out.println("*****");
}
```

Unfortunately the emboldened expression "REPEAT 5 times" is *not* a valid command in Java. Instead, if we wish to repeat a section of code a fixed number of times (five in the example above) we would use Java's **for** loop.

The **for** loop is usually used in conjunction with a **counter**. A counter is just another variable (usually integer) that has to be created. We use it to keep track of how many times we have been through the loop so far. We do this by carrying out three tasks:

1. Set the counter to some initial value (usually zero or one).
2. Check the value of the counter before each new repetition of the loop in order to determine when to stop.
3. Change the value of the counter (usually by adding one to the counter) each time it goes around the loop to indicate that another repetition has occurred.

Task number one is usually referred to as setting the **start condition** of the loop.

Task number two sets the **boolean condition** that we met when discussing selections. When used with loops, this condition is often referred to as the **while condition** as the code continues to loop *while* this condition is **true**.

Task number three is referred to as the **action** that takes place at the end of each repetition of the loop.

These items are assembled as follows to construct the **for** loop:

```
for( /* start condition */ ; /* while condition */ ; /* action */)
{
    // instruction(s) to be repeated go here
}
```

Let's assume that a variable called *i* has been declared for use as a loop counter:

```
int i;
```

We can construct a loop to display a square of stars as follows:

```
for(i = 1; i <= 5; i = i+1)
{
    System.out.println("*****");
}
```

Note that we started our loop counter at one (**i = 1**). Each time the loop repeats we add one to the counter, and we continue repeating while the counter is less than or equal to five.

This is one way of saying "repeat 5 times" in Java. Note that if we had chosen to start the loop counter at zero (i = 0) then our **while condition** would have been (i < 5) and not (i <= 5).

The action associated with this **for** loop is a very common one: add one to the loop counter. It is so common that a shorthand exists for this expression in Java:

```
i++;
```

The operator ++ is known as the **increment operator** of Java and can be used *whenever* you wish to add one to a value. Similarly there exists a **decrement operator** (--) that allows you to reduce the value of a variable by one. Thus

```
i--;
```

is equivalent to the following assignment:

```
i = i - 1;
```

As an example of the use of this operator, program 3.6 prints out the numbers from 10 down to 1.

Program 3.6

```
class Countdown
{
  public static void main(String[] args)
  {
    int i;   // declare loop counter
    System.out.println("***Numbers from 10 to 1***");
    for (i=10; i>=1; i--)   // counter moving from 10 down to 1
    {
      System.out.println(i);
    }
    EasyIn.pause();
  }
}
```

Note that it is perfectly acceptable to refer to the loop counter inside the loop body as we did in the body of the **for** loop of program 3.6:

```
System.out.println(i); // counter 'i' used here
```

When you do this, however, be careful not to *change* the loop counter within the loop body as this can throw your loop condition off track!

Finally, before moving on to look at another form of loop in Java, a reminder that the loop body can contain any number of instructions, including another loop. In other words, you may nest loops just as you nested **if**s. As an example of this, consider again the **for** loop we constructed to display a square of stars.

```
for(i = 1; i <= 5; i = i+1)
{
        System.out.println("*****");
}
```

The body of this loop has an output statement that displays five stars on the screen in a row. We could, if we had wanted, have displayed only a *single* star on the screen as follows:

```
System.out.print("*");
```

Now, to get the program to display a row of five of these stars we could put this statement in another loop. We will need another loop counter for this new loop. Let's assume we have declared an integer variable 'j' for this purpose. The inner loop would look like this:

```
for (j = 1; j<=5; j++)
{
        System.out.print("*");
}
```

Now to display our square:

```
for(i = 1; i <= 5; i++) // outer loop control
{
    for (j = 1; j<=5; j++) // inner loop control
    {
        System.out.print("*");
    } // inner loop ends here
    System.out.println();
} // outer loop ends here
```

For now let's look at how the control in this program flows.

1.   The outer loop has its start condition set (i =1).
2.   The while condition (i <= 5) of the outer loop is then checked and found to be **true** so the body of the outer loop is entered.

Now, the body of the outer loop itself contains a loop. We have already told you that when any loop is entered, instructions in the body of that loop are executed. This means that the *entire* inner loop is executed before we finish one cycle of the outer loop. So we effectively print five stars out in a row (moving the inner *j* counter from one through to five in the process) giving us the following output:

```
*****
```

3.   After completing the inner loop the program moves the cursor to a new line, then returns to the action of the outer loop (i++).

Steps two and three are then repeated until the **while condition** of the outer loop is made **false**. Notice that it is also possible to declare the variables *i* and *j* within the round brackets of the **for** loop. This would give us the following version:

```
for(int i = 1; i <= 5; i++) // counter 'i' declared in loop control
{
    for (int j = 1; j<=5; j++) // counter 'j' declared in loop control
    {
        System.out.print("*");
    }
    System.out.println();
}
```

Finally, although a **for** loop is used to repeat something a fixed number of times, you don't necessarily need to know this fixed number when you are writing the program. This fixed number could be a value given to you by the user of your program, for example. Program 3.7 asks the user to determine the size of the square of stars.

Program 3.7

```
class DisplayStars
{
  public static void main(String[] args)
  {
      int num; // to hold user response
      // prompt and get user response
      System.out.println("Size of square?");
      num = EasyIn.getInt();
      // display square
      for(int i = 1; i <= num; i++) // loop fixed to 'num'
      {
        for (int j = 1; j<=num; j++) // loop fixed to 'num'
        {
              System.out.print("*");
        }
        System.out.println();
      }
      EasyIn.pause();
  }
}
```

In this program you cannot tell from the code exactly how many times the loops will iterate, but you can say that they will iterate *num* number of times – whatever the user may have entered for 'num'. So in this sense the loop is still fixed. Here is a sample run of program 3.7:

```
Size of square?
8
* * * * * * * *
* * * * * * * *
* * * * * * * *
* * * * * * * *
* * * * * * * *
* * * * * * * *
* * * * * * * *
* * * * * * * *
```

3.3.2   The 'while' loop

As we have already said, much of the power of computers comes from the ability to ask them to carry out repetitive tasks, so iteration is a very important form of program control. The **for** loop is an often used construct to implement fixed repetitions.

Sometimes, however, a repetition is required that is *not fixed* and a **for** loop is not the best one to use in such a case. Consider the following scenarios, for example:

- a racing game that repeatedly moves a car around a track until the car crashes;
- a ticket issuing program that repeatedly offers tickets for sale until the user chooses to quit the program;
- a password checking program that does not let a user into an application until he or she enters the right password.

Each of the above cases involves repetition; however, the number of repetitions is not fixed but depends upon some condition. The **while** loop offers one type of non-fixed iteration. The syntax for constructing this loop in Java is as follows:

```
while ( /* test goes here */ )
{
      // instruction(s) to be repeated go here
}
```

As you can see, this loop is much simpler to construct than a **for** loop. As this loop is not repeating a fixed number of times, there is no need to create a counter to keep track of the number of repetitions. This means there is no need for a start condition or an end of loop action.

When might this kind of loop be useful? The first example we will explore is the use of the **while** loop to check data that is input by the user. Checking input data for errors is referred to as **input validation**.

For example, look back at program 3.2, which asked the user to enter an exam mark:

```
System.out.println("What exam mark did you get?");
mark = EasyIn.getInt();
if (mark > 39)
// rest of code goes here
```

The mark that is entered should never be greater than 100. At the time we assumed that the user would enter the mark correctly. However, good programmers never make this assumption!

Before accepting the mark that is entered and moving on to the next stage of the program, it is good practice to check that the mark entered is indeed a valid one. If it is not, then the user will be allowed to enter the mark again. This will go on until the user enters a valid mark.

We can express this using pseudocode as follows:

```
DISPLAY prompt for mark
ENTER mark
KEEP REPEATING WHILE mark typed in is > 100
BEGIN
      DISPLAY error message to user
      ENTER mark
END
// REST OF PROGRAM HERE
```

This is an example of an iteration as the user may make many errors. However, the number of iterations is not fixed as it is impossible to say how many, if any, mistakes the user will make.

This sounds like a job for the **while** loop!

```
System.out.println("What exam mark did you get?");
mark = EasyIn.getInt();
while (mark > 100) // check for invalid input
{
   // display error message plus allow for re-input
   System.out.println("invalid mark: Re-enter!");
   mark = EasyIn.getInt();
}
if (mark > 39)
// rest of code goes here
```

Actually, the mark should also never be less than zero. So an invalid input is a mark that's too high or too low. This requires a more complicated test condition; we want our test condition to say (mark > 100 OR mark < 0).

The word 'OR' in the previous sentence is not a valid Java word. We actually have to write the following symbol:

$$||$$

Symbols like OR and AND, which are used with boolean conditions, are known as **logical** (or **boolean**) **operators**. Table 3.2 lists the Java counterparts to the three most common of these logical operators. We will see many examples of their use as we progress through the book.

Table 3.2 The logical operators of Java	
Logical operator	**Java counterpart**
AND	&&
OR	||
NOT	!

With this in mind we can rewrite the **while** loop as follows:

```
while (mark < 0 || mark > 100)
{
      // instruction(s) to be repeated go here
}
```

Program 3.8 below shows the whole of the previous program rewritten out to include the input validation. Notice how this works – we ask the user for the mark; if it is within the acceptable range the **while** loop is not entered and we move past it to the other instructions. But if the mark entered is less than zero or greater than 100 we enter the loop, display an error message and ask the user to input the mark again. This continues until the mark is within the required range.

Program 3.8

```
class DisplayResult3
{
  public static void main(String[] args)
  {
    int mark;
    System.out.println("What exam mark did you get?");
    mark = EasyIn.getInt();
    // input validation
    while (mark < 0 || mark > 100) // check if mark is invalid
    {
      // display error message
      System.out.println("Invalid mark: please re-enter");
      // mark must be re-entered
      mark = EasyIn.getInt();
    }
    // by this point loop is finished and mark will be valid
    if (mark > 39)
    {
      // executed when test is true
      System.out.println("Congratulations, you passed");
    }
    else
    {
      // executed when test is false
      System.out.println("I'm sorry, but you failed");
    }
    System.out.println("Good luck with your other exams");
    EasyIn.pause();
  }
}
```

Here is a sample test run:

```
What exam mark did you get?
101
Invalid mark: please re-enter
-10
Invalid mark: please re-enter
10
I'm sorry, but you failed
Good luck with your other exams
```

3.3.3   The do...while loop

There is one more loop construct in Java that we need to tell you about: the **do...while** loop.

The **do...while** loop is another variable loop construct, but unlike the **while** loop, the **do...while** loop has its while condition at the *end* of the loop rather than at the *beginning*.

The syntax of a **do...while** loop is given below:

```
do
{
    // instruction(s) to be repeated go here
}while ( /* test goes here */ ); // note the semi-colon
```

You are probably wondering what difference it makes if the while condition is at the end or the beginning of the loop. Well, there is one subtle difference. If the while condition is at the end of the loop, the loop will iterate *at least once*. If the condition is at the beginning of the loop, however, there is a possibility that the condition will be false to begin with and the loop is never executed. A **while** loop therefore executes *zero or more times* whereas a **do...while** loop executes *one or more times.*

To make this a little clearer, look back at the **while** loop we just showed you for validating exam marks. If the user entered a valid mark initially (such as 66), the test to trap an invalid mark (mark <0 || mark > 100) would be **false** and the loop would be skipped altogether. A **do...while** loop would not be appropriate here as the possibility of never getting into the loop should be left open.

When would a **do...while** loop be suitable? Well, any time you wish to code a non-fixed loop that must execute at least once. Usually, this would be the case when the **while** condition can be tested only *after* the loop has been entered.

Think about all the programs you have written so far. Once the program has done its job it terminates – if you want it to perform the same task again you have to go through the whole procedure of running that program again.

In many cases a better solution would be to put your whole program in a loop that keeps repeating until the user chooses to quit your program. This would involve asking the user each time if he or she would like to continue repeating your program, or to stop.

A **for** loop would not be the best loop to choose here as this is more useful when the number of repetitions can be predicted. A **while** loop would be difficult to use as the test that checks the user's response to a question cannot be made at the beginning of the loop. The answer is to move the test to the end of the loop and use a **do...while** loop as follows:

```
char response; // variable to hold user response
do// place code in loop
{     // program instructions go here
      System.out.println("another go (y/n)?");
      response = EasyIn.getChar(); // get user reply
} while (response == 'y'); // test must be at the end
```

A simple program that uses this technique is developed in tutorial question 3. However, another way to allow a program to be run repeatedly using a **do...while** loop is to include a *menu* of options within the loop (this was very common in the days before windows and mice!). One of the options in the menu list would be the option to quit, and this option is checked in the while condition of the loop. Program 3.9 is a reworking of program 3.5 using this technique.

Program 3.9

```
class TimetableWithLoop
{
  public static void main(String[] args)
  {
      char group, response;
      System.out.println("***Lab Times***");
      do // put code in loop
      {  // offer menu of options
        System.out.println(); // create a blank line
        System.out.println("[1] TIME FOR GROUP A");
        System.out.println("[2] TIME FOR GROUP B");
        System.out.println("[3] TIME FOR GROUP C");
        System.out.println("[4] QUIT PROGRAM");
        System.out.print("enter choice [1,2,3,4]: ");
        response = EasyIn.getChar(); // get response
        System.out.println(); // create a blank line
        switch(response)   // process response
        {
          case '1': System.out.println("10.00 a.m ");break;
          case '2': System.out.println("1.00 p.m ");break;
          case '3': System.out.println("11.00 a.m ");break;
          case '4': System.out.println("Goodbye ");break;
          default:  System.out.println("Options 1-4 only!");
        }
      } while (response != '4'); // test for Quit option
    }
}
```

Here is a sample test run of this program:

```
***Lab Times***

[1] TIME FOR GROUP A
[2] TIME FOR GROUP B
[3] TIME FOR GROUP C
[4] QUIT PROGRAM
enter choice [1,2,3,4]:  2


1.00 p.m

[1] TIME FOR GROUP A
[2] TIME FOR GROUP B
[3] TIME FOR GROUP C
[4] QUIT PROGRAM
enter choice [1,2,3,4]:  5


Options 1-4 only!

[1] TIME FOR GROUP A
[2] TIME FOR GROUP B
[3] TIME FOR GROUP C
[4] QUIT PROGRAM
enter choice [1,2,3,4]:  1
10.00 a.m

[1] TIME FOR GROUP A
[2] TIME FOR GROUP B
[3] TIME FOR GROUP C
[4] QUIT PROGRAM
enter choice [1,2,3,4]:  3


11.00 a.m

[1] TIME FOR GROUP A
[2] TIME FOR GROUP B
[3] TIME FOR GROUP C
[4] QUIT PROGRAM
enter choice [1,2,3,4]:  4


Goodbye
```

Tutorial exercises

1. Look back at program 3.9 and the test run that follows it. Now assume that the **break** statements are removed from the **switch** command in program 3.9. What results would you see now if you ran the program with the same values entered in the original test run?

2. Which kind of loop would be the most suitable to use for the following purposes:

    a)   to validate a user's password?

    b)   to display the details of all the employees in a company?

    c)   to display the details of employees one by one till the user decides to quit?

3. Program 3.10 asks the user to enter two numbers and displays the sum of these two numbers. It then gives the user the opportunity to have another go or to quit the program; this continues until the user chooses to quit. Study the program, then answer the questions that follow:

Program 3.10

```
class Arithmetic
{
  public static void main(String[] args)
  {
    int num1, num2;
    char choice;
    do
    {
        System.out.print("Enter a number: ");
        num1 = EasyIn.getInt();
        System.out.print("Enter another number: ");
        num2 = EasyIn.getInt();
        System.out.println("The sum of the two numbers is "
                        + (num1 + num2));
        System.out.print("Do you want another go (y/n): ");
        choice = EasyIn.getChar();
      }while(choice == 'y');
    }
  }
```

a)   What happens if the user presses a character other than 'y' or 'n' when asked if he or she wants another go?

b)   What happens if the user presses an upper case 'Y' in response to the question?

c)   How would you adapt the program so that the user would be given another go irrespective of whether or not an upper case or lower case 'y' is entered?

4.   What is the purpose of a **default** statement in a **switch** command?

5.   Consider a vending machine that offers the following options:

```
[1] Get gum
[2] Get chocolate
[3] Get popcorn
[4] Get juice
[5] Display total sold
```

Design a program that continually allows users to select from these options. When options 1–4 are selected an appropriate message is to be displayed acknowledging their choice. For example, when option 3 is selected the following message could be displayed:

```
Here is your popcorn
```

The program terminates when option 5 is selected, at which point the total number of each type of item sold is displayed. For example:

```
3 items of gum were sold
2 items of chocolate were sold
6 items of popcorn were sold
9 items of juice were sold
```

If an option other than 1–5 is entered an appropriate error message should be displayed, such as:

```
Error, options 1-5 only!
```

Practical work

1. Type, compile and run program 3.10, and then

    a) make the changes that you considered in tutorial question 3c;

    b) instead of displaying the sum of the numbers, ask the user to enter the sum. Then, if the user answers correctly, a congratulatory message is displayed; if the user's answer is incorrect then the correct answer is displayed.

2. Implement the program you designed in tutorial question 5.

3. a) Using a **for** loop, write a program that asks the user to type in three numbers and then displays the total of those numbers;

    b) rewrite the program (using a **do..while** loop instead of a **for** loop) so that the user is allowed to type in numbers continually until he or she chooses to finish.

4. a) Using a **for** loop, write a program that displays a "6 times" multiplication table; the output should look like this:

```
 1 × 6 = 6
 2 × 6 = 12
 3 × 6 = 18
 4 × 6 = 24
 5 × 6 = 30
 6 × 6 = 36
 7 × 6 = 42
 8 × 6 = 48
 9 × 6 = 54
10 × 6 = 60
11 × 6 = 66
12 × 6 = 72
```

b) Adapt the program so that instead of a "6 times" table, the user chooses which table is displayed.

c) Adapt the program further, so that the user can choose whether to have another go or to quit.

4 Classes and objects

Learning objectives

By the end of this chapter you should be able to:

- explain the meaning of the term **object-oriented**;
- explain the concept of **encapsulation**;
- explain the terms **class**, **object**, **attribute** and **method**;
- declare objects in Java and create new objects;
- call the methods of an object in Java;
- declare and use `Strings` in Java;
- create a simple `Frame` in Java.

4.1   Introduction

Now at last it is time to find out what we really mean by this phrase *object-oriented*. We have been using it already, and hinting at what it is all about; and you have probably heard it being used in all sorts of contexts, since object-oriented development has become very popular over the course of the 1990s.

The object-oriented way of doing things is the most recent development in the building of software systems, and is concerned very much with the production of reusable components; it is arguable that the sophisticated graphical interfaces that are now universal would never have been developed without an object-oriented approach. Object-oriented development also lends itself to the Rapid Application Development approach that you learnt about in the first chapter, because it allows us to move much more smoothly between analysis and design. In addition, because of the technique of **encapsulation** or **information-hiding** that you will learn about soon, object-orientation allows us to build much more secure systems.

4.2   What is object-orientation?

First some background. As computers become more and more powerful the software needed to control them becomes more and more complex. Thirty or so years ago the demands on software developers were nothing compared to the demands on today's programmers. As the complexity of software increased it became clear that large, unstructured programs were becoming increasingly difficult to develop and that a **modular** approach was required, whereby programs were broken up into smaller units.

This was referred to as **structured** programming. Structured programming was the first attempt at formally modularizing program code. Now the program was no longer considered one large task, but a collection of smaller tasks (often called **procedures** or **functions** in programming languages). This is illustrated in figure 4.1. The main program is broken down into four tasks; the second task is broken down further into two tasks, and so on.

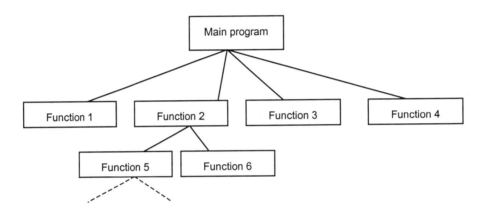

Fig 4.1   A structured approach to modular design

For some time this approach to modular design dealt adequately with the increased complexity of software. But then, with the rapid microchip advances of the 1980s and the growth of the Internet in the 1990s, the demands on software developers increased again and the structured approach was found to be deficient. The reason for this is that the approach focuses on the actions (functions) but not *the things acted on* – the data. The data becomes spread throughout the system in a very unstructured way (figure 4.2).

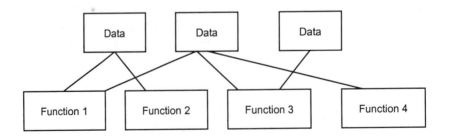

Fig 4.2   A complex web of links between data and functions arises in the structured approach

However, the *data* is central to the program's existence – so an approach such as that shown in figure 4.2 can lead to the following problems:

- data is subject to change by many functions, and data can therefore become unexpectedly corrupted, leading to unreliable programs that are difficult to debug;
- revising the data requires rewriting every function that interacts with it, leading to programs that are very difficult to maintain;
- functions and the data they act upon are not closely tied together, leading to code that is very difficult to reuse since there is a complex web of links to disentangle.

Let us assume, for example, that we wish to write a car-chase game and that we already have a driving game written. We may wish to use the cars from the first game in our new program. The code we are interested in using is not just the functions that control the car (brake, accelerate etc.) but also the data related to the car (speed, colour etc.).

The "old-fashioned" structured approach does not match well with our own view of the world. We do not see the world as a set of functions alone; the data that the functions act upon is equally important (as is the case in the car example above). The structured way of looking at things makes it difficult to conceptualize problems.

From these issues it became clear that functions and the data they act upon should be grouped together. This higher unit of organization was called an **object** (figure 4.3).

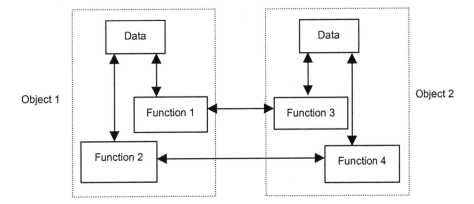

Fig 4.3   An object-oriented approach to modular design

Closely related to the idea of an object is a **class**. A class is the blueprint from which objects are generated. In other words, if we have six cars in our car-chase game we do not need to define a car six times. We will define a car once (in a class) and then generate as many **objects** as we want from this class blueprint. In one program we may have many classes as we probably wish to generate many kinds of objects (cars, tracks, players etc.).

Object-oriented programming therefore consists of defining one or more classes that may interact with each other. To exploit the full power of object-orientation requires us to use an object-oriented programming language. There are many object-oriented languages such as C++, SmallTalk, Eiffel, Object Pascal and of course Java!

4.3   Attributes and methods

We have seen that the term "object-oriented" means that we organize software as a collection of objects that incorporate both data and behaviour (the functions); objects belong to a **class**, which we can think of as the template for all the objects (and potential objects) that can belong to that class.

Let's consider another example, a `Student` class. The individual objects in that class could be John, Abdul, Ayotunde, Susan, Abiola and other students who will join the university in the future. We often describe the individual objects of the class as **instances** of the class.

Now that you know a little more about classes you are in a better position to understand what you learnt in the first chapter, namely that a class consists of:

- a set of **attributes** (the data);
- a set of **methods** which can access or change those attributes (the functions).

Together the attributes and methods are often referred to as the **members** of a class.

What might be the attributes and methods of a `Student` class? Let's keep it fairly simple and suggest five attributes, and two methods which we have specified in figure 4.4, using the UML notation that we introduced in the first chapter:

Student
studentNumber   *studentName*   *markForMaths*   *markForEnglish*   *markForScience*
enterMarks   *calculateAverageMark*

Fig 4.4   A Student class

4.4 Encapsulation

As we shall see, when we design our classes we normally arrange things so that the attributes of an object can be manipulated only by methods of that object – in this way we "close off" our classes and protect the attributes from outside interference. This is referred to as **encapsulation**.

Any object-oriented programming language will provide us with the facility of defining a class and restricting access to the members (that is, the attributes and the methods of that class). The usual way of doing things is to define the attributes of the class as **private** and the methods as **public**. By doing this we ensure that the only way that the attributes of an object can be accessed is by the methods of that object, and not by the methods of any other object; in this way encapsulation is achieved.

Let us think about our Student example. Say an object of another class – a StudentReport class for example – needed to know the student's average mark. If we have implemented our class sensibly then the only way that we will be able to access the student's marks is by calling one of the methods. In this case the calculateAverageMark method would be the one we needed. An object of the StudentReport class would invoke the calculateAverageMark method of a Student object. It could then use the result in any way it chose. This process of one object using another object's methods is a bit like sending a message and getting a reply, and is therefore often referred to as **message passing**.

This is illustrated in figure 4.5, which shows an object of the StudentReport class passing a message to an object of the Student class, and getting a message back.

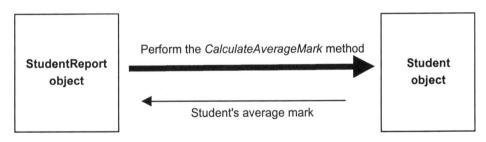

Fig 4.5 An object passing a message and getting a reply

It is not necessary that there is a reply every time a message is sent. For example, consider a class called Admin, which might provide methods for dealing with administrative functions of the system. An object of the Admin class might send a message to a Student object which calls the enterMarks method. In this case the Admin object would need to call the enterMarks method, and will need to *send* information to the method in order for it to be able to do its job.

This is shown in figure 4.6.

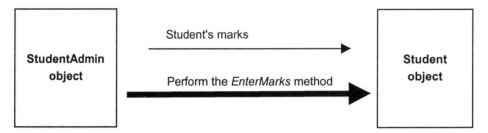

Fig 4.6   An object passing a message with the necessary information

As we shall see later, it is perfectly possible for a method both to receive information and to send some information back; or there could be cases where a method needs no information and returns none – it just has to perform some internal function, which requires no data to be sent in. So you can see that any class method can be set up so that it can receive data or can send data back, or both, or neither. It is the class methods that provide the means by which we can access the attributes of an object (by passing a message) and together they form the **interface** of the class. In describing the interface, the crucial information that we have to specify is the type (or types) of data that the methods can receive (the **inputs**) and the type of data they can send back (the **output**).

It is important to understand here that the internal details of the methods of a class are not of any significance to other classes. The `StudentReport` class had no idea how the `calculateAverageMark` method of the `Student` class did its job – all it cared about was the result. This is important – it means that we can change the internal details of one part of a system without affecting another part. This helps us make our systems more secure, and also encourages us to reuse classes in other systems rather than starting from scratch each time. These are some of the principal benefits of encapsulation.

4.5   Classes and objects in Java

You have already seen that all Java programs must be made up of classes, and now you can see why. The notion of a class is fundamental to the object-oriented approach, and by declaring a class in Java we are able to bring into being the classes that we identified when we analysed the system. We can then declare the **instances** or **objects** that belong to that class; you will see how to do that in a moment.

In this chapter, in order to help you understand the notion of encapsulation, we are going to see how to use classes that have already been created; creating our own classes will be left till the next chapter. You will see that we do not need to know very much about the details of these classes – all we need to know about is the interface. The classes that you need can be downloaded from the website or copied from chapter 5. In order to run the programs we are developing in this chapter you don't need look at the detail of these classes, you just have to download them and use them – that is what encapsulation is all about!

4.5.1   The *Oblong* class

Let's consider a situation in which we wanted a program that created and used oblongs; maybe it is for the purposes of drawing oblongs on the screen, or for school children to use in order to practise their understanding of geometry.

Instead of writing a new Oblong class it would be very useful if we could use a ready-made class (Oblong.java) for you and you can download it from the website. We have of course made sure that the attributes of the class are not directly accessible. In order to use the class you do not need to know the specific names of the attributes, although you do need to know that they exist.

So, you need to be aware that any Oblong object can hold information about the length and the height of the oblong and that the type **double** is used for this data. An Oblong might also have other attributes that it uses for its own purpose, but anyone using the class doesn't need to know about this.

You also need to know what the class can do – its methods; but of course you do not need to know how these methods work. What you really need to know are the **inputs** and **outputs**. These are listed in table 4.1.

Table 4.1 The methods of the *Oblong* class			
Method	Description	Inputs	Output
setLength	Sets the value of the length attribute	An item of type **double**	None
setHeight	Sets the value of the height attribute	An item of type **double**	None
getLength	Sends back the value of the length attribute	None	An item of type **double**
getHeight	Sends back the value of the height attribute	None	An item of type **double**
calculateArea	Calculates and sends back the area of the oblong	None	An item of type **double**
calculatePerimeter	Calculates and sends back the perimeter of the oblong	None	An item of type **double**
Oblong	A special method called a **constructor** (see below)	Two items of data, both of type **double**, representing the length and height of the oblong respectively	

You can see from the table that one of the available methods is a special method called a **constructor**, *which always has the same name as the class*. When you create a new object this special method is always called; its function is to reserve some space in the computer's memory just big enough to hold the required object (in our case an object of the Oblong class). The person developing the class doesn't have to worry about defining the constructor if this is all that he or she wants the constructor to do. However, it is very common to find that you want the constructor to do a bit more than this when a new object is created. In the case of our Oblong class the constructor has been defined so that every time a new Oblong object is created the length and the height are set – and they are set to the values that the user of the class "sends in"; so every time you create an Oblong you have to specify its length and its height at the same time. You will see how to do that in the program below.

4.5.2   Using the *Oblong* class

Program 4.1 shows how the oblong class can be used by another class, in this case a class called OblongTester. You should make sure that your Oblong class is in the same directory as the OblongTester class, in which case your compiler will find it.

Program 4.1

```
class OblongTester
{
 public static void main(String[] args)
  {
      /* declare two variables to hold the length and height
      of the oblong as input by the user */
      double oblongLength, oblongHeight;
      // declare a reference to an Oblong object
      Oblong myOblong;
      // now get the values from the user
      System.out.print("Please enter the length of your oblong: ");
      oblongLength = EasyIn.getDouble();
      System.out.print("Please enter the height of your oblong: ");
      oblongHeight = EasyIn.getDouble();
      // create a new Oblong object
      myOblong = new Oblong(oblongLength, oblongHeight);
      /* use the various methods of the Oblong class to display
      the length, height, area and perimeter of the Oblong */
      System.out.println("Oblong length is " + myOblong.getLength());
      System.out.println("Oblong height is " + myOblong.getHeight());
      System.out.println("Oblong area is " + myOblong.calculateArea());
      System.out.println("Oblong perimeter is "
                                     + myOblong.calculatePerimeter());
      EasyIn.pause("Press <Enter> to quit");
  }
}
```

Let's analyse this program line by line. The first line is the declaration of the class, which is followed by the heading for the `main` method. The first line of the `main` method declares two variables:

```
double oblongLength, oblongHeight;
```

As you can see, these are of type **double** and they are going to be used to hold the value that the user chooses for the length and height of the oblong.

The next line introduces something new:

```
Oblong myOblong;
```

You can see that this line is similar to a declaration of a variable; however, what we are doing here is not declaring a variable of a scalar type such as **int**, but declaring the name of an *object* (`myOblong`) of the *class* (`Oblong`).

You need to be sure that you understand what this line actually does; all it does in fact is to create something called a **reference**. A reference is simply a *name* for a location in memory. At this stage we have *not* reserved space for our new `Oblong` object; all we have done is named a memory location `myOblong`, as shown in figure 4.7.

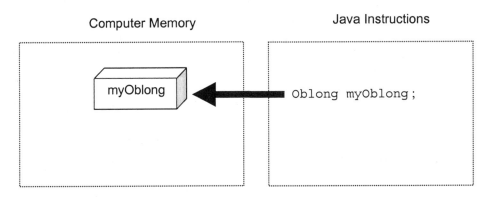

Fig 4.7   Declaring an object reference

Now of course you will be asking the question "What is going to be held in the memory location called myOblong?". We will see the answer in a moment.

Let us look at the next few lines first, though.

```
System.out.print("Please enter the length of your oblong: ");
oblongLength = EasyIn.getDouble();
System.out.print("Please enter the height of your oblong: ");
oblongHeight = EasyIn.getDouble();
```

This should be fairly familiar to you by now; we are prompting the user to enter a value for the length of the oblong, then reading the user's chosen value from the keyboard, and then doing the same thing for the height. The values entered are stored in oblongLength and oblongHeight respectively.

Now we can return to the question of what is going to be stored in the memory location myOblong. Look at this line of code:

```
myOblong = new Oblong(oblongLength, oblongHeight);
```

This is the statement that reserves space in memory for a new Oblong object. As you can see, this is done by using the keyword **new**, in conjunction with the name of the class (in this case Oblong) and some stuff in brackets. Remember what we said a while ago about a special method called a *constructor*? Well, using the class name in this way, with the keyword **new**, calls the constructor, and memory is reserved for a new Oblong object. Now, in the case of the Oblong class the people who developed it (okay, that was us!) defined their own constructor method. This method requires that two items of data get sent in, both of type **double**. You can see that they have to be put in the brackets and separated by a comma. The values in brackets are referred to as the **actual parameters** of the method (you will find out more about this in chapter 5). The Oblong constructor was defined so that when the new object is created the length and the height attributes are set − in that order − to the values that are sent in via the brackets. In our program the values that we are sending in are oblongLength and oblongHeight, the values entered by the user of the program.

There are all sorts of ways that we can define constructors (for example, in a BankAccount class we might want to start the balance at zero when the account is created) and we shall see examples of these as we go along.

But wait a minute − how do we know the location in memory where the new object is stored? Well, now we have the answer to our previous question! The location of the new object is stored in the named reference myOblong. This is illustrated in figure 4.8.

Computer Memory   Java Instructions

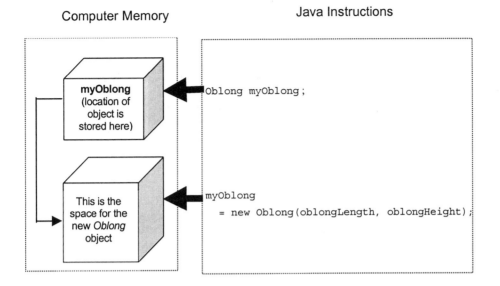

Fig 4.8   Creating a new object

In some programming languages a location like myOblong is often referred to as a pointer, because it "points" to the location of something. Now every time we want to refer to our new Oblong we can use the variable name myOblong. You may have realized that this variable does not have to stay pointing at the Oblong we just created – for example, we could create a different oblong with the **new** keyword, and make myOblong point to that.

Two things are worth noting at this point. Firstly, the process of creating a new object is often referred to as **instantiation**, because we are creating a new *instance* of a class. Secondly, you should note that, in Java, when a reference is first created it is given a special value of **null**; a **null** value indicates that no storage is allocated. We can assign a **null** value to references and test for it as in the following example:

```
Oblong myOblong;

// more code goes here

myOblong = null;
if(myOblong == null)
{
      System.out.println("No storage is allocated to this object");
}
```

Now let's look at the next line of program 4.1:

```
System.out.println("Oblong Length is " + myOblong.getLength());
```

This line displays the length of the oblong. It uses the method of Oblong called getLength. We say we are **calling** the method. When we call a method of an object we are in fact sending a message to that object as we described in section 4.4. You can see how we do this now – we use the name of the object (in this case myOblong) together with the name of the method (getLength) separated by a full stop. Notice that this time there is nothing in the brackets – we are not sending in any data, as we did when we used the constructor method. As we can see from table 4.1, the getLength method sends back **(returns)** a value (of type **double**); the value sent back from a method is called the **return value**. Because it sends back a value we can use it in the way we have here, simply placing the call to the method – myOblong.getLength() – directly in the output statement, just as if it were a variable or a fixed value. There are other ways we could have used the return value too, such as assigning it to a variable; for example, if we had declared a variable x of type double, we could assign the return value to x with the following statement:

```
x = myOblong.getLength();
```

The next three lines are similar to the first:

```
System.out.println("Oblong height is " + myOblong.getHeight());
System.out.println("Oblong area is " + myOblong.calculateArea());
System.out.println("OblongPerimeter is "+ myOblong.calculatePerimeter());
```

We have called the `getHeight` method, the `calculateArea` method and the `calculatePerimeter` method to display the height, area and perimeter of the oblong on the screen. You might have noticed that we haven't used the `setLength` and `setHeight` methods – that is because in this program we didn't wish to change the length and height once the oblong had been created – but this is not the last you will see of our `Oblong` class – and in future programs these methods will come in useful.

Finally, we use one of the `pause` methods of `EasyIn` to terminate the program.

Now we can move on to look at using some other classes. The first is not one of our own, but the built-in `String` class provided with all versions of Java.

4.6   Using the *String* class

A **string** is a sequence of any characters – letters of the alphabet, numbers, punctuation marks etc. Clearly strings are going to be very important to us in our programming – we are often going to have to store people's names and addresses, a description of a stock item, or countless other things. Ideally we would like to be able to declare variables of type `String`, just like we can with **int**s or **double**s; however, a string is not a simple scalar value like an integer so it is a bit more complicated than that. But the Java people have come to the rescue with a special `String` class.

Obviously the most important attribute of a `String` object will be the string itself, for example "hello", "goodbye", "020 8223 3000", "YP190088A" and so on. But the most interesting thing about the `String` class is the methods that are provided. We will discuss a few of them here.

Firstly, there are a number of constructors. Remember that a constructor is the method that comes into action every time we create a new object. Remember also that we can define lots of different constructors, which are distinguished from each other by what we place in the brackets.

The first constructor we will look at simply creates an empty string, so there is nothing to put in the brackets when we use it:

```
String str;
str = new String();
```

In fact it is more usual to combine these two statements into one line:

```
String str = new String();
```

Do remember, however, that this one line does two things: it names an object (`str`) and creates space in memory for it.

Now why would anyone want to create an empty string? Well, that is a good question, and it can be asked on many occasions about other objects. The answer is that it is best, if possible, to avoid leaving a reference with a `null` value. Pointing our reference to a location as soon as we declare it will prevent us from doing silly things like creating an uninitialized object and trying to use its methods (although most Java compilers would warn us about this when we tried to compile our code!).

A more useful constructor is the one that allows us to give a value to the string at the time we create it:

```
String str = new String("Hello");
```

Now we have a string with the value "Hello". Actually there is an even quicker way to create this string. As we explained in chapter 2, the assignment operator (=) is *overloaded*. You have seen that it can be used for **double**s, **int**s, **float**s and so on; each of these operations is different because, for example, the way in which **double**s are stored in the computer's memory is different to the way in which **int**s are stored. Now this has also been extended to strings – so we can conveniently use the assignment operator to create a new string as follows:

```
String str = "Hello";
```

The *String* class has a number of interesting and useful methods, and we have listed some of them in table 4.2.

Table 4.2 Some *String* methods			
Method	**Description**	**Inputs**	**Output**
length	Returns the length of the string	None	An item of type int
charAt	Accepts an integer and returns the character at the position in the string of that integer. Note that indexing starts from zero, not 1!	An item of type int	An item of type char
substring	Accepts two integers (for example m and n) and returns a chunk of the string. The chunk starts at the m and finishes at the one before n. Remember that indexing starts from zero. (Study the example below).	Two items of type int.	A String object
concat	Accepts a string and joins this to the end of the original string. The new string is then returned.	A String object	A String object
toUpperCase	Returns the original string, all upper case.	None	A String object
toLowerCase	Returns the original string, all lower case.	None	A String object
compareTo[1]	Accepts a string (say str) and compares it to the original string. It returns zero if the strings are identical, a negative number if the original string comes before str in the alphabet, and a positive number if it comes later.	A String object	An item of type int
equals[1]	Accepts an object and compares this to the original string. It returns true if these are identical, otherwise returns false.	An object of any class	A boolean value
equalsIgnoreCase[1]	Accepts a String object and compares this to the original string. It returns true if the strings are identical (ignoring case), otherwise returns false.	A String object	A boolean value
startsWith	Accepts a string (say str) and returns true if the original string starts with str and false if it does not (e.g. "hello world" starts with "h" or "he" or "hel" and so on).	A String object	A boolean value
endsWith	Accepts a string (say str) and returns true if the original string ends with str and false if it does not (e.g. "hello world" ends with "d" or "ld" or "rld" and so on).	A String object	A boolean value

---

[1]   You must never use the equality operator (==) when comparing strings; always use compareTo, equals or equalsIgnoreCase.

There are many other useful methods of the `String` class which you can look up. Program 4.2 provides examples of how you can use some of the methods listed above; the last three are left for you to experiment with in your tutorial and practical sessions.

Program 4.2

```java
class StringTest
{
  public static void main(String[] args)
  {
    // create a new string
    String str = new String();
    // get the user to enter a string
    System.out.print("Enter a string: ");
    str = EasyIn.getString();
    // display the length of the user's string
    System.out.println("The length of the string is " + str.length());
    // display the third character of the user's string
    System.out.println("The character at position 3 is "+ str.charAt(2));
    // display a selected part of the user's string
    System.out.println("Characters 2 to 4 are " + str.substring(1,4));
    // display the user's string joined with another string
    System.out.println(str.concat(" was the string entered"));
    // display the user's string in upper case
    System.out.println("This is upper case: " + str.toUpperCase());
    // display the user's string in lower case
    System.out.println("This is lower case: " + str.toLowerCase());
    EasyIn.pause("Press <Enter> to quit");
  }
}
```

A sample run from program 4.2:

```
Enter a string: Mary had a little bear
The length of the string is 22
The character at position 3 is r
Characters 2 to 4 are ary
Mary had a little bear was the string entered
This is upper case: MARY HAD A LITTLE BEAR
This is lower case: mary had a little bear
Press <Enter> to quit
```

We will now move on to explore another class that we have defined ourselves.

4.7 The *BankAccount* class

We have created a class called `BankAccount`, which you can download from the website (`BankAccount.java`), or copy from chapter 5.

This could be a very useful class in the real world, for example as part of a financial control system. Once again you do not need to look at the details of how this class is coded in order to use it. You do need to know, however, that the class has three attributes, which record the account number, the account name and the account balance. The first two of these will be `String` objects and the final one will a variable of type **double**.

The methods are listed in table 4.3.

Table 4.3 The methods of the *BankAccount* class			
Method	Description	Inputs	Output
BankAccount	A constructor. It accepts two strings and assigns them to the account number and account name respectively. It also sets the account balance to zero.	Two `String` objects	None
getAccountNumber	Returns the value of the `accountNumber` attribute	None	An item of type **double**
getAccountName	Returns the value of the `accountName` attribute	None	An item of type **double**
getBalance	Returns the value of the `balance` attribute	None	An item of type **double**
deposit	Accepts an item of type **double** and adds it to the balance	An item of type **double**	None
withdraw	Accepts an item of type **double** and subtracts it from the balance	An item of type **double**	None

A short program which uses the `BankAccount` class is shown in program 4.3. More interesting ways of using this class are left for the tutorial and practical work at the end of the chapter.

Program 4.3

```
class BankAccountTester
{
 public static void main(String[] args)
 {
   BankAccount account1
                  = new BankAccount("99786754","Martin Luther King");
   account1.deposit(1000);
   System.out.println("Account number: " + account1.getAccountNumber());
   System.out.println("Account name: " + account1.getAccountName());
   System.out.println("Current balance: " + account1.getBalance());
   EasyIn.pause("Press <Enter> to quit");
 }
}
```

The output from this program is:

```
Account number: 99786754
Account name: Martin Luther King
Current balance: 1000.0
Press <Enter> to quit
```

Finally, here's one to whet your appetite for the future!

4.8   The *SmileyFace* class

This class – `SmileyFace.java` – is rather different, and we have included it in order to give you your first taste of graphics programming. It has one method only, a special method called `paint`. This method is associated with graphical applications and is automatically called when the application starts. So you won't see a statement that calls the `paint` method in our program.

As you can imagine, there is quite a lot to graphical programming, and this is really just a first opportunity to see what might be possible in the future. The `paint` method of `SmileyFace` has been defined – as you might expect – to draw a smiley face like the one in figure 4.9.

Fig 4.9   The *SmileyFace* class running in a frame

Program 4.4 below is used to test out the `SmileyFace` class. You will need to download `SmileyFace.java` in order to run it (or copy it from chapter 5).

Program 4.4

```
import java.awt.*;

class RunFace
{
    public static void main(String[] args)
    {
        Frame frame = new Frame();
        SmileyFace face = new SmileyFace();
        frame.setSize(260,200);
        frame.setBackground(Color.yellow);
        frame.add(face);
        frame.setVisible(true);
    }
}
```

Let's take a look at this. First we have something called an **import** statement:

```
import java.awt.*;
```

This line tells the compiler that we want it to compile, along with our own program, the contents of a Java **package**. A package is the name that Java gives to its libraries. Packages keep together a number of different but related files, and you are able to create your own packages if you wish; some of you, depending on what compiler you are using, will have noticed that the compiler puts all your work into a package for you. Using the asterisk at the end means that everything in that package is imported. This particular package, java.awt, is the **Abstract Window Toolkit (AWT)**. It contains lots of stuff that you need for graphics programming and you will learn much more about it in chapter 9. But we are interested in it now because it contains a class called Frame, an instance of which we have created with the following line:

```
Frame frame = new Frame();
```

A Frame is a standard graphic component; whenever we create a graphical application we need to create a frame to run it in (this is not the case with an *applet* because this can run in the browser window).

One problem with the Frame class is that it doesn't provide a built-in method to close the window when we click on the little "x" in the top right-hand corner. Now, it is perfectly possible to write our own code for this, but it is not easy to understand unless you have learnt a lot more about Java programming than you have so far; so at this stage we haven't included it as we are trying to keep things simple for now. Therefore – if you are in a Windows environment – just close the frame by clicking on the black text screen and pressing Ctrl+C (or use equivalent commands if you are not using Windows)[2].

The next line creates a new SmileyFace object:

```
SmileyFace face = new SmileyFace();
```

We then set the size for our frame:

```
frame.setSize(260,200);
```

---

[2]   Some Java compilers provide an extension of the Frame class with a built-in method to close the window.

This sends the width and height of the frame (measured in pixels[3]), in that order, into the setSize method of Frame.

The next line sets the background colour of our frame to yellow.

```
frame.setBackground(Color.yellow);
```

The SmileyFace class has been designed in such a way as to allow an object of this class to be added to a frame. We do that with this line which uses the add method of Frame:

```
frame.add(face);
```

Finally we make our frame visible with the setVisible method.

```
frame.setVisible(true);
```

---

[3]   Pixels are the little coloured dots that make up any video display or graphics screen.

Tutorial exercises

1. Identify two reasons why object-oriented development is rapidly taking the place of structured methods for developing software.

2. With the help of pseudocode, design a program that performs in the following way:

    *   when the program starts two bank accounts are created, using names and numbers which are written into the code;
    *   the user is then asked to enter an account number, followed by an amount to deposit in that account;
    *   the balance of the appropriate account is then updated accordingly – or if an incorrect account number was entered a message to this effect is displayed;
    *   the user is then asked if he or she wishes to make more deposits;
    *   if the user answers 'yes', the process continues;
    *   if the user answers 'no', then both account details (account number, account name and balance) are displayed;
    *   the program then waits for a press of the *Enter* key before terminating.

Practical work

You will need to have downloaded the following classes (or you can copy them from chapter 5):

*   Oblong.java
*   BankAccount.java
*   SmileyFace.java

1. Adapt program 4.1 so that the user inputs the length and height of two oblongs, and sees a message on the screen saying which one, if any, has the greater area.

2. Write a program that asks the user to input two strings, and then tests the strings to see whether they are identical or, if not, which comes first in the alphabet.

3. a) Write a program that asks the user to input a string, followed by a single character, and then tests whether the string starts with that character.

    b) Make your program work so that the case of the character is irrelevant.

4. Implement the program you designed in question 2 of the tutorial exercises.

5. Type, compile and run the RunFace program (program 4.4).

5 Implementing classes

Learning objectives

By the end of this chapter you should be able to:

- write the Java code for a specified class;
- explain the meaning of the term **polymorphism**;
- code simple graphic shapes in Java;
- describe the use of the **static** keyword;
- explain how **parameters** are passed to class methods in Java;
- use the type conversion methods of **wrapper** classes.

5.1 Introduction

This chapter is arguably the most important so far, because it is here that you are going to learn how to develop the classes that you need for your programs. You are already familiar with the concept of a class, and the idea that we can create objects that belong to a class; in the last chapter you saw how to create and use objects; you saw that we could hide or encapsulate information in a class; and you saw how we could use the methods of a class without knowing anything about how they work.

In this chapter you will look inside the classes you have studied to see how they are constructed, and how you can write classes of your own.

5.2 Implementing classes in Java

In the last chapter you saw that a class consists of:

- a set of **attributes** (the data);
- a set of **methods** which can access or change those attributes.

To help you to understand how we actually implement this in Java we are going to look at the code for the classes we used in chapter 4.

5.2.1 The *Oblong* class

We will start with the Oblong class. You should recall the notation for specifying classes that we introduced in the very first chapter.

Let's use this notation to specify our `Oblong` class, as shown in figure 5.1.

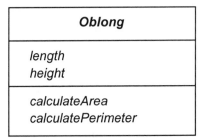

Fig 5.1   The specification of the *Oblong* class

Now we can go on to *design* this class (if you have forgotten the difference between specification and design then look back at the first chapter). This is shown in figure 5.2.

Oblong
length *height*
Oblong *setLength* *setHeight* *getLength* *getHeight* *calculateArea* *calculatePerimeter*

Fig 5.2   The design of the *Oblong* class

Notice that when we design our classes we tend to enter more detail then we do when we are initially specifying them. So when we drew the class diagram for the `Student` class discussed in the previous chapter (figure 4.4) we didn't bother to include such methods as `getStudentName` or `getStudentNumber`. These "basic" methods that do nothing more than access the attributes are normally not listed until we start to think about the design of our class; the same is true for the constructor.

So now that we are designing our `Oblong` class for implementation we can include the following in our class diagram:

- the constructor (`Oblong`);
- some methods that allow us to assign values (in other words **write**) to the attributes – these are the methods `setLength` and `setHeight`;
- some methods to send back (in other words **read**) the values of the attributes – these are the methods `getLength` and `getHeight`.

It is not always the case that we choose to supply methods such as `setLength` or `setHeight`, which allow us to *change* the attributes. Sometimes we set up our class so that the only way that we can assign values to the attributes is via the constructor. This would mean that the values of the `length` and `height` could be set only at the time a new `Oblong` object was created, and could not be changed after that. Whether or not you want to provide a means of writing to individual attributes depends on the nature of the system you are developing and should be discussed with potential users. However, we believe that it is a good policy to provide write access to only those attributes that clearly require to be changed during the object's lifetime, and we have taken this approach throughout this book. In this case we have included "set" attributes for `length` and `height` because we are going to need them in chapter 9.

Now that we have the basic design of the `Oblong` class we can go ahead and write the Java code for it:

The *Oblong* class

```java
class Oblong
{
    // the attributes are declared first
    private double length;
    private double height;

    // then the methods

    // the constructor
    public Oblong(double lengthIn, double heightIn)
    {
        length = lengthIn;
        height = heightIn;
    }



    // the next method allows us to "read" the length attribute
    public double getLength()
    {
        return length;
    }

    // the next method allows us to "read" the height attribute
    public double getHeight()
    {
        return height;
    }
```

```java
        // the next method allows us to "write" to the length attribute
        public void setLength(double lengthIn)
        {
            length = lengthIn;
        }

        // the next method allows us to "write" to the height attribute
        public void setHeight(double heightIn)
        {
            height = heightIn;
        }

        // this method returns the area of the oblong
        public double calculateArea()
        {
            return length * height;
        }

        // this method returns the perimeter of the oblong
        public double calculatePerimeter()
        {
            return 2 * (length + height);
        }
    }
```

Let's take a closer look at this. The first line declares the `Oblong` class. Once this is done, we declare the attributes. An `Oblong` object will need attributes to hold values for the length and the height of the oblong, and these will be of type **double**.

The declaration of the attributes in the `Oblong` class is as follows:

```java
private double length;
private double height;
```

You can now see how, in Java, the keyword **private** is used to restrict access to these attributes. Once they are declared as **private**, the only way to get at them is via the class methods. Take a look back at table 4.1 to remind yourself of the class methods that we are now going to define within our `Oblong` class.

First comes the constructor. You should recall that it has the same name as the class.

```
public Oblong(double lengthIn, double heightIn)
{
    length = lengthIn;
    height = heightIn;
}
```

The first thing to notice is that this method is declared as **public**. Unlike the attributes, we want our methods to be accessible from outside so that they can be called by methods of other classes.

Do you remember our saying in chapter 4 that this constructor is a *user-defined*[1] constructor? We are defining it so that when a new Oblong object is created (with the keyword **new**) then not only do we get some space reserved in memory, but we also get some other stuff occurring; in this case two assignment statements are executed. The first assigns the value lengthIn to the length attribute, and the second assigns the value heightIn to the heightIn attribute.

But what exactly are these variables lengthIn and heightIn? You can see that the first time they appear is in the brackets. The variables in the brackets are called the **formal parameters** of the method, and they are the variables that *receive* the values that we send into the method when we call it. Cast your mind back to program 4.1, the OblongTester program, when we used the following line to call the constructor:

```
myOblong = new Oblong(oblongLength, oblongHeight);
```

The user of the OblongTester program had been asked to enter values for oblongLength and oblongHeight and with the line above we call the constructor and send in these values by placing them in the brackets. As we told you in chapter 4, the variables oblongLength and oblongHeight are referred to as the **actual parameters** (also known as **arguments**) of the calling method; their values are copied to the formal parameters lengthIn and heightIn in that order.

You should be able to see that the order in which we send values to the parameters of a method is important; they are copied in the order they are sent. You can see that the Oblong constructor has been defined so that it requires the length followed by the height – if we sent them the other way round, then the length would be copied to the height attribute and vice versa.

---

[1] Here the word *user* is referring to the person *writing* the program, not the person using it!

Notice also that it is possible to send values into a method only by listing the right number of variables of the right type. With the single constructor defined for `Oblong`, we would get compiler error messages if we tried to call the constructor with any of the following lines:

```
// all these would result in compiler errors:

myOblong = new Oblong(oblongLength);
// one variable too few

myOblong = new Oblong(10.0, 20.0, 30.0);
// one variable too many

myOblong = new Oblong(10.0, 'c');
// second variable of wrong type (char instead of double)
```

One more thing about constructors: in chapter 4 we told you that if you don't define your own constructor then a "default" constructor is provided – which does nothing more than reserve space in memory for the new object. It is called by using the constructor name (which is the same as the class name) with empty brackets. Now once we have defined our own constructors, this default constructor is no longer automatically available. If we want it to be available then we have explicitly to re-define it. In the `Oblong` case we would define it as:

```
public Oblong()
{
}
```

You may be wondering how the program knows which constructor to call, since we now have two of them. The answer is simple – it knows by matching the actual parameters in the brackets of the calling function to the formal parameters in the constructor.

So this statement would call our original constructor:

```
myOblong = new Oblong(10.0, 20.0);
```

whereas this one would call our newly defined default constructor:

```
myOblong = new Oblong();
```

This idea of having two or even more methods in the same class with the same name is not confined to constructors. We can have as many methods as we like with the same name as long as each one has a different set of parameters. This technique is a very important feature of object-oriented programming languages and is called **polymorphism**, which means *having many forms*. We are not done with polymorphism here – we will come across it again in future chapters.

Now let's take a look at the definition of the next method, getLength. The purpose of this method is simply to send back the value of the length attribute:

```
public double getLength()
{
    return length;
}
```

Once again you can see that the method has been declared as **public**, enabling it to be accessed by methods of other classes.

After the word **public** comes the word **double**, which states the *type* of the method. At first you may wonder why a method should have a type. The answer is that as we have seen, a method can send back or *return* a value, and the *type* of the method (which must be stated before the method name) is the type of the value it returns, in this case **double**. If a method does not return anything, its return type is declared as **void**.

After the word **double** comes the name of the method, getName, followed by a pair of brackets. There is nothing in these brackets (that is, the method has no parameters) because we do not need to pass any information into this method.

The body of the method is defined between the curly brackets. In this case the code consists of the single line:

```
return length;
```

This line sends the value of the length attribute back to the calling function. Notice also that the word **return** performs another very important function as well as sending back the value; it also ends the method! So whenever a **return** statement is encountered in a method, the method ends and control of the program goes back to the function that called it.

Let's just remind ourselves how we called this method in program 4.1. We did it with the following line:

```
System.out.println("Oblong Length is " + myOblong.getLength());
```

The next method is the getHeight method, which is defined in exactly the same way. This is followed by the setLength method:

```
public void setLength(double lengthIn)
{
    length = lengthIn;
}
```

This method does not return a value, so its return type is **void**. However, it does require a parameter of type **double** that it will assign to the length attribute. We have called this parameter lengthIn.[2] The body of the method consists of a single line which assigns the value of lengthIn to the length attribute.

The next method, setHeight, behaves in the same way in respect of the height attribute. After this comes the calculateArea method:

```
public double calculateArea()
{
    return length * height;
}
```

---

[2] We are going to adopt the convention of ending all our parameter names with the suffix In.

Once again there are no formal parameters, as this method does not need any data in order to do its job; it is of type **double** since it returns an item of this type. The actual code is just one line, namely the statement that returns the area of the oblong, calculated by multiplying the value of the length attribute by the value of the height attribute.

The calculatePerimeter method is similar.

In a moment we shall take a look at some of the other classes we encountered in chapter 4. But before we do that we can take a minute to think about the way we design our classes. In figure 5.2 we added some detail to the specification of an oblong by including in our class diagram all the methods of the Oblong class that were going to be implemented – even the "basic" ones.

As our understanding has increased we can now include more information, namely the types of the attributes, as well as the return types of the method and the types of the parameters that we pass to the method. Figure 5.3 shows the specification of the Oblong class with this detail added. As we explained in chapter 1, we are going to make our diagrams conform to the standard UML notation for specifying and designing classes. Thus for each method, the parameters are shown in the brackets and the return types appear after the brackets, separated by a colon.

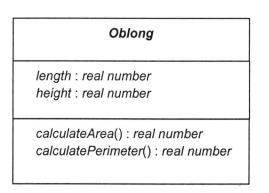

Fig 5.3   The UML specification of the *Oblong* class

Notice that when we are specifying the class we do not use Java-specific type names like **int**, **double** or **float**, because type names vary from one programming language to the next, and, although *we* will be using Java, a good specification should lend itself to being implemented in more than one programming language.

However, at the design stage we can make the decision that we will be using a specific language – Java in our case – so it is okay to use Java type names as shown in figure 5.4.

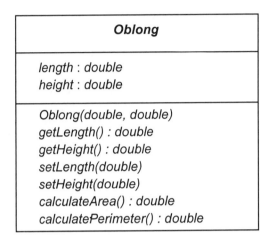

Fig 5.4   The detailed design of the *Oblong* class

5.2.2   The *BankAccount* class

Cast your mind back to program 4.3, which used our *BankAccount* class. The design is shown in figure 5.5.

BankAccount
accountNumber : String accountName : String balance : double
BankAccount (String, String) getAccountNumber() : String getAccountName() : String getBalance() : double deposit(double) withdraw(double)

Fig 5.5 The *BankAccount* class

We can now inspect the code for this class:

The *BankAccount* class

```java
class BankAccount
{
    // the attributes
    private String accountNumber;
    private String accountName;
    private double balance;

    // the methods

    // the constructor
    public BankAccount(String numberIn, String nameIn)
    {
        accountNumber = numberIn;
        accountName = nameIn;
        balance = 0;
    }

    // methods to read the attributes
    public String getAccountName()
    {
        return accountName;
    }
    public String getAccountNumber()
    {
        return accountNumber;
    }
    public double getBalance()
    {
        return balance;
    }

    // methods to deposit and withdraw money
    public void deposit(double amountIn)
    {
        balance = balance + amountIn;
    }
    public void withdraw(double amountIn)
    {
        balance = balance - amountIn;
    }
}
```

Now that we are getting the idea of how to define a class in Java, we do not need to go into so much detail in our analysis and explanation.

The first three lines declare the attributes of the class, and are as we would expect:

```
private String accountNumber;
private String accountName;
private double balance;
```

One thing to notice, however, is that accountNumber and accountName are declared as Strings; it is perfectly possible for the attributes of one class to be objects of another class.

Now the constructor method, which has an interesting additional feature:

```
public BankAccount(String numberIn, String nameIn)
{
    accountNumber = numberIn;
    accountName = nameIn;
    balance = 0;
}
```

You can see that when a new object of the BankAccount class is created, the accountName and accountNumber will be assigned the values of the parameters passed to the method and also the balance will be assigned the value zero; this makes sense because when someone opens a new account there is a zero balance until a deposit is made.

The next three methods, getAccountNumber, getAccountName and getBalance, are all set up so that we can read the values of the corresponding attributes (which of course have been declared as **private**).

After these we have the deposit method:

```
public void deposit(double amountIn)
{
    balance = balance + amountIn;
}
```

Notice that this method does not return a value; it is therefore declared to be of type **void**. It does however require that a value is sent in (the amount to be deposited), and therefore has one parameter – of type **double** – in the brackets. As you would expect with this method, the action consists of adding the deposit to the `balance` attribute of the `BankAccount` object.

The withdraw method behaves in a similar manner, but the amount is subtracted from the current balance.

5.2.3   The *SmileyFace* class

If you remember, when we ran this class in a frame we got the graphic shown in figure 5.6.

Fig 5.6   The *SmileyFace* class running in a frame

Take a look at the code:

The *SmileyFace* class

```java
import java.awt.*;
import java.applet.*;

class SmileyFace extends Applet
{
    public void paint(Graphics g)
    {
        g.setColor(Color.red);
        g.drawOval(85,45,75,75); // the face
        g.setColor(Color.blue);
        g.drawOval(100,65,10,10); // the right eye
        g.drawOval(135,65,10,10); // the left eye
        g.drawArc(102,85,40,25,-0,-180); // the mouth
        g.drawString("Smiley Face",90,155);
    }
}
```

There are a number of new concepts here. First, let's look at the import clauses:

```java
import java.awt.*;
import java.applet.*;
```

As we saw in chapter 4, the first of these imports the standard Java **Abstract Window Toolkit** (java.awt) which supplies the graphical components that we need; as we have said, you will find out much more about this in chapter 9.

The second package, java.applet, supplies support for *applets*; remember, applets are applications which run in a browser; they do not need a **main** method to run them, and they have special methods which are invoked when they become visible – more about this in chapter 12.

In this book we will make all our graphical applications kinds of applets. By doing this we can easily add them to a frame and run them as applications, or alternatively run them as applets in a browser, as we shall see in chapter 12.

This brings us to the next line:

```java
class SmileyFace extends Applet
```

Our normal class declaration has the words **extends** Applet after it. The word **extends** has a special meaning that you will learn about in chapter 7, but for now it is good enough just to understand that our SmileyFace class is taking the standard Java Applet class and adding stuff to it.

Now we come to the paint method:

```
public void paint (Graphics g)
{
    g.setColor(Color.red);
    g.drawOval(85,45,75,75); // the face
    g.setColor(Color.blue);
    g.drawOval(100,65,10,10); // the right eye
    g.drawOval(135,65,10,10); // the left eye
    g.drawArc(102,85,40,25,0,-180); // the mouth
    g.drawString("Smiley Face",90,155);
}
```

This special method is a method of a basic graphics class called Component, of which Applet itself is an extension; you will find out a lot more about this in chapter 9 when we study graphics programming in detail.

When the window that displays the component becomes visible, the paint method is called. When this happens, an object of a core Java class called Graphics (which comes with the AWT package) is automatically sent in to this method. A Graphics object has lots of useful methods.

The first one sets the foreground colour:

```
g.setColor(Color.red);
```

Then we use the drawOval method of the Graphics class to draw our circles. The first of these draws the big circle for the face itself:

```
g.drawOval(85,45,75,75);
```

The drawOval method takes four integer parameters. Referring to these as x, y, l, h, the oval that gets drawn fits into an imaginary rectangle that starts at position (x,y), and is l pixels long and h pixels high. This is illustrated in figure 5.7.

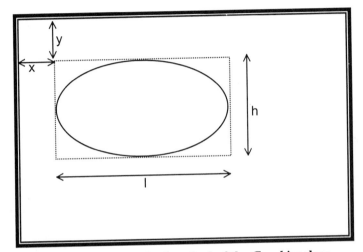

Fig 5.7   The _drawOval_ method of the _Graphics_ class

Notice that since we want a circle, we have made the values of l and h equal.

After we have drawn the big circle, we set the colour to blue and draw the right eye and left eye respectively:

```
g.setColor(Color.blue);
g.drawOval(100,65,10,10);
g.drawOval(135,65,10,10);
```

The next line draws the mouth:

```
g.drawArc(102,85,40,25,0,-180);
```

This requires some explanation. As you can see, this method requires six parameters, all integers. We shall call them x, y, 1, h, α, θ. The first four define an imaginary rectangle as above. The arc is drawn so that its centre is the centre of this rectangle, as shown in figure 5.8.

The next two parameters, α and θ, represent angles. The first, α, is the start angle – measured from an imaginary horizontal line pointing to the "quarter-past-three" position (representing zero degrees). The next, θ, is the finish angle. If θ is positive then the arc is drawn by rotating from the start position in an anti-clockwise direction; if it is negative we rotate in a clockwise direction. If this is not clear, you should try some experiments; play about with the SmileyFace class and see what happens.

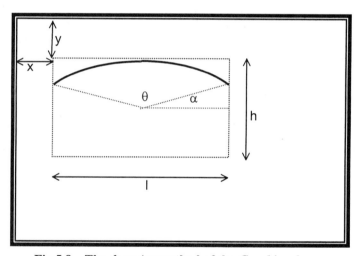

Fig 5.8   The *drawArc* method of the *Graphics* class

The final line draws the string "Smiley Face" in the graphics window at the coordinates (90,155).

```
g.drawString("Smiley Face",90,155);
```

Look back at program 4.4 to remind yourself how we show this graphic in a frame.

You now have the basics of how to write the code for a Java class, and you can now move on to learn some important new concepts that will help you to refine your classes.

5.3   The *static* keyword

You might already have noticed the keyword **static** in front of the names of methods or attributes in some Java classes. A word such as this (as well as the words **public** and **private**) is called a **modifier**.

Let's explore what this **static** modifier does. Consider the BankAccount class that we discussed earlier in the chapter. Say we wanted to have an additional method which added interest, at the current rate, to the customer's balance. It would be useful to have an attribute called interestRate to hold the value of the current rate of interest. But of course the interest rate is the same for any customer – and if it changes we want it to change for every customer in the bank; in other words for every object of the class. We can achieve this by declaring the variable as **static**. An attribute declared as **static** is a *class* attribute; any changes that are made to it are made to all the objects in the class.

We have rewritten our BankAccount class as shown below; the new items have been emboldened. Notice that we have included three new methods as well as the new **static** variable interestRate. The first two of these – setInterestRate and getInterestRate – are the methods that allow us to read and write to our new attribute. The third – addInterestRate – is the method that adds the interest to the customer's balance.

The modified *BankAccount* class

```
class BankAccount2
{
    private String accountNumber;
    private String accountName;
    private double balance;
    private static double interestRate;

    public BankAccount(String numberIn, String nameIn)
    {
            accountNumber = numberIn;
            accountName = nameIn;
            balance = 0;
    }
```

```
        public String getAccountName()
        {
                return accountName;
        }
        public String getAccountNumber()
        {
                return accountNumber;
        }
        public double getBalance()
        {
                return balance;
        }
        public void deposit(double amountIn)
        {
                balance = balance + amountIn;
        }
        public void withdraw(double amountIn)
        {
                balance = balance - amountIn;
        }
        public void setInterestRate(double rateIn)
        {
                interestRate = rateIn;
        }
        public double getInterestRate()
        {
                return interestRate;
        }
        public void addInterest()
        {
                balance = balance + (balance * interestRate)/100;
        }
}
```

Program 5.1 uses this modified version of the BankAccount class.

Program 5.1

```java
class BankAccountTester2
{
    public static void main(String[] args)
    {
        // create a bank account
        BankAccount account1 = new BankAccount("99786754","Nelson Mandela");
        // create another bank account
        BankAccount account2 =  new BankAccount("99887776","Marie Curie");
        // make a deposit into the first account
        account1.deposit(1000);
        // make a deposit into the second account
        account2.deposit(2000);
        // set the interest rate - we could have chosen account1
        account2.setInterestRate(10);
        // add interest to account 1
        account1.addInterest();
        // display the account details
        System.out.println("Account number: " + account1.getAccountNumber());
        System.out.println("Account name: " + account1.getAccountName());
        System.out.println("Interest Rate " + account1.getInterestRate());
        System.out.println("Current balance: " + account1.getBalance());
        System.out.println(); // blank line
        System.out.println("Account number: " + account2.getAccountNumber());
        System.out.println("Account name: " + account2.getAccountName());
        System.out.println("Interest Rate " + account2.getInterestRate());
        System.out.println("Current balance: " + account2.getBalance());
        System.out.println();
        EasyIn.pause("Press <Enter> to quit");
    }
}
```

Take a closer look at the first four lines of the main method of program 5.1. We have created two new bank accounts which we have called account1 and account2, and have assigned account numbers and names to them at the time they were created (via the constructor). We have then deposited amounts of 1000 and 2000 respectively into each of these accounts.

Now look at the next two lines:

```
account2.setInterestRate(10);
account1.addInterest();
```

The first of these lines sets the interest rate to 10. We have called the setInterestRate method from account2. However, because interestRate has been declared as a **static** variable this change is effective for any object of the class. So we should expect the interest rate to change for account1 as well. Therefore, when we add interest to this account as we do with the next line we should expect it to be calculated with an interest rate of 10, giving us a new balance of 1100.

This is exactly what we get, as can be seen from the output below:

```
Account number: 99786754
Account name: Nelson Mandela
Interest rate: 10.0
Current balance: 1100.0

Account number: 99887776
Account name: Marie Curie
Interest rate: 10.0
Current balance: 2000.0

Press <Enter> to quit
```

The above example shows that it doesn't matter which object's setInterestRate method is called – the same effect is achieved whether it is account1 or account2, because they are changing a **static** attribute. It would make more sense if there were a way to invoke this method without reference to a specific object; and so there is!

All we have to do is to declare our setInterestRate method as **static** as shown below:

```
public static void setInterestRate(double rateIn)
{
     interestRate = rateIn;
}
```

This turns our method into a *class* method; it does not refer to any specific object. We can call a class method by using the class name instead of the object name. So to set the interest rate to 15, for example, for all objects of the BankAccount class, we could do the following:

```
BankAccount.setInterestRate(15);
```

The getInterestRate method could also be declared as static:

```
public static double getInterestRate()
{
      return interestRate;
}
```

Class methods can very useful indeed and we shall see further examples of them in this chapter. You should notice, by the way, that you have already been using **static** methods extensively – all the methods of the EasyIn class are **static** methods – and that is why you have been using the class name – EasyIn – to call them! And of course we have always declared our main method as **static** – because this method obviously belongs to the class and to a specific object.

Incidentally, it is conventional when producing UML diagrams to underline the names of class attributes and methods; you will see an example of this in our case study in chapter 10.

5.4   More on parameter passing

We talked about the notion of passing parameters to methods in section 5.2. There are a couple of very important points that you need to take note of here. Firstly, you should be clear that when a parameter is passed to a method all that is happening is that a copy is made of the value of this parameter somewhere else in the computer's memory, and this value can be used by the method for whatever purpose is required – the original value of the variable is *not* changed.

This is illustrated by the following example, where we have defined a class called ParameterTest that has a single method called treble. This method (which has been declared as static so that we just have to use the class name) accepts an integer i and multiplies it by 3.

The *ParameterTest* class

```
class ParameterTest
{
    public static void treble(int i)
    {
        i = 3 * i;
    }
}
```

Program 5.2 uses this class. It has a `main` method in which an integer `testInteger` is declared and given the value 20; this variable is then sent to the `treble` method of `parameterTest`. The value of `testInteger` is then displayed.

Program 5.2

```
class RunParameterTest
{
    public static void main(String[] args)
    {
        int testInteger = 20;
        ParameterTest.treble(testInteger);
        // will the integer now be trebled?
        System.out.println("The value of the integer is " + testInteger);
        EasyIn.pause("Press <Enter> to quit");
    }
}
```

If you run this program you will see that the integer has not been changed, and we get the following output, showing that the value of `testInteger` is unaltered:

```
The value of the integer is 20
```

It is interesting, however, to note that some methods receive objects rather than intrinsic variables. Let's write another method for our `ParameterTest` class which takes an object of the `BankAccount` class which we defined earlier, and which we will call `objectTest`. This method deposits an amount of 1000 into the account.

```
public static void objectTest (BankAccount account)
{
     account.deposit(1000);
}
```

Program 5.3 creates a *BankAccount* object and sends it to this method.

Program 5.3

```
class RunParameterTest2
{
   public static void main(String[] args)
   {
      BankAccount testAccount = new BankAccount ("1", "Muhammad Ali");
      /* now we send the object to the objectTest method of
      ParameterTest */
      ParameterTest.objectTest (testAccount);
      System.out.println("Account Number: "
                                       + testAccount.getAccountNumber());
      System.out.println("Account Name: " + testAccount.getAccountName());
      System.out.println("Balance: " + testAccount.getBalance());
      EasyIn.pause("Press <Enter> to finish");
   }
}
```

The output from this program is as follows:

```
Account Number: 1
Account Name: Muhammad Ali
Balance: 1000
```

You can see that the deposit has successfully been made. This is because what was sent to the method was, of course, a reference to a BankAccount object. The object in question can be "traced" and its methods invoked in the usual way.

5.5 Wrapper classes

The final topic of this chapter has the seemingly strange name of **wrapper** classes. There are times when instead of wanting to use a basic scalar type to represent such things as integers and real numbers you might want to use a class instead. For every intrinsic type, Java provides a corresponding class – the name of the class is similar to the basic type, but begins with a capital letter – for example `Integer`, `Character`, `Float`, `Double`. They are called *wrappers* because they "wrap" a *class* around the basic *type*. So an object of the **`Integer`** class, for example, holds an integer value, and also has some useful methods.

You might be wondering why such classes are necessary. One of the main reasons is for their methods. There are a number of methods provided with each wrapper, some of which are class methods, and the most common use of these is to convert from one type to another. You will find that the most often-needed conversion is from strings to numbers and vice versa, particularly when writing graphics programs. This is because when a user enters something in a box on the screen this is always read as a `String`. If whatever is entered is a number that needs to be used in a calculation, then we first have to convert it to the appropriate type such as **int** or **double**. The methods of the wrapper classes are used for this purpose. Examples of these methods are provided in the programs that follow.

Program 5.4 uses the `parseInt` method of the `Integer` class to convert a `String` to an **int**; to prove that it really is an integer, the program computes its square and displays it!

Program 5.4

```
class StringToInteger
{
    public static void main(String[] args)
    {
        String s;
        int i;
        s = "10";
        i = Integer.parseInt(s); // convert the string to an integer
        System.out.print(i * i); // 100 will be displayed
        EasyIn.pause();
    }
}
```

To convert a `String` to a **double** you can use the `parseDouble` method of the `Double` class – *but*, for some reason, this is only available in the latest version of Java. If you are using an earlier version you have to do it as shown in program 5.5.

Program 5.5

```
class StringToDouble
{
   public static void main(String[] args)
   {
        String s;
        double d;
        Double D;
        s = "10.0";
        D = new Double(s); // create a new object of the Double class
        d = D.doubleValue(); // get the actual double value
        System.out.print(d * d); // 100.0 will be displayed
        EasyIn.pause();
   }
}
```

You can see that we have first to create a new object of the class `Double`. We do this with one of the constructors of the `Double` class:

```
D = new Double(s);
```

This constructor accepts a `String` object and creates a `Double` object which holds the number represented by the `String`.

Now we can use the `doubleValue` method of the `Double` class to send us the actual value that the object holds and assign this to an ordinary **double** variable:

```
d = D.doubleValue();
```

If this seems like a bit of a business then at least there is a quicker way of doing it the other way round. If for any reason we need to convert an **integer** or a **double** to a string we can cheat! We can just concatenate the number onto an empty string – because using the "+" operator acting upon a `String` and a scalar type converts the scalar type to a `String`. So we could write:

```
String s = "" + 3;
```

or:

```
String s = "" + 3.12;
```

or even:

```
double d = 10.3;
int i = 20;
String s = "" + i + d;
```

Tutorial exercises

1. Explain how encapsulation is achieved in the Java language.

2. Explain the meaning of the following terms:

   - polymorphism;
   - a **static** attribute;
   - a **static** method;
   - actual parameters;
   - formal parameters;
   - wrapper classes.

3. Imagine that a developer requires a class called Circle. An object of this class must hold the value of its radius and its position on the screen – these values, which are all whole numbers, should be set only at the time a circle is created and need not be changed thereafter. A Circle object must be capable of reporting its area and its circumference. It should also have a paint method which draws the specified circle on a graphics screen, with the area and circumference printed below it as shown:

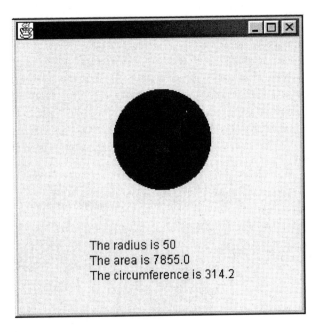

The radius is 50
The area is 7855.0
The circumference is 314.2

Design the class using UML notation.

Practical work

1. The diagram below represents the design for the *Student* class that we discussed in chapter 4.

Student
studentNumber : String studentName : String markForMaths : int markForEnglish : int markForScience : int
Student(String, String) getNumber() : String getName() : String enterMarks(int, int, int) getMathsMark() : int getEnglishMark() : int getScienceMark() : int calculateAverageMark() : double

   a) Write the code for the Student class. You should note that in order to ensure that a **double** is returned from the calculateAverageMark method you should specifically divide the total of the three marks by 3.0 and not simply by 3 (look back at chapter 2 to remind yourself why this is the case).

   b) Write a tester class to test out your student class; it should create two or three students, and use the methods of the student class to test whether they work according to the specification.

2. Implement the Circle class that you designed in tutorial question 3. To draw the circle you should use the fillOval method which works in the same way as drawOval. You can run the class in a frame with the code shown below. We suggest that you display your first string at (75, 210) – after you have your program working you can try changing some of the settings.

```java
import java.awt.*;
class RunCircle
{
    public static void main(String[] args)
    {
        Frame frame = new Frame();
        Circle myCircle = new Circle(100,50,50);
        frame.setSize(300,300);
        frame.setBackground(Color.yellow);
        frame.add(myCircle);
        frame.setVisible(true);
    }
}
```

6 Arrays and collection classes

Learning objectives

By the end of this chapter you should be able to:

- create arrays of scalar types;
- create arrays of objects;
- use the `length` attribute of arrays;
- use arrays as parameters to methods;
- develop collection classes using arrays of scalar types and arrays of objects.

6.1   Introduction

In the previous chapters we have shown you how to create simple variables from the basic scalar types (such as **int** and **char**), and objects from classes (such as String and Student). In each case we created as many variables or objects as we needed. How, though, would you deal with the situation in which you had to create and handle a very large number of variables or objects?

An obvious approach would be just to declare as many variables or objects as you need. This sounds reasonable – but it is not as straightforward as it might seem. Let's assume that these items are closely related to each other, like the maximum daily temperature readings in a week or details of all students in a group. You'd probably wish to process these items together. For example entering all the temperature readings, or displaying details of all students.

Declaring a larger number of variables or objects is a nuisance but simple enough. For example, let's start to consider a very simple application that records seven temperature readings (one for each day of the week). As this application is quite small we will just develop it within a `main` method for now.

```
class TemperatureReadings
{
    public static void main(String[] args)
    { // declare 7 variables to hold readings
        double temperature1, temperature2, temperature3, temperature4,
                            temperature5, temperature6, temperature7;

     // more code will go here

    }
}
```

Here we have declared seven variables each of type **double** (as temperatures will be recorded as real numbers). So far so good. Now to write some code that allows the user to enter these temperatures. Getting one temperature is easy:

```
System.out.println("max temperature for day 1 ?");
temperature1 = EasyIn.getDouble( );
```

But how would you write the code to get the second temperature, the third temperature and all the remaining temperatures? Well, you could repeat the above pair of lines for each temperature entered, but surely you've got better things to do with your time!

Essentially you want to repeat the same pair of lines seven times. You already know that a **for** loop is useful when repeating lines of code a fixed number of times. Maybe you could try using a **for** loop here?

```
for (int i=1; i<=7; i++)// try this?
{
    System.out.println("max temperature for day " +i);
    temperature1 = EasyIn.getDouble( );
}
```

This looks like a neat solution. Unfortunately it won't do what you want it to do. Can you see what the problem is?

The problem is that each time a temperature is entered, it is placed in the same variable, temperature1.

```
temperature1 = EasyIn.getDouble( );
```

When the loop finishes, this variable will contain only the last temperature entered, and all the other variables will not have a temperature stored in them at all! As things stand there is no way around this, as each variable has a *distinct* name.

Ideally we would like each variable to be given the *same* name (temperature, say) so that we could use a loop here, but we would like some way of being able to distinguish between each variable, say by means of an index (temperature[1], temperature[2] and so on). In fact, this is exactly what an **array** allows us to do.

6.2   Creating an array

An **array** is a special kind of object in Java and is used to hold a *collection of items all of the same type*. For example, an array object could hold a collection of temperatures, or a collection of students. It couldn't hold a few students and a few temperatures as this is a collection involving two types.

Actually, an array doesn't quite fit perfectly with the idea of an object that we have met already. For example, there is no obvious class from which it is generated, and the syntax for method calls is peculiar to arrays. For this reason an array is often thought of as a type all of its own – not a scalar type and not quite an object.

However, we aren't going to worry too much about how arrays are categorized – we are far more interested in showing you how to use them in your programs. Firstly you need to know how to create an array. Just as with the creation of objects, array creation is a two-stage process:

1.   Declare an array.
2.   Create memory to store the array.

For convenience, let's say every element in the array is of type `ArrayType` (where `ArrayType` may be any type such as **int, char,** `String`, `Student`); then an array is declared as follows:

```
ArrayType [] arrayName;
```

Note that this declaration is just like the declaration of a simple variable or an object except that square brackets '[ ]' are included after the type name. These brackets indicate that the data item called `arrayName` is in fact an array.

So, to declare an array `temperature` of **double** values you would write the following:

```
double [] temperature;
```

At the moment this simply defines `temperature` to be a *reference* to an array. The memory that will eventually hold the array has not been allocated. This is done as before with the **new** operator. This time, however, as well as using the **new** operator, you must state how big your array will be – that is, how many elements you want your array to hold.

```
arrayName = new ArrayType [sizeOfArray];
```

The variable sizeOfArray is some integer value. So, for the temperature example above, if you wanted the array to hold seven temperatures you would allocate memory as follows:

```
temperature = new double [7];
```

Just like the creation of objects, we could have combined the two procedures of declaring and creating an array in one step as follows:

```
double [ ] temperature = new double [7];
```

We have already said that arrays can be used to hold *any* collection of items as long as they are of the same type. This type can be a simple scalar type such as **int** or **char** or a class such as String or Student. In other words, you can create an array of simple scalar items or an array of objects. The effect of the **new** operator differs slightly depending upon whether you are creating an array of simple scalar items (as in this case) or an array of objects. We will return to look at an array of objects later. For now, let's see what effect the **new** operator has when creating this array temperature in figure 6.1.

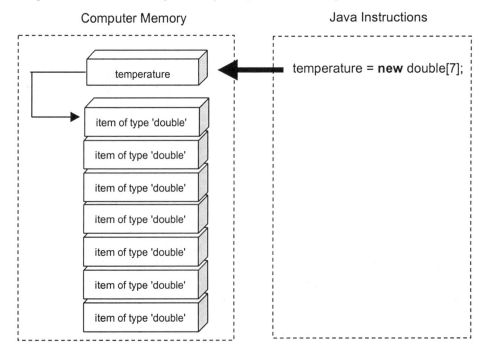

Fig 6.1   The effect on computer memory of declaring an array of values of type 'double'

As can be seen from figure 6.1, the array creation creates a reference, `temperature`, that points to seven other memory locations that have also been created. As this array was declared to hold values of type **double**, each of the seven memory locations is big enough to hold a value of type **double**. In effect the array reference, `temperature`, points to seven *new variables*. These variables are often referred to as the **elements** of the array.

You may be wondering: what names have each of these elements been given? Well, each element in an array shares *the same name as the array*, so in this case each element is called `temperature`. The individual elements are then *uniquely identified* by an additional **index value**. An index value acts rather like a street number to identify houses on the same street. Like a street number, these index values are always continuous integers. Note carefully that, in Java, *array indices start from 0 and not from 1*. This index value is always enclosed in square brackets, so the first temperature in the list is identified as `temperature[0]`, the second temperature by `temperature[1]` and so on.

This means that the size of the array and the last index value are not the same thing. In this case the size is 7 and the last index is 6. There is no such value as `temperature[7]`, for example. Remember this, as it is a common cause of error in programs!

Usually, when an array is created, values will be added into it as the program runs. If, however, all the values of the array elements are known beforehand, then an array can be created without use of the **new** operator by initialization as follows.

```
double [] temperature = {9, 11.5, 11, 8.5, 7, 9, 8.5} ;
```

Here each initial value is placed in braces and separated by commas. The compiler determines the length of the array by the number of initial values (in this case 7). Each value is placed into the array in order, so `temperature[0]` is set to 9, `temperature[1]` to 11.5 and so on. This is the only instance in which *all the elements* of an array can be assigned explicitly by listing out the elements in a single assignment statement. Once an array has been created, elements must be accessed *individually*.

6.3 Accessing array elements

Once an array has been created, its elements can be used like any other variable of the given type in Java. If you look back at the temperature example, initializing the values of each temperature when the array is created is actually quite unrealistic. It is much more likely that temperatures would be entered into the program as it runs. Let's look at how to achieve this.

Whether an array is initialized or not, values can be placed into the individual array elements. We know that each element in this array is a variable of type **double**. As with any variable of a scalar type, the assignment operator can be used to enter a value.

The only thing you have to remember when using the assignment operator with an array element is to specify *which* element to place the value in. For example, to allow the user of the program to enter the value of the first temperature, the following assignment could be used:

```
temperature[0] = EasyIn.getDouble();
```

We know we have to use the `getDouble` method of the `EasyIn` class here as every element of the `temperature` array is of type **double**. Note again that, since array indices begin at 0, the first temperature is not at index 1 but index 0.

Array elements can also be printed on the screen; for example, the following command prints out the value of the *sixth* array element:

```
System.out.println(temperature[5]); // index 5 is the sixth element!
```

Note that an array index (such as 5) is just used to *locate* a position in the array; it is *not* the item at that position.

For example, let's assume that the user enters a value of 69.5 for the first temperature in the array; the following statement:

```
System.out.println ("temperature for day 1 is "+ temperature[0]);
```

would then print out the message:

```
temperature for day 1 is 69.5
```

Statements like the `println` command above might seem a bit confusing at first. The message refers to "temperature for day **1**" but the temperature that is displayed is `temperature[0]`. Remember though that the temperature at index position 0 *is* the first temperature!

After a while you will get used to this rather unfortunate indexing system of Java. Later on in this chapter we will look at ways to overcome this difference between the natural way of indexing lists (1,2,3 etc.) and array indices (0,1,2 etc.).

As you can see from the examples above, you can use array elements in exactly the same way you can use any other kind of variable of the given type. Here are a few more examples:

```
temperature[4] = temperature[4] * 2; //doubles the fifth temperature
if (temperature[2]>=18)      // checks if day 3 was a hot day
{
     System.out.println("it was hot today");

}
```

So far so good, but if you are just going to use array elements in the way you used regular variables, why bother with arrays at all?

The reason is that the indexing system of arrays is in fact a very powerful programming tool. The index value does not need to be a literal number such as 5 or 2 as in the examples we have just shown you; it can be *any expression that returns an integer value.*

More often than not an integer *variable* is used, in place of a fixed index value, to access an array element. For example, if we assume that i is some integer variable, then the following is a perfectly legal way of accessing an array element:

```
System.out.println(temperature[i]); // index is a variable
```

Here the array index is not a literal number (like 2 or 5) but the variable i. The *value* of i will determine the array index. If the value of i is 4 then this will display temperature[4], if the value of i is 6 then this will display temperature[6], and so on.[1]

The advantage of using a variable in place of a fixed number as an array index is that the name of each array element can be *computed.* One useful application of this is to place the array instructions within a loop (usually a **for** loop), with the loop counter being used as the array index.

In this way *entire* arrays can be processed by writing the code to process a *single* array element and placing that code within a loop. For example, returning to the original problem in section 6.1 of entering all seven temperature readings, the following loop could now be used:

---

[1] Note that the array index value must always be a *valid* value. In this case it must be a number from zero to six. If it is not, for example if i is 7, then your program will terminate when this line is executed with a message ArrayIndexOutOfBounds. We will look at approaches to guard against this kind of error in chapter 8.

```
for(int i = 0; i<7; i++) // note, loop counter runs from 0 to 6
{
    System.out.println("max temperature for day "+(i+1));
    temperature[i] = EasyIn.getDouble(); // use loop counter
}
```

Note carefully the following points from this loop:

- Unlike the previous examples of **for** loop counters that started at 1, this counter starts at 0. Since the counter is meant to track the array indices, 0 is the natural number to start from.
- The counter goes up to, but does not include, the number of items in the array. In this case this means the counter goes up to 6 and not 7. Again this is because the array index for an array of size seven stops at six.
- The println command uses the loop counter to display the number of the given day being entered. The loop counter starts from 0, however. We would not think of the first day of the week as being day 0! In order for the message to be more meaningful for the user, therefore, we have displayed (i+1) rather than i.

Effectively this loop implies that the following statements are executed:

```
System.out.println("max temperature for day 1 ");      } 1st time round loop
temperature[0] = EasyIn.getDouble();

System.out.println("max temperature for day 2 ");      } 2nd time round loop
temperature [1] = EasyIn.getDouble();

//as above but with indices 2-5                          } 3rd - 6th time round
                                                           loop

System.out.println("max temperature for day 7 ");      } 7th time round loop
temperature [6] = EasyIn.getDouble();
```

You should now be able to see the value of an array. This loop can be made more readable if we make use of a built-in feature of all arrays. That is the **public attribute** length. This attribute of an array holds the **number of elements** that can be placed in the array.

As with any public component of an object, you access it with the dot operator. For example:

```
System.out.print("number of temperatures = ");
System.out.println(temperature.length);
```

which displays the following on to the screen:

```
number of temperatures = 7
```

Note that length is an *attribute* of an array, not a *method*, so it is not accessed with round brackets as temperature.length(). This attribute can be used in place of a fixed number in the **for** loop as follows:

```
for (int i = 0; i < temperature.length, i++)
{
     // code for loop goes here
}
```

To see this technique being exploited, look at program 6.1 to see the completed TemperatureReadings class, which stores and displays the maximum daily temperatures in a week.

Program 6.1

```
class TemperatureReadings
{
     public static void main(String[] args)
     {   // create array
         double [ ] temperature = new double[7];
         // enter temperatures
         for (int i = 0; i < temperature.length; i++)
         {
             System.out.println("max temperature for day " + (i+1));
             temperature[i] = EasyIn.getDouble();
         }
         // display temperatures
         System.out.println(); // blank line
         System.out.println("***TEMPERATURES ENTERED***");
         for (int i = 0; i < temperature.length; i++)
         {
             System.out.println("day "+(i+1)+" "+ temperature[i]);
         }
         EasyIn.pause("Press <Enter> to quit");
     }
}
```

Note how the `length` attribute was used to control the two **for** loops. Here is a sample test run.

```
max temperature for day 1 12.2
max temperature for day 2 10.5
max temperature for day 3 13
max temperature for day 4 15
max temperature for day 5 13
max temperature for day 6 12.5
max temperature for day 7 12

***TEMPERATURES ENTERED***
day 1 12.2
day 2 10.5
day 3 13.0
day 4 15.0
day 5 13.0
day 6 12.5
day 7 12.0
Press <Enter> to quit
```

Note that as each temperature is stored as a **double** value, this value will be displayed with a decimal point. This means, for example, that a temperature of 12 will be displayed as 12.0.

6.4   Passing arrays as parameters

We have said that an array is a kind of object in Java. Apart from a few discrepancies that we told you about, you can pretty much treat an array as you would any other object. In particular you can use an array as a parameter to a method just as you would use an object as a parameter to a method.

As an example of passing an array to a method, consider once again program 6.1 which processes temperature readings. That program contains all the processing within the main method. As a result, the code for this method is becoming a little difficult to read. Let's do something about that.

Up until now we have always declared attributes of classes as **private** and methods of classes as **public**. Most of the time that is exactly what you need to do – keep your data hidden and make your methods accessible. Sometimes, however, you may not wish to keep an attribute **private**, or a method **public**. For instance, arrays (as you have already seen) have an attribute, `length`, that is **public**.

When might you choose to declare a method as **private**? One answer is when this method is just being used by *other methods within the class*. For this reason, these methods are sometimes called **worker methods**; they simply carry out some work for other methods within the class – they themselves are not publicly accessible.

We will use this idea to relieve the main method of all the hard work it is being asked to carry out. We will create two worker methods, enterTemps and displayTemps, to enter and display temperatures respectively. As a first attempt you might consider the following code for enterTemps:

```
private void enterTemps( ) // try this ?
{
    for (int i = 0; i < temperature.length; i++)
    {
        System.out.println("max temperature for day " +(i+1));
        temperature[i] = EasyIn.getDouble();
    }
}
```

Here, we have taken the code for entering temperature readings from the main method and placed it in this worker method. This is fine, but there are a few problems with the method header.

```
private void enterTemps( ) // what is wrong ?
```

The first problem is that this worker method is going to be called by the main method. The main method, however, is an example of a *class* method that we discussed in the last chapter. You can see that because it is declared as **static**. Class methods can call only *other* class methods. This means that any worker method that main calls upon *must* be declared as **static**.

```
private static void enterTemps( ) // a bit better
```

There is still something wrong with this method header. Look back at the code within this method. There are two items of data being accessed, the loop counter i and the array temperature.

```
for (int i = 0; i < temperature.length; i++)
{
    System.out.println("max temperature for day " + (i+1)):
    temperature[i] = EasyIn.getDouble();
}
```

There is no problem with the loop counter as it is declared within the loop and so is local to the worker method. The problem is the array, temperature, as it was declared within the main method. When an item of data is declared within one method, it is not (by default) visible *outside of this method*.[2] Therefore, this worker method *does not have access to the array* and so cannot refer to it. To give this worker method access to the array it must receive it as a parameter as follows:

```
private static void enterTemps( double[] temperatureIn )
```

Notice that when a parameter is declared as an array type, the size of the array is not required. This array can now be accessed by the body of the method. The name of this parameter is entirely up to you. In this case we have called it temperatureIn. Remember that, like any other object, an array is a reference type, so the parameter temperatureIn is a copy of that reference. Any changes you make to the contents of the array temperatureIn you make to the original array. In other words, when this method is called from within main, temperatureIn is just another name for the array that is sent from main.

Having created this worker method, main can now call upon this method to carry out its work. Since worker methods live in the same class as the methods that call upon them, a dot operator is not necessary to associate the method with a particular object or class. This is how main would call the method enterTemps:

```
public static void main(String[] args)
{
    double [] temperature = new double [7]; // create array
    enterTemps (temperature); // call worker with array temperature
    // more code goes here
}
```

---

[2] The visibility of a variable is often referred to as the **scope** of a variable.

Notice that (just as with any other parameter) when you call a method that is expecting an array, you plug in only the array *name*, in this case `temperature`; you do not include the array *type*. Program 6.2 rewrites program 6.1 by giving the `main` method two worker methods.

Program 6.2

```
class TemperatureReadings2
{
    public static void main(String[] args)
    {
        double [ ] temperature = new double[7];
        enterTemps(temperature); // call static enter method
        displayTemps(temperature); // call static display method
        EasyIn.pause("press <Enter> to Quit");
    }


    // worker method to enter temperatures
    private static void enterTemps(double [] temperatureIn)
    {
        for (int i = 0; i < temperatureIn.length; i++)
        {
            System.out.println("max temperature for day " + (i+1));
            temperatureIn[i] = EasyIn.getDouble();
        }
    }


    // worker method to display temperatures
    private static void displayTemps(double[] temperatureIn)
    {
        System.out.println(); // blank line
        System.out.println("***TEMPERATURES ENTERED***");
        for (int i = 0; i < temperatureIn.length; i++)
        {
            System.out.println("day "+(i+1)+" "+ temperatureIn[i]);
        }
    }
}
```

Notice how the `main` method now becomes much more readable. Although we have written this program differently, it produces exactly the same results as program 6.1.

6.5   Collection classes

So far we have used an array only as a variable within a method. However, an array can also be used as an *attribute* of a class. In this way we can hide some of the inconveniences of the array type (such as remembering to start array indices at zero) by providing our own methods to control array access. A class that contains many items of the same type is said to be a **collection** class. In our everyday lives we can see many examples of collections:

- a train contains a collection of passengers;
- a post bag contains a collection of letters;
- a letter contains a collection of words.

As can be seen from the examples above, some collections can themselves contain other collections.

6.5.1   Types of collections

Collections must have some *internal structure,* which determines the relationship between the members of the collection, and some access rules. For example:

- **a set** is an *unordered* collection of elements, from which any item may be removed;
- **a list** (figure 6.2) is an *ordered* collection of elements, from which any item may be removed;
- **a stack** (figure 6.3) is a restrictive form of list that obeys a last-in-first-out (LIFO) rule, like a stack of plates that are stored after being washed, then used again – the last one to join the stack is the first one to leave;
- **a queue** (figure 6.4) is also a restrictive form of list that obeys a first-in-first-out (FIFO) rule, like the queue at a bus-stop – the first one to join the queue is the first one to leave (imagine the arguments at the post office if a queue obeyed a LIFO rule!).

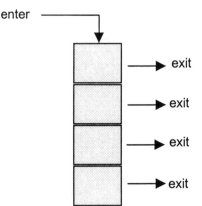

Fig 6.2   Items may leave from any point in a list

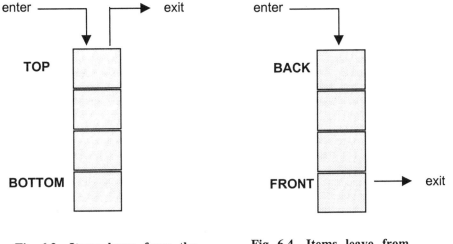

Fig 6.3 Items leave from the top of a stack

Fig 6.4 Items leave from the front of a queue

In practice we can implement collection classes in a number of ways.[3] For the purpose of this chapter we will show you how to use an array to implement a collection class. We will begin with a stack of integers.

6.5.2 The *IntegerStack* class

As we have already said, a stack is defined as a LIFO collection. Computer texts refer to the operation that places an item on the stack as a **push** operation, and the operation to remove an item as a **pop** operation. We will use the same convention here.

Unlike the array we used in programs 6.1 and 6.2, the number of elements in a stack shrinks and grows over time. One of the limitations of an array is that, once it is created, its maximum size is *fixed*. This means that most of the time the array will have many positions empty.

We have already shown you that loops are useful when processing arrays and that the length attribute can be used to help track array indices. Let's assume that a stack is fixed at size five. If the array is partially filled with only two elements, the length attribute is no longer of any use when checking these elements as it just returns the *maximum* capacity (see figure 6.5).

---

[3] In some texts the term *container* class is used in place of *collection* class.

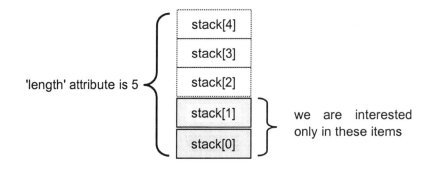

Fig 6.5   The length attribute is not as useful with a partially filled array

Note that we are viewing the first element of the array, stack[0], as being the *bottom* of the stack. To be able to process a partially filled array we will need to keep track of the actual number of elements entered by introducing a new attribute. If we call this attribute total, we will also need to provide a method to read this value, getTotal say.

Now, before we show you the UML diagram for the IntegerStack class, let's go back to the problem of arrays needing to be of a fixed size. While there is nothing we can do about that, we can at least allow the user of our class to decide what this size should be, rather than size the array ourselves.

How will we go about doing this? Well, remember that we told you that creating an array is a two-stage process: first you declare and then you allocate memory. You have to fix a size for the array only *when you allocate memory for it*. If we put off the array creation in the IntegerStack constructor, we can allow the size of the array to be set to the value of some parameter.

Now, let's have a look at the UML diagram for the design of the IntegerStack class in figure 6.6.

IntegerStack
stack: int [ ] *total : int*
IntegerStack(int) *push (int): boolean* *pop( ): boolean* *isEmpty(): boolean* *isFull(): boolean* *getItem(int): int* *getTotal(): int*

Fig 6.6   The *IntegerStack* class

The *push* operation will require one parameter (a value of type **int**), which is the value to be pushed onto the stack; the *pop* operation will not require any parameters, as the item removed will always be the last one that was pushed onto the stack. Both of these operations return a **boolean** value to indicate whether or not the operation was processed successfully. A *push* operation will not be successful if the stack is already full and a *pop* will be unsuccessful if the stack is empty. Notice that we have also included three additional methods:

- IsEmpty, which reports on whether or not the stack is empty;
- IsFull, which reports on whether or not the stack is full;
- getItem, which returns the value of the item at a given position in the stack.

The code for this class is given in the box below. Have a look at the code and read the comments carefully.

The *IntegerStack* class

```
class IntegerStack
{
    private int[] stack ; // to hold the stack of integers
    private int total; // to track number of items

    public IntegerStack(int sizeIn)
    {   // size array with parameter
        stack = new int[sizeIn];
        // set number of items to zero
        total = 0;
    }


    // add an item to the array
    public boolean push(int j)
    {
        if( isFull() == false ) // checks if space in stack
        {
            stack[total] = j; // add item
            total++; // increment item counter
            return true; // to indicate success
        }
        else
        {
            return false; // to indicate failure
        }
    }
```

```java
// remove an item by obeying LIFO rule
public boolean pop()
{
    if( isEmpty() == false) // makes sure stack is not empty
    {
        total--; // reduce counter by one
        return true; // to indicate success
    }
    else
    {
        return false; // to indicate failure
    }
}


// checks if array is empty
public boolean isEmpty()
{
    if(total==0)
    {
        return true;
    }
    else
    {
        return false;
    }
}


// checks if array is full
public boolean isFull()
{
    if(total==stack.length)
    {
        return true;
    }
    else
    {
        return false;
    }
}
```

```
    // returns the ith item
    public int getItem(int i)
    {
        return stack[i-1]; // ith item at position i-1
    }


    // return the number of items in the array
    public int getTotal()
    {
        return total;
    }
}
```

All these methods should be easy to follow. Look again at the getItem method. Do you see what we've done? We said earlier that arrays have an unfortunate indexing system where the fourth element, for example, is at index number 3. Here, we have allowed the getItem method to take a natural index, 4 for the fourth element, 3 for the third and so on, and we have taken one off this index within the method.

Below is program 6.3 which tests the IntegerStack class.

Program 6.3

```
class IntegerStackTester
{
    public static void main(String[] args)
    {
        char choice;
        int size;
        // ask user to fix maximum size of stack
        System.out.print("Maximum number of items on stack?");
        size = EasyIn.getInt();
        // create new stack
        IntegerStack stack = new IntegerStack(size);
        // offer menu
        do
        {
            System.out.println();
            System.out.println("1. Push number onto stack");
            System.out.println("2. Pop number from stack");
            System.out.println("3. Check if stack is empty");
            System.out.println("4. Check if stack is full");
            System.out.println("5. Display numbers in stack");
```

```java
                System.out.println("6. Quit");
                System.out.println();
                System.out.print("Enter choice [1-6]: ");
                choice = EasyIn.getChar();
                System.out.println();
                // process choice
                switch(choice)
                {   // call static methods
                      case '1': option1(stack); break;
                      case '2': option2(stack); break;
                      case '3': option3(stack); break;
                      case '4': option4(stack); break;
                      case '5': option5(stack); break;
                      case '6': break;
                      default : System.out.println("Invalid entry");
                }
        }while(choice!='6');
}


// static method to push item onto stack
public static void option1(IntegerStack stack)
{
    System.out.print("Enter number: ");
    int num = EasyIn.getInt();
    boolean ok = stack.push(num); // attempt to push
    if(!ok) // check if push was unsuccessful
    {
        System.out.println("Push unsuccessful");
    }
}


// static method to pop item onto stack
public static void option2(IntegerStack stack)
{
    boolean ok = stack.pop(); // attempt to pop
    if(!ok)// check if pop was unsuccessful
    {
        System.out.println("Pop unsuccessful");
    }
}


// static method to check if stack is empty
public static void option3(IntegerStack stack)
{
```

```java
        if(stack.isEmpty())
        {
            System.out.println("Stack empty");
        }
        else
        {
            System.out.println("Stack not empty");
        }
    }


    // static method to check if stack is full
    public static void option4(IntegerStack stack)
    {
        if(stack.isFull())
        {
            System.out.println("Stack full");
        }
        else
        {
            System.out.println("Stack not full");
        }
    }


    // static method to display stack
    public static void option5(IntegerStack stack)
    {
        if(stack.isEmpty())
        {
            System.out.println("Stack empty");
        }
        else
        {
            System.out.println("Numbers in stack are: ");
            System.out.println();
            for(int i = 1; i<=stack.getTotal(); i++)
            {
                System.out.println(stack.getItem(i));
            }
            System.out.println();
        }
    }
}
```

Again, most of the techniques used in this program you have met before. We will just point out one or two things that you should note.

Both the **static** option1 method (to *push* an item) and the **static** option2 method (to *pop* an item) involve checking whether the associated IntegerStack methods completed their task successfully. Recall that both push and pop in the IntegerStack class return a **boolean** value. This value is set to **true** to indicate that the operation was successful and **false** otherwise. Now, take a look at the call to the pop method:

```
boolean ok = stack.pop();
```

The **boolean** value is returned and placed into a variable that we have called ok. The **if** statement that follows then checks the value of this variable:

```
if(!ok) // check if pop was unsuccessful
{
      System.out.println("Pop unsuccessful");
}
```

If you look at the test associated with this selection, it is expressed in a very intuitive way:

```
if(!ok)
```

This is equivalent to the following longer and not so intuitive test:

```
if (ok == false)
```

Secondly, notice how the loop used in the displayItems method is also more intuitive than the **for** loops we used earlier to process arrays.

```
for(int i = 1; i<=stack.getTotal(); i++)
{
    System.out.println(stack.getItem(i));
}
```

Here the loop can start from 1 and go up to the number of items in the stack. That is because the getItem method takes one off this index for us to translate back into true array indices. Now, here is a test run of this program; study it carefully.

```
Maximum number of items on stack? 5

1. Push number onto stack
2. Pop number from stack
3. Check if stack is empty
4. Check if stack is full
5. Display numbers in stack
6. Quit
Enter choice [1-6]:2

Pop unsuccessful

1. Push number onto stack
2. Pop number from stack
3. Check if stack is empty
4. Check if stack is full
5. Display numbers in stack
6. Quit

Enter choice [1-6]:3

Stack is empty

1. Push number onto stack
2. Pop number from stack
3. Check if stack is empty
4. Check if stack is full
5. Display numbers in stack
6. Quit

Enter choice [1-6]:4

Stack not full
```

```
1. Push number onto stack

2. Pop number from stack

3. Check if stack is empty

4. Check if stack is full

5. Display numbers in stack

6. Quit


Enter choice [1-6]:1



enter number: 22


1. Push number onto stack

2. Pop number from stack

3. Check if stack is empty

4. Check if stack is full

5. Display numbers in stack

6. Quit


Enter choice [1-6]:1



enter number: 9


1. Push number onto stack

2. Pop number from stack

3. Check if stack is empty

4. Check if stack is full

5. Display numbers in stack

6. Quit


Enter choice [1-6]:1



enter number: 15


1. Push number onto stack

2. Pop number from stack

3. Check if stack is empty

4. Check if stack is full

5. Display numbers in stack

6. Quit


Enter choice [1-6]:5
```

```
22
9
15

1. Push number onto stack
2. Pop number from stack
3. Check if stack is empty
4. Check if stack is full
5. Display numbers in stack
6. Quit

Enter choice [1-6]:2

1. Push number onto stack
2. Pop number from stack
3. Check if stack is empty
4. Check if stack is full
5. Display numbers in stack
6. Quit

Enter choice [1-6]:5
22
9

1. Push number onto stack
2. Pop number from stack
3. Check if stack is empty
4. Check if stack is full
5. Display numbers in stack
6. Quit

Enter choice [1-6]:6
```

This `IntegerStack` class is an example of the use of an array to model a collection of scalar types. Collection classes are, however, most commonly required to hold objects.

6.5.3   The *StringList* class

Consider an object that contains a simple collection of fruit names, where each fruit name is implemented as a `String`. These names will be added to and deleted from the collection freely. A stack is too restrictive a collection here as only the *last* name added could be deleted. A much more suitable type of collection would be a *list*. We will develop a collection class, `StringList`, to be a list of `String` objects.

When one object itself consists of other objects, this relationship is called **aggregation**. This association is often referred to as a *part-of* relationship. For example, the association between a car object and wheel objects is one of *aggregation*: wheels are *part-of* a car. **Containment** is a special form of aggregation where the one object exists in its own right, regardless of the number of objects it contains. For instance, the association between a car object and passenger objects is one of *containment* as a car exists whether or not it contains any passengers. A collection class is an implementation of this containment relationship.

The association between the container object, `StringList`, and the contained object, `String`, is shown in the UML diagram of figure 6.7.

Fig 6.7   The *StringList* object can contain many *String* objects

The diamond indicates aggregation. The asterisk at the other end of the joining line indicates that the `StringList` object contains *zero or more* `String` objects. The design for the `StringList` class is now given in figure 6.8.

StringList
list: String [] *total : int*
StringList(int) *add (String):boolean* *remove(int):boolean* *isEmpty():boolean* *isFull():boolean* *getItem(int):String* *getTotal():int*

Fig 6.8   The *StringList* class

As you can see, the design for this class looks very like the `IntegerStack` class that we have already developed. One important difference is that our array will contain objects (of type `String`) as opposed to scalar types. You create an array of simple scalar types or objects in the same way. To declare an array of four `String` objects, for example, you could do the following:

```
String [ ] list;
list = new String [4];
```

We have already illustrated the effect of the **new** operator on arrays in figure 6.1. Then, the **new** operator created enough memory for the given array. As we indicated earlier though, the **new** operator behaves slightly differently when creating an array of objects. Instead of setting up an array of the given objects, it sets up an array of *references* to such objects (see figure 6.9).

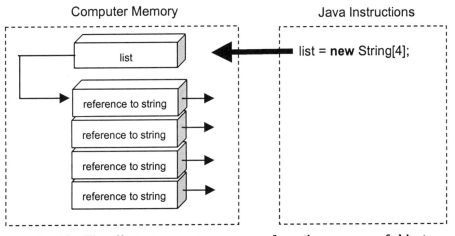

Fig 6.9   The effect on computer memory of creating an array of objects

At the moment, space has been reserved for the four `String` references only, *not* the four `String` objects. As we told you in chapter 4, when a reference is initially created it points to the constant **null**, so at this point each reference in the array points to **null**.

This means that memory would still need to be reserved for individual `String` objects each time we wish to link a `String` object to the array. For example, if we wanted to associate a `String` object with the first element in the array, the following instructions could be used:

```
String [ ] list; // sets up a single array reference
list = new String [4]; // sets up space for four String references
list[0] = new String("Strawberry"); // creates space for the string
```

Here, in the last line, a `String` object has been created with value of "Strawberry" and the reference at `list[0]` is set to point to it (see figure 6.10).

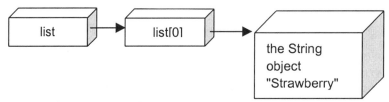

Figure 6.10   Objects are linked to arrays by reference

Apart from the fact that the `StringList` class is a collection of objects whereas the `IntegerStack` class was a collection of integers, the only other real difference between the two classes is that the `pop` method of the `IntegerStack` class is replaced by a `remove` method in the `StringList` class.

Removing an item from any point in a list is a bit more complicated than just taking something off the top of a stack. For this reason we will present the code for the `StringList` class, but leave the `remove` method incomplete for now. Examine the code for this class closely and then we'll pick up the discussion of the `remove` method.

The *StringList* class with *remove* method left incomplete

```
class StringList
{
    // attributes
    private String[] list ;
    private int total ;


    // methods
    public StringList (int sizeIn)
    {   // equivalent to the constructor of IntegerStack
        list = new String[sizeIn];
        total = 0;
    }


    public boolean add(String s)
    {   // equivalent to the push method of IntegerStack
        if(!isFull())
        {
            list[total] = s;
            total++;
            return true;
        }
        else
        {
```

```
                return false;
        }
    }

    public boolean isEmpty()
    {   // equivalent to the isEmpty method of IntegerStack
        if(total==0)
        {
            return true;
        }
        else
        {
            return false;
        }
    }

    public boolean isFull()
    {   // equivalent to the isFull method of IntegerStack
        if(total==list.length)
        {
            return true;
        }
        else
        {
            return false;
        }
    }

    public String getItem(int i)
    {   // equivalent to the getItem method of IntegerStack
        return list[i-1];
    }

    public int getTotal()
    {   // same as the getTotal method of IntegerStack
        return total;
    }

    public boolean remove(int numberIn)
    {
        // to be completed!!!
    }
}
```

As you can see, the interface for the `remove` method is given as follows:

```
public boolean remove (int numberIn)
```

This method accepts an integer value, `numberIn`, which represents *the position of the item to be removed*, and it returns a **boolean** value to indicate whether or not that item was removed successfully. One reason why an item might not be removed from a given list would be that there was no item at the given position.

Effectively this means that the position of the item to be removed, `numberIn`, must lie between the range of 1 and the value of `total`. We can check whether or not this is the case and return a value of **true** or **false** to indicate whether or not an attempt to remove an item has been successful. This can easily be coded into an **if-else** statement as follows:

```
if (numberIn >= 1 && numberIn <= total())
{
    // code to remove item from list goes here
    return true; // remove successful
}
else
{
    return false; // remove unsuccessful
}
```

Now let's look at a strategy to remove the given item from a list. One very common approach is to shuffle the previous items in the list along so that the given item is *overwritten* (see figure 6.11).

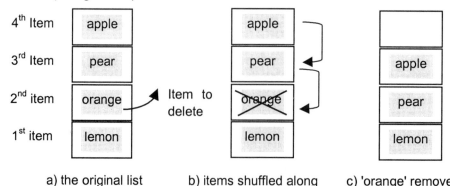

a) the original list   b) items shuffled along   c) 'orange' removed

Fig 6.11 An item can be deleted from a list by shuffling adjacent items along

In the case of figure 6.11, the item to be removed ('orange') was the second item in the list. The items to be shuffled ('pear' and 'apple') were the third and fourth items in the list respectively. Remembering that this list is implemented as an array and that array indices begin at zero, the following assignments could be used to achieve this shuffling:

```
list[1] = list[2]; // overwrite 'orange' with 'pear'
list[2] = list[3]; // overwrite 'pear' with 'apple'
```

This is fine for the small list given in figure 6.11 but what if we had to shuffle 50 items rather than just two? Writing 50 assignment statements is going to be an awful waste of effort. Can you see an easier way to deal with the general case?

As each assignment statement is basically the same apart from the value of the array indices, a much more concise approach would be to use a loop rather than a long series of assignments, and then to use the loop counter in place of the array indices.

We can express this using pseudocode as follows:

```
LOOP FROM index of item to delete TO index of last but one item
BEGIN
        SET current item TO next item
END
```

We already know that the *position* of the item to delete is given by the parameter numberIn. Since array indices begin at zero we must take one off this attribute to get the array index of the item to delete. This gives us so far:

```
LOOP FROM numberIn-1 TO index of last but one item
BEGIN
        SET current item TO next item
END
```

Now, the *position* of the *last* item in the list is the same as the total number of items in the list (stored in the total attribute). Therefore the position of the *last but one* item is given as total−1. Again, since array indices start at zero, we must remember to take one off *this* value to arrive at the array index, giving us:

```
LOOP FROM numberIn-1 TO total-2
BEGIN
        SET current item TO next item
END
```

Having thought that through carefully using pseudocode, it is relatively easy to code this into a **for** loop in Java as follows:

```
// loops from item to delete to last but one item
for (int i=numberIn-1; i<= total-2; i++)
{    // overwrite current item with next item
    list[i]= list[i+1];
}
```

This isn't quite the whole story! If we used this loop on the initial list of fruit, to delete 'orange', the array would be left as depicted in figure 6.12.

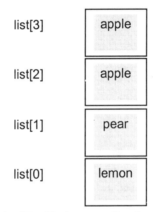

list[3]   apple

list[2]   apple

list[1]   pear

list[0]   lemon

Fig 6.12   The 'list' array after 'orange' has been deleted

As you can see, 'apple' is in two positions in the array. There is still an 'apple' in the last position of the list as it hasn't been overwritten with anything. We don't really want that 'apple' in the last position. One way to achieve this is simply to ignore it!

If we wish to ignore it we must remember to reduce the total number of elements in the list, as stored in the `total` attribute, by one. We can achieve this simply as follows:

```
total--;
```

Now the extra 'apple' is effectively hidden from the list.[4] Putting all this back together gives us the following code for the remove method:

```
public boolean remove(int numberIn)
{    // check if index is valid before removing
     if(numberIn >= 1 && numberIn <= total())
     {   // overwrite items by shifting other items along
         for(int i = numberIn-1; i<= total-2; i++)
         {
             list[i] = list[i+1];
         }
         total--; // decrement total number of objects
         return true; // remove successful
     }
     else
     {
         return false; // remove unsuccessful
     }
}
```

Program 6.4 is a tester class for the StringList collection. As you would expect, it is very similar to the tester class for IntegerStack.

Program 6.4

```
class StringListTester
{
public static void main(String[] args)
{
        char choice;
        int size;
        System.out.print("Maximum number of items in list?");
        size = EasyIn.getInt();
        // create StringList object to test
        StringList fruit = new StringList(size);
```

---

[4] In fact when a new item is added into the list it will overwrite this extra 'apple' item.

```
        // offer menu
        do
        {
                System.out.println();
                System.out.println("1. Add fruit to list");
                System.out.println("2. Remove fruit from list");
                System.out.println("3. Check if list is empty");
                System.out.println("4. Check if list is full");
                System.out.println("5. Display list of fruit");
                System.out.println("6. Quit");
                System.out.println();
                System.out.print("Enter choice [1-6]: ");
                // get choice
                choice = EasyIn.getChar();
                System.out.println();
                // process menu options
                switch(choice)
                 {
                        case '1': option1(fruit); break;
                        case '2': option2(fruit); break;
                        case '3': option3(fruit); break;
                        case '4': option4(fruit); break;
                        case '5': option5(fruit);break;
                        case '6': break;
                        default : System.out.println("Invalid entry");
                 }
        }while(choice!='6');
}


// add fruit
public static void option1 (StringList fruit)
{
        System.out.print("Enter name of fruit: ");
        // create String object to add to list
        String name = EasyIn.getString();
        // add string to list
        boolean ok = fruit.add(name);
        if(!ok)
        {
                System.out.println("Can't add to a full list");
        }
}
```

```java
// remove fruit
public static void option2 (StringList fruit)
{
    // get position of item
    System.out.print("Enter position to remove: ");
    int position = EasyIn.getInt();
    // delete item if it exists
    boolean ok = fruit.remove(position);
    if(!ok)
    {
        System.out.println("No such position");
    }
}


// check if empty
public static void option3 (StringList fruit)
{
    if(fruit.isEmpty())
    {
        System.out.println("list is empty");
    }
    else
    {
        System.out.println("list is not empty");
    }
}


// check if full
public static void option4 (StringList fruit)
{
    if(fruit.isFull())
    {
        System.out.println("list is full");
    }
    else
    {
        System.out.println("list is not full");
    }
}

// display list
public static void option5 (StringList fruit)
{
    if(fruit.isEmpty()) // no need to display if list is empty
```

```
        {
            System.out.println("list is empty");
        }
        else
        {
            System.out.println("Fruits in list are: "); // header
            System.out.println();
            // loop through list
            for(int i = 1; i<= fruit.getTotal(); i++)
            {
                System.out.println("item " + i +": " +fruit.getItem(i));
            }
        }
    }
}
```

Here is a sample test run; examine it closely and make sure you understand how the underlying StringList class is working.

```
Maximum number of items in list? 5

1. Add fruit to list
2. Remove fruit from list
3. Check if list is empty
4. Check if list is full
5. Display list of fruit
6. Quit
Enter choice [1-6]: 3

list is empty

1. Add fruit to list
2. Remove fruit from list
3. Check if list is empty
4. Check if list is full
5. Display list of fruit
6. Quit

Enter choice [1-6]: 4

list is not full
```

```
1. Add fruit to list
2. Remove fruit from list
3. Check if list is empty
4. Check if list is full
5. Display list of fruit
6. Quit
Enter choice [1-6]: 1

Enter name of fruit: Apple

1. Add fruit to list
2. Remove fruit from list
3. Check if list is empty
4. Check if list is full
5. Display list of fruit
6. Quit
Enter choice [1-6]: 1

Enter name of fruit: Orange

1. Add fruit to list
2. Remove fruit from list
3. Check if list is empty
4. Check if list is full
5. Display list of fruit
6. Quit
Enter choice [1-6]: 1

Enter name of fruit: Pear

1. Add fruit to list
2. Remove fruit from list
3. Check if list is empty
4. Check if list is full
5. Display list of fruit
6. Quit
Enter choice [1-6]: 5

Fruits in list are:

item 1: Apple
item 2: Orange
item 3: Pear
```

```
1. Add fruit to list
2. Remove fruit from list
3. Check if list is empty
4. Check if list is full
5. Display list of fruit
6. Quit

Enter choice [1-6]: 2

Enter position to remove: 4
No such position

1. Add fruit to list
2. Remove fruit from list
3. Check if list is empty
4. Check if list is full
5. Display list of fruit
6. Quit

Enter choice [1-6]: 2

Enter position to remove: 2

1. Add fruit to list
2. Remove fruit from list
3. Check if list is empty
4. Check if list is full
5. Display list of fruit
6. Quit

Enter choice [1-6]: 5

Fruits in list are:
item 1: Apple
item 2: Pear

1. Add fruit to list
2. Remove fruit from list
3. Check if list is empty
4. Check if list is full
5. Display list of fruit
6. Quit

Enter choice [1-6]: 6
```

Tutorial exercises

1.   Consider the following explicit creation of an array:

```
int [] someArray = {2,5,1,9,11};
```

      a)   What would be the value of `someArray.length` ?

      b)   What is the value of `someArray[2]` ?

      c)   Create the equivalent array by using the **new** operator and then assigning the value of each element individually.

      d)   Write a loop that will double the value of every item in `someArray`.

      e)   Write a loop that will display all those items in the array greater than or equal to 5.

2.   How do the creation of an array of scalar values and an array of objects differ?

3.   Look back at program 6.2 which read in and displayed a series of temperature readings. Now define another **static** method, `wasHot`, which displays all days that recorded temperatures of 18 degrees or over.

4.   Assume a class has been written, `Book`, to model the details of a library book. The constructor for this class takes a book title, author name(s) and a book number (each as strings) respectively to create a new book. Now write the code to:

      a)   declare a variable `library` to be an array of books;

      b)   allocate memory for this array to hold 300 books;

      c)   add the book ("*Java the First Semester*", "*Charatan & Kans*", "*0-07-709757-2*") into the 50th element in the array;

      d)   display the title of the 10th book in the array by using the `Book` method `getTitle`;

      e)   display the titles of all 300 books.

Practical work

1. Implement program 6.2 and add the `wasHot` method you developed in tutorial question 3 (remember to include a call to this method in your `main` method).

2. The `StringList` class was an example of the use of an array to hold a collection of objects. An array can be used to hold not only objects created from built-in predefined classes, like `String`, but also objects created from your own user-defined classes. For example, look back at the first practical task we gave you at the end of chapter 5. There we defined a `Student` class for you to implement. Take this implementation of the `Student` class and use an array to develop a `StudentList` class. The UML diagram depicting the association between a `StudentList` object and a `Student` object is given in figure below:

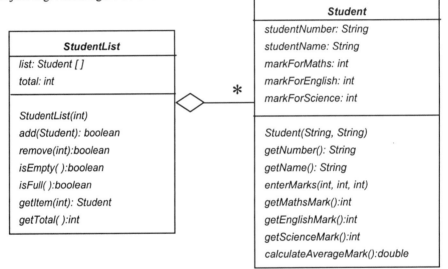

3. Develop a `StudentListTester` class to test the `StudentList` class you defined in practical task 2 above.

4. Look back at figure 6.4 depicting a *queue*. A queue is very similar to a stack apart from the fact that items leave from the *front* of a queue, not the *back*. Use an array to help you implement an `IntegerQueue` class to store a queue of integers. This class should have the same methods as the `IntegerStack` class except that the `push` and `pop` methods should be renamed `addToQueue` and `removeFromQueue` respectively.

5. Develop a program to test your `IntegerQueue` class.

6. Develop a `StringQueue` class to hold a queue of `String` objects.

7. Develop a program to test your `StringQueue` class.

7 Extending classes with inheritance

Learning objectives

By the end of this chapter you should be able to:

- explain the term **inheritance**;
- specify and design inheritance structures using UML notation;
- implement inheritance relationships in Java;
- explain the term **method overriding**;
- explain the term **type cast** and implement this in Java;
- create and use a generic collection class.

7.1   Introduction

One of the greatest benefits of the object-oriented approach to software development is that it offers the opportunity for us to *reuse* classes that have already been written – either by ourselves or by someone else. Let's look at a possible scenario. Say you wanted to develop a software system and you have, during your analysis, identified the need for a class called `Employee`. You might be aware that a colleague in your organization has already written an `Employee` class; rather than having to write your own class, it would be easier to approach your colleague and ask her to let you use her `Employee` class.

So far so good, but what if the `Employee` class that you are given doesn't quite do everything that you had hoped? Maybe it was written to deal with full-time employees whereas you want a class that can also handle the sort of attributes and methods that are relevant to part-time employees. For example, you might want your class to have an attribute like `hourlyPay`, or methods like `calculateWeeklyPay` and `setHourlyPay`; and these attributes and methods do not exist because they are not applicable to full-time employees.

You may think it would be necessary to go into the old class and start messing about with the code. But there is no need, because object-oriented programming languages provide the ability to extend existing classes by adding attributes and methods to them. This is called **inheritance**.

7.2   Defining inheritance

Inheritance is the sharing of attributes and methods among classes. We take a class, and then define other classes based on the first one. The new classes *inherit* all the attributes and methods of the first one, but also have attributes and methods of their own. Let's try to understand this by thinking about the `Employee` class.

Say our `Employee` class has three attributes, number, name and `annualSalary`, and one method, `calculateMonthlyPay`. We now define our `PartTimeEmployee` class; this class will *inherit* these attributes and methods, but can also have attributes and methods of its own. We will give it one additional attribute, `hourlyPay`, and one new method, `calculateWeeklyPay`.

This is illustrated in figure 7.1 which uses the UML notation for inheritance, namely a triangle.

You can see from this diagram that an inheritance relationship is a *hierarchical* relationship. The class at the top of the hierarchy – in this case the `Employee` class – is referred to as the **superclass** (or **base class**) and the `PartTimeEmployee` as the **subclass** (or **derived class**).

The inheritance relationship is also often referred to as an *is-a-kind-of* relationship; in this case a `PartTimeEmployee` *is a kind of* `Employee`.

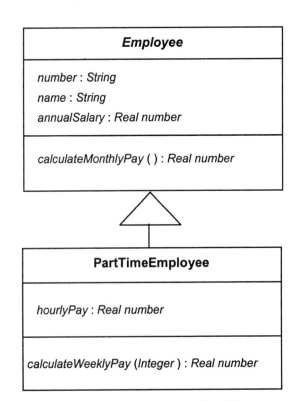

Fig 7.1   An inheritance relationship

7.3   Implementing inheritance in Java

Let's think about the design of our classes by filling in some more detail.

First, the Employee class. In addition to the calculateMonthlyPay method, we need to think about how we are going to access the attributes. We will certainly need to be able read all three attributes – but what about writing to them? It would seem like a good idea to set the employee's name and number at the time an Employee is created (that is, via a constructor), but not to allow the number to be changed thereafter. We should, however, allow the user to change the employee's name or set the salary.

The complete design of the Employee class is shown in figure 7.2; the program code then follows.

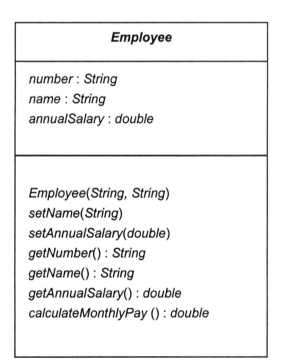

Fig 7.2   The design of the *Employee* class

The *Employee* class

```
class Employee
{
    private String number;
    private String name;
    private double annualSalary;

    public Employee(String numberIn, String nameIn)
    {
        number = numberIn;
        name = nameIn;
    }

    public void setName(String nameIn)
    {
        name = nameIn;
    }

    public void setAnnualSalary(double salaryIn)
    {
        annualSalary = salaryIn;
    }

    public String getNumber()
    {
        return number;
    }

    public String getName()
    {
        return name;
    }

    public double getAnnualSalary()
    {
        return annualSalary;
    }

    public double calculateMonthlyPay()
    {
        return annualSalary/12;
    }
}
```

There is nothing new here, so let's get on and design our `PartTimeEmployee` class. We will do the same thing as before with the constructor – send in the number and name when a new `PartTimeEmployee` object is created. We'll also need "set" and "get" methods for the `hourlyPay` attribute as well as the `calculateMonthlyPay` method that we identified earlier. The design is shown in figure 7.3.

PartTimeEmployee
hourlyPay : double
PartTimeEmployee(String, String) *setHourlyPay(double)* *getHourlyPay() :double* *calculateWeeklyPay(int) :double*

Fig 7.3   The design of the *PartTimeEmployee* class

Now we can code our `PartTimeEmployee` class. We will present the code first and analyse it afterwards.

The *PartTimeEmployee* class

```
class PartTimeEmployee extends Employee
{
    private double hourlyPay;
    public PartTimeEmployee(String numberIn, String nameIn)
    {
        super(numberIn, nameIn);
    }

    public double getHourlyPay()
    {
        return hourlyPay;
    }

    public void setHourlyPay(double hourlyPayIn)
    {
        hourlyPay = hourlyPayIn;
    }

    public double calculateWeeklyPay(int noOfHoursIn)
    {
        return noOfHoursIn * hourlyPay;
    }

}
```

The first line of interest is the class header itself:

```
class PartTimeEmployee extends Employee
```

Here we see the use of the keyword **extends**. Using this word in this way means that the PartTimeEmployee class (the *subclass*) inherits all the attributes of the Employee class (the *superclass*). So although we haven't coded them, any object of the PartTimeEmployee class will have, for example, an attribute called name and a method called getNumber.

But can you see a problem here? The attributes have been declared as private in the superclass so although they are now part of our PartTimeEmployee class, none of the PartTimeEmployee class methods can directly access them – the subclass has only the same access rights as any other class!

There are a number of possible ways around this:

1. We could declare the attributes as **public** – but this would take away the whole point of encapsulation!

2. We could use the special keyword **protected** instead of **private**. The effect of this is that anything declared as **protected** is accessible to the methods of any subclasses. There are, however, two problems with this. The first is that you have to anticipate in advance when you want your class to be able to be inherited. The second problem is that it weakens your efforts to encapsulate information within the class, since, in Java, **protected** attributes are also accessible to any other class in the same package.

3. The other solution is the one that we like best – and this is the one that we will be using in this book. This is to leave the attributes as **private**, but to plan in advance how we code the methods that provide access to these attributes. You will see examples of this as we proceed.

After the class header we have the following declaration:

```
private double hourlyPay;
```

This declares an attribute, `hourlyPay`, which is unique to our subclass – but remember that the attributes of the superclass, `Employee`, will be inherited, so in fact any `PartTimeEmployee` object will have four attributes.

Next comes the constructor. As we said before, we want to be able to assign values to the number and name at the time that the object is created, just as we do with an `Employee` object; so our constructor will need two parameters, which will be assigned to the `number` and `name` attributes.

But wait a minute! How are we going to do this? The `number` and `name` attributes have been declared as private in the superclass – so they aren't accessible to objects of the subclass. Luckily there is a way around this problem. We can call the constructor of the superclass by using the keyword **super**. Look how this is done:

```java
public PartTimeEmployee(String numberIn, String nameIn)
{
    // call the constructor of the superclass
    super(numberIn, nameIn);
}
```

The remaining methods are new methods specific to the derived class:

```java
public double getHourlyPay()
{
    return hourlyPay;
}

public void setHourlyPay(double hourlyPayIn)
{
    hourlyPay = hourlyPayIn;
}

public double calculateWeeklyPay(int noOfHoursIn)
{
    return noOfHoursIn * hourlyPay;
}
```

The first two provide read and write access respectively to the `hourlyPay` attribute. The third one receives the number of hours worked and calculates the pay by multiplying this by the hourly rate. Program 7.1 demonstrates the use of the `PartTimeEmployee` class.

Program 7.1

```
class PartTimeEmpTester
{
    public static void main(String[] args)
    {
        String number, name;
        double pay;
        int hours;
        PartTimeEmployee emp;
        // get the details from the user
        System.out.print("Employee Number? ");
        number = EasyIn.getString();
        System.out.print("Employee's Name? ");
        name = EasyIn.getString();
        System.out.print("Hourly Pay? ");
        pay = EasyIn.getDouble();
        System.out.print("Hours worked this week? ");
        hours = EasyIn.getInt();
        // create a new part-time employee
        emp = new PartTimeEmployee(number, name);
        // set the employee's hourly pay
        emp.setHourlyPay(pay);
        // display employee's details, including the weekly pay
        System.out.println();
        System.out.println(emp.getName());
        System.out.println(emp.getNumber());
        System.out.println(emp.calculateWeeklyPay(hours));
        EasyIn.pause();
    }
}
```

Here is a sample test run:

```
Employee Number? A103456
Employee's Name? Walter Wallcarpeting
Hourly Pay? 15.50
Hours worked this week? 20

Walter Wallcarpeting
A103456
310.0
```

We can now move on to look at another inheritance example; let's choose the `Oblong` class from chapter 5.

7.3.1   Extending the *Oblong* class

We are going to define a new class called `ExtendedOblong`, which extends the `Oblong` class. Firstly, let's remind ourselves of the `Oblong` class itself.

The *Oblong* class

```java
class Oblong
{
    // the attributes are declared first
    private double length;
    private double height;

    // then the methods

    // the constructor
    public Oblong(double l, double h)
    {
        length = l;
        height = h;
    }

    // the next method allows us to "read" the length attribute
    public double getLength()
    {
        return length;
    }

    // the next method allows us to "read" the height attribute
    public double getHeight()
    {
        return height;
    }

    // the next method allows us to "write" to the length attribute
    public void setLength(double lengthIn)
    {
        length = lengthIn;
    }
```

```
        // the next method allows us to "write" to the height attribute
        public void setHeight(double heightIn)
        {
            height = heightIn;
        }


        // this method returns the area of the oblong
        public double calculateArea()
        {
            return length * height;
        }


         // this method returns the perimeter of the oblong
        public double calculatePerimeter()
        {
            return 2 * (length + height);
        }
    }
```

The original Oblong class had the capability of reporting on the perimeter and area of the oblong. Our extended class will have the additional capability of drawing a text oblong on the screen by repeatedly displaying a symbol such as an asterisk.

So we will need an additional attribute, which we will call symbol, to hold the character that is to be used to draw the oblong. We will also provide a setSymbol method, and of course we will need a draw method. The new constructor will accept values for the length and height as before, but will also receive the character to be used for drawing the oblong.

The design is shown in figure 7.4.

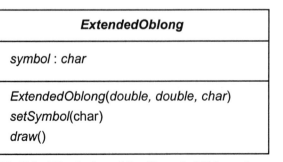

Fig 7.4   The design of the *ExtendedOblong* class

Now for the implementation. As well as those aspects of the code that relate to inheritance, there is an additional new technique used in this class – this is the technique known as **type casting**. Take a look at the complete code first – then we can discuss this new concept along with some other important features of the class.

The *ExtendedOblong* class

```java
class ExtendedOblong extends Oblong
{
   private char symbol;

   // the constructor
   public ExtendedOblong(double lengthIn, double heightIn, char symbolIn)
   {
       /* the 'super' method must be called before any other methods
       in the constructor */
       super(lengthIn, heightIn);
       symbol = symbolIn;
   }

   public void setSymbol(char symbolIn)
   {
       symbol = symbolIn;
   }

   public void draw()
   {
       int l, h, i, j;
       /* in the next two lines we type cast from double to
       integer so that we are able to count how many times we
       print the symbol */
       l = (int) getLength();
       h = (int) getHeight();
       for(i = 1; i <= h; i++)
       {
           for(j = 1; j <=l; j++)
           {
               System.out.print(symbol);
           }
           System.out.println();
       }
   }
}
```

So let's take a closer look at all this. After the class header – which **extend**s the
Oblong class – we declare the additional attribute, symbol, and then define our
constructor:

```
public ExtendedOblong(double lengthIn, doubleheightIn,char symbolIn)
{
    super(lengthIn, heightIn);
    symbol = symbolIn;
}
```

Once again we call the constructor of the superclass with the keyword **super**, but this
time we need to perform one more task – namely to assign the third parameter, symbolIn,
to the symbol attribute. Notice, however, that the line that calls **super** has to be the first
one!

After the constructor comes the setSymbol method – which allows the symbol to be
changed during the oblong's lifetime – and then we have the draw method, which
introduces the new concept of **type casting**.

```
public void draw()
{
    int i, j, l, h;
    // in the next two lines we type cast from double to integer
    l = (int) getLength();
    h = (int) getHeight();
    for(i = 1; i <= h; i++)
    {
        for(j = 1; j <=l; j++)
        {
            System.out.print(symbol);
        }
        System.out.println();
    }
}
```

Inspect the code carefully – notice that we have declared four local variables of type
int. The first two, i and j, are simply to be used as loop counters. But to understand the
purpose of the last two, l and h, we need to explore this business of type casting, which
means forcing an item to change from one type to another.

The draw method is going to draw the oblong by displaying one or more rows of stars or crosses or whatever symbol is chosen. Now the dimensions of the oblong are defined as **doubles**. Clearly our draw method needs to be dealing with whole numbers of rows and columns – so we must convert the length and height of the oblong from doubles to ints. There will obviously be some loss of precision here, but that won't matter in this particular case.

As you can see from the above code, type casting is achieved by placing the new type name in brackets before the item you wish to change. A further example appears in section 7.7.

Program 7.2 uses the ExtendedOblong class. It creates an oblong of length 10 and height 5, with an asterisk as the symbol; it then draws the oblong, changes the symbol to a cross, and draws it again.

Program 7.2

```
class ExtendedOblongTester
{
    public static void main(String[] args)
    {
        ExtendedOblong extOblong = new ExtendedOblong(10,5,'*');
        extOblong.draw();
        System.out.println();
        extOblong.setSymbol('+');
        extOblong.draw();
        EasyIn.pause();
    }
}
```

The output from program 7.2 is shown below:

```
* * * * * * * * *
* * * * * * * * *
* * * * * * * * *
* * * * * * * * *
* * * * * * * * *

+++++++++
+++++++++
+++++++++
+++++++++
+++++++++
```

7.4   Overriding class methods

Let's write another class that is derived from Oblong. This time we will develop a class that represents a three-dimensional oblong (a cuboid) as shown in figure 7.5. We will call this class ThreeDOblong.

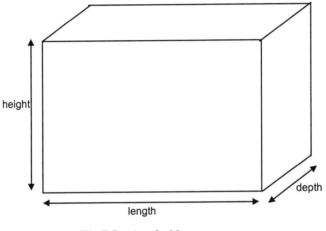

Fig 7.5   A cuboid

Clearly we are going to need another attribute, depth, to represent the additional dimension. We will also include a calculateVolume method. So far so good. But wait a second – the ThreeDOblong is going to inherit *all* the attributes and methods from the Oblong class. This includes the calculateArea method. And if we were to invoke this method for a ThreeDOblong object we would get the value of the length times the height – in other words, the area of one face of the oblong. In actual fact, finding the surface area of a three-dimensional oblong involves adding up the areas of all six faces. So the means of calculating the area differs according to whether the object is an Oblong object or a ThreeDOblong object.

Do you remember the term *polymorphism*? If not, look back at chapter 5 and remind yourself. It means we can use the same name for two different methods. In chapter 5 the program knew which method to call because the parameter list was different for each method. We are going to use a different form of polymorphism here. In our ThreeDOblong class we are going to re-define the calculateArea method. This is called **overriding** the method of the superclass. Look at the code for the ThreeDOblong class below. Notice how we have declared and defined a `calculateArea` method for that class.

The *ThreeDOblong* class

```
class ThreeDOblong extends Oblong
{
    private double depth;

    public ThreeDOblong(double l, double h, double d)
    {
        super(l,h);
        depth = d;
    }

    public void setDepth(double depthIn)
    {
        depth = depthIn;
    }

    public double getDepth()
    {
        return depth;
    }

    public double calculateVolume()
    {
        return getLength() * getHeight() * depth;
    }

    public double calculateArea()
    {
        /* Notice that we cannot access the length and height
        attributes directly as they are declared as private in
        the superclass, so we must use the getLength and
        getHeight methods. The depth attribute is accessible as
        it is declared in the subclass */
        return 2 *( getLength() * getHeight()
                    + getLength() * depth
                    + getHeight() * depth );
    }
}
```

So how does the program know which method we mean when we call `calculateArea`? Well, it knows because the call to the method will always be associated with a particular object – and the `calculateArea` method of the corresponding object will be called. This is illustrated in program 7.3, the output of which is displayed after the program. The two calls to the `calculateArea` method have been emboldened to help you understand it.

Program 7.3

```
class ThreeDOblongTester
{
    public static void main(String[] args)
    {
        Oblong oblong = new Oblong(5,10);
        ThreeDOblong threeDOblong = new ThreeDOblong(5,10,20);
        System.out.println("Area of the oblong is: "
        + oblong.calculateArea());
        System.out.println("Surface area of the 3D oblong is: "
        + threeDOblong.calculateArea());
        EasyIn.pause();
    }
}
```

The output from this program is:

```
Area of the oblong is: 50.0
Surface area of the 3D oblong is: 700.0
```

7.5   Abstract classes

Let's think again about our `Employee` class. Imagine that we had been developing our system from scratch – it might well have occurred to us at that time that there could be two types of employee, full-time and part-time. We might also have thought about the fact that in the future, as our business expands, there could be other types of employee (maybe "casual" or "fractional"). It would make sense to create a generalized `Employee` class, so that we can easily create other kinds of `Employees` later.

Figure 7.6 shows the structure of an employee **hierarchy** with the two types of employee that we already know about, the full-time and the part-time employee. We have gone straight into the design and have included all the basic access methods here – including a new method in the `Employee` class, called `getStatus`. We will discuss this method later.

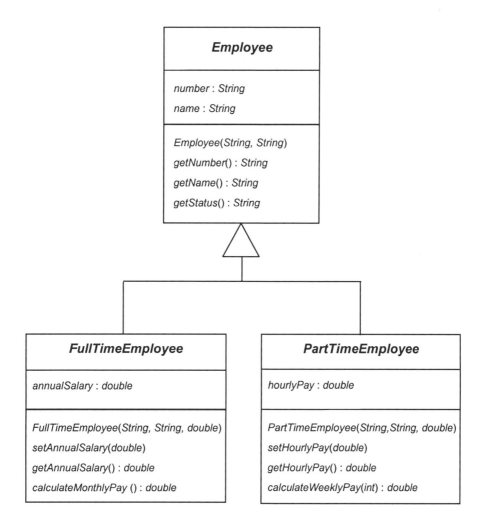

**Fig 7.6   An inheritance relationship showing the superclass _Employee_
and the subclasses _FullTimeEmployee_ and _PartTimeEmployee_**

Notice how the two subclasses now both contain the appropriate attributes and methods. If you think about this a bit more, it will occur to you that _any_ employee will always be either a full-time employee or a part-time employee. There is never going to be a situation in which an individual is just a plain old employee! So users of a program that included all these classes would never find themselves creating objects of the Employee class. In fact it would be a good idea to prevent people from doing this – and, as you might have guessed, there is a way to do so, and that is to declare the class as **abstract**. Once a class has been declared in this way it means that you are not allowed to create objects of that class. The Employee simply acts a basis on which to build other classes.

The code for the Employee appears below. If you inspect it you will notice something else interesting. Do you see that the getStatus method has also been declared **abstract**? Not only that, it also has a header but no body! Study the class for a moment and then we will tell you what this is all about.

The *Employee* class

```
abstract class Employee // the class is declared abstract
{
    private String number;
    private String name;

    public Employee(String numberIn, String nameIn)
    {
        number = numberIn;
        name = nameIn;
    }

    public String getNumber()
    {
        return number;
    }

    public String getName()
    {
        return name;
    }

    abstract public String getStatus(); // an abstract method
}
```

The purpose of declaring a *method* as **abstract** is to force all subclasses of our class to implement this method. In this case, a FullTimeEmployee and a PartTimeEmployee – and any future subclasses of Employee – will have to have a method called getStatus. The purpose of the getStatus method is to enable an object to report on what kind of employee it is – it will send back a String saying either "Full-time" or "Part-time" accordingly. Each subclass will *override* the getStatus method in a slightly different way.

We shall now implement the two derived classes. First the FullTimeEmployee:

The *FullTimeEmployee* class

```
class FullTimeEmployee extends Employee
{
    private double annualSalary;

    public FullTimeEmployee(String numberIn,
                                      String nameIn, double salaryIn)
    {
        super(numberIn,nameIn);
        annualSalary = salaryIn;
    }


    public void setAnnualSalary(double salaryIn)
    {
        annualSalary = salaryIn;
    }


    public double getAnnualSalary()
    {
        return annualSalary;
    }

    public double calculateMonthlyPay()
    {
        return annualSalary/12;
    }


    public String getStatus()
    {
        return "Full-Time";
    }
}
```

And now the PartTimeEmployee:

The *PartTimeEmployee* class

```
class PartTimeEmployee extends Employee
{
    private double hourlyPay;

    public PartTimeEmployee(String numberIn,
    String nameIn, double hourlyPayIn)
    {
        super(numberIn, nameIn);
        hourlyPay = hourlyPayIn;
    }

    public void setHourlyPay(double hourlyPayIn)
    {
        hourlyPay = hourlyPayIn;
    }

    public double getHourlyPay()
    {
        return hourlyPay;
    }

    public double calculateWeeklyPay(int noOfHoursIn)
    {
        return hourlyPay * noOfHoursIn;
    }

    public String getStatus()
    {
        return "Part-Time";
    }
}
```

You may be thinking that abstract classes and abstract methods are quite interesting, but is it worth all the bother? Well, there is another really useful thing we can do with abstract classes and methods.

Say a method of some class somewhere expects to receive as a parameter a particular class – an `Employee` class for example; and inside this method there is some code that calls a particular method of `Employee` – for example a method called `getStatus`. The marvellous thing about inheritance is that an object of any subclass of `Employee` is *a kind of* `Employee` and can therefore be passed as a parameter into a method that expects an `Employee` object. However, this subclass *must* have a `getStatus` method for it to be able to be passed as a parameter into a method that calls `getStatus`. By declaring the abstract method `getStatus` in the superclass we can *insist* that every subclass must have a `getStatus` method. We can tell anyone who is going to use a derivative of `Employee` to go right ahead and call a `getStatus` method because it will definitely be there – and what is more, it will behave differently for each object that it applies to.

If you think this sounds a bit complicated then an example will help. We have written a very simple class called `StatusTester`, whose sole purpose is to test out this abstract method stuff:

The *StatusTester* class

```
class StatusTester
{
    public static void tester(Employee employeeIn)
    {
        System.out.println(employeeIn.getStatus());
    }
}
```

You can see that this class has a single method, `tester`, which receives an `Employee` object, `employeeIn`, as a parameter. It then calls the `getStatus` method of `employeeIn`. Now, because objects of the class `FullTimeEmployee` and objects of the class `PartTimeEmployee` are both kinds of `Employee`, we can pass either of them to this `tester` method. We have made this a **static** method, so it can be called by using the class name.

In program 7.4 objects of both of these types are sent to the `tester` method.

```
Program 7.4

class RunStatusTester
{
    public static void main(String[] args)
    {
      // create a FullTimeEmployee object
      FullTimeEmployee fte = new FullTimeEmployee ("100", "Patel", 30000);
      // create a PartTimeEmployee object
      PartTimeEmployee pte = new PartTimeEmployee ("101", "Jones", 12);
      // call tester with the full-time employee
      StatusTester.tester(fte);
      // now call tester with the part-time employee
      StatusTester.tester(pte);
      EasyIn.pause("Press <enter> to quit");
    }
}
```

The tester method will call the appropriate getStatus method according to the type of object it receives. Thus the output from this program will be:

```
Full-Time
Part-Time
```

7.6   The *final* modifier

You have already seen the use of the keyword **final** in chapter 2, where it was used to modify a variable and turn it into a constant. It can also be used to modify a class and a method. In the case of a class it is placed before the class declaration, like this:

```
final class SomeClass
{
      // code goes here
}
```

This means that the class cannot be subclassed. In the case of a method it is used like this:

```
public final someMethod
{
    // code goes here
}
```

This means that the method cannot be overridden.

7.7   Generic collection classes

In the last chapter we constructed collection classes to hold specific items (for example integers or students). Sometimes it is desirable to have a collection class that can hold *any* item, and inheritance can help us to achieve this.

Remember the StudentList class you developed in your second practical task at the end of chapter 6. Apart from the type of the array elements, the code you wrote should have been exactly the same as the code for the StringList class that we developed in that chapter. Rather than write many lists, each to hold a different type, it would be much more productive to develop a list that could contain *any* type.

A collection that can contain items of any type is called a **generic collection class**. We will rewrite the StringList collection class from chapter 6 so that it can be used to contain items of *any* class, not just a String class. In some programming languages this is difficult; but in Java it is relatively easy because every object is in fact a subclass of a basic class called an **Object** class. In other words, any object in Java *is a kind of* **Object**! So all we have to do to make our list class generic is to use the type **Object** rather than a specific type like Student.

Below is the code for this generic class, which we have called ObjectList.

The *ObjectList* class

```
class ObjectList
{
    private Object[] object ;
    private int total ;

    public ObjectList(int sizeIn)
    {
        object = new Object[sizeIn];
        total = 0;
    }
```

```
    public boolean add(Object objectIn)
    {
        if(!isFull())
        {
            object[total] = objectIn;
            total++;
            return true;
        }
        else
        {
            return false;
        }
    }

    public boolean isEmpty()
    {
        if(total==0)
        {
            return true;
        }
        else
        {
            return false;
        }
    }


    public boolean isFull()
    {
        if(total==object.length)
        {
            return true;
        }
        else
        {
            return false;
        }
    }

    public Object getObject(int i)
    {
        return object[i-1];
    }
```

```
    public int getTotal()
    {
        return total;
    }


    public boolean remove(int numberIn)
    {
        // check that a valid index has been supplied
        if(numberIn >= 1 && numberIn <= total)
        {   // overwrite object by shifting following objects along
            for(int i = numberIn-1; i <= total-2; i++)
            {
                object[i] = object[i+1];
            }
            total--; // Decrement total number of objects
            return true;
        }
        else // remove was unsuccessful
        {
            return false;
        }
    }
}
```

As you can see, apart from changing the type of the array elements from `String` to `Object`, this code is identical to the `StringList` class that we developed in chapter 6. The advantage it has, however, is that this class can be used to hold objects of *any* type.

For example, you could use it to hold a list of `BankAccount` objects or a list of `Student` objects. You just have to be careful of one thing. That is, when an object is returned from a method in a generic collection class such as this, the type of that object will be `Object`. This collection class has one such method, `getObject`.

```
public Object getObject(int i) // returns Object type
{
    return object[i-1];
}
```

This item of type `Object` must be converted back into the actual type used within the list. That is, back to a `BankAccount` if the list was used to hold `BankAccount` objects, back to `String` if the list was used to hold `String` objects and so on. This is easily done – by **type casting**.

For example, assume an object of type `ObjectList` has been created and named `list`. If the list was used to hold `Student` objects, the second student in the list could be accessed as follows:

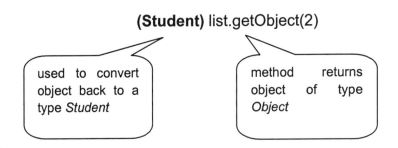

Program 7.5 is an `ObjectListTester` class, which illustrates the generic list being used to hold items of type `String`. Since the code is almost identical to the `StringListTester` in chapter 6, most lines have been replaced by comments, with only the changes highlighted.

Program 7.5

```
class ObjectListTester
{
    public static void main(String[] args)
    {
        char choice;
        int size;
        System.out.println("Maximum number of items in list?");
        size = EasyIn.getInt();
        // create generic list
        ObjectList list = new ObjectList(size);
        // menu control goes here as before
    }
    public static void option1 (ObjectList list)
    {
        // code for adding object, as before
    }
```

```
    public static void option2 (ObjectList list)
    {
        // code for removing item,as before
    }
    public static void option3 (ObjectList list)
    {
        // code for checking if list is empty, as before
    }
    public static void option4 (ObjectList list)
    {
        // code for checking if list is full, as before
    }
    public static void option5 (ObjectList list) // displays items
    {
        // as before up to loop
        for(int i = 1; i<= list.getTotal(); i++)
        {
            // remember to type cast back
            System.out.println((String)list.getObject(i));
        }
        System.out.println();
    }
}
```

Of course, if you were to run this program it would behave exactly the same as program 6.4. The advantage with the ObjectList class is that you could reuse it to hold objects of other types simply by replacing String in the tester above with another class!

This all sounds great, but what are you going to do if you want a generic collection class to hold values of the simple scalar types? Unfortunately, you can't just write a tester class and replace the String class in program 7.5 with the type **int**.

Can you see why you can't do this?

The reason you can't use the generic list to hold items of type **int** is that the generic class can hold values of any type, *as long as they are objects* and not simple intrinsic types like **double**s.

All is not lost, however. At the end of chapter 5 we told you about a special group of classes that would be ideal for our purposes right now – **wrapper classes**.

If you remember, wrapper classes provide a class wrapper for simple scalar types. Each scalar type has a class wrapper. Once we put a scalar value into its wrapper class we can pass it into the ObjectList for storage.

The wrapper class for integers is Integer. Look at the following example to see how to place a value of type **int** into an Integer wrapper.

```
// create a simple variable
int x = 10;
// create wrapper object from the value of x
Integer value = new Integer (x);
System.out.println("object has an integer value of " + value.intValue());
```

In this example x is a simple variable of type **int**. The value of x is initialized to 10. A new object, value, of type Integer (a wrapper class) is then created to contain the value of x by using the **new** operator. The final output then displays the value of the Integer object as follows:

```
object has value of 10
```

We have used the intValue method of Integer to extract the **int** value that the object holds.[1]

Program 7.6 illustrates another tester program that uses the ObjectList as a list of integers. Once again, only those parts of the class that have changed from program 7.5 have been highlighted.

Program 7.6

```
class ObjectListTester2
{
        public static void main(String[] args)
        {
                char choice;
                boolean ok;
                int size;
                System.out.println("Maximum number of items in list?");
                size = EasyIn.getInt();
                // create generic list
                ObjectList list = new ObjectList(size);
                // offer menu for an integer list
                do
                {
                        System.out.println();
                        System.out.println("1. Add integer to list");
```

---

[1] Actually, the concatenation operator allows you to join an Integer object with a string, so we could have got away with just using value instead of value.intValue().

```
                System.out.println("2. Remove integer from list");
                System.out.println("3. Check if list is empty");
                System.out.println("4. Check if list is full");
                System.out.println("5. Display integers in list");
                System.out.println("6. Quit");
                System.out.println();
                System.out.print("Enter choice [1-6]: ");
                choice = EasyIn.getChar();
                System.out.println();
                // process choice
                switch(choice)
                {
                    case '1': option1(list); break;
                    case '2': option2(list); break;
                    case '3': option3(list); break;
                    case '4': option4(list);break;
                    case '5': option5(list);break;
                    case '6' : break;
                    default : System.out.println("Invalid entry");
                }
        }while(choice!='6');
    }


    public static void addInteger (ObjectList list)
    {
        System.out.print("Enter an integer number: ");
        int number = EasyIn.getInt(); // enter value
        Integer item = new Integer (number); // place in wrapper
        boolean ok = list.add(item); // add object
        // other code same as before
    }

    public static void removeInteger (ObjectList list)
    {
        // as before
    }



    public static void checkEmpty (ObjectList list)
    {
        // as before
    }
```

```
        public static void checkFull (ObjectList list)
        {
            // as before
        }


        public static void displayIntegers (ObjectList list)
        {
            if(list.isEmpty())
            {
                // as before
            }
            else
            {
                System.out.println("Integers in list are: ");
                System.out.println();
                for(int i=1; i<= list.getTotal(); i++)
                { // Type cast back to Integer
                    System.out.println((Integer)list.getObject(i));
                }
                System.out.println();
            }
        }
    }
```

7.8   Pros and cons of generic collections

The idea of a generic collection class sounds good – and so it is; however, as with most things in life there are drawbacks as well as advantages. One obvious drawback is that we have to remember to type cast every time we retrieve an item from the collection. Another disadvantage is that we are limited as to what we can do with the methods of a generic collection class, since we cannot anticipate in advance the sort of objects it is going to contain.

The choice of whether to use a generic collection class (which might well mean we can reuse an existing class) or to use a specialized class is one of the many decisions that we have to make at the design stage, and will depend on the application we are building and the way we want it to work. In chapter 10, when we develop our case study, you will be able to see how we take our generic ObjectList class from this chapter and develop it using inheritance.

Tutorial exercises

1. Explain the meaning of the following terms:

   - inheritance;
   - method overriding;
   - type casting;
   - generic collection.

2. A class called Vehicle is required by a programmer who is writing software for a car dealer. An object of the class Vehicle will consist of a registration number, the make of the vehicle, the year of manufacture and the current value of the vehicle. The first three of these will need to be set only at the time an object is created. The current value will also be set at the time of creation, but may need to be changed during the vehicle's lifetime.

   It will be necessary to have a means of reading the values of all the above data items. A method should also be provided which accepts a year as input, and returns the age of the vehicle.

   a) Design the Vehicle class using UML notation and then write the code for this class.

   b) Design and code a subclass of Vehicle called SecondHandVehicle. The subclass will have an additional attribute, numberOfOwners, which will need to be set at the time a new vehicle is created, and will also need to have read access to it. An additional method is also required which will report on whether or not the vehicle has had more than one previous owner.

3. Explain why it is not possible to use a generic collection class to store items of type char, and describe what you would need to do in order to use a generic class to store characters.

Practical work

1. Implement the Vehicle and the SecondHandVehicle classes from tutorial question 2 above.

2. Write a tester class to test out all the methods of the SecondHandVehicle class.

3. Write a menu-driven program that uses a generic collection class to hold Vehicles. The menu should offer the following options:

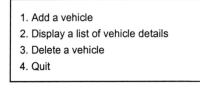

```
1. Add a vehicle
2. Display a list of vehicle details
3. Delete a vehicle
4. Quit
```

4. a) Implement a generic ObjectQueue class. Test this out by using it to hold firstly characters and then integers (refer back to tutorial question 3 before you do this).

    b) Repeat the above with a generic ObjectStack class.

8 Software quality

Learning objectives

By the end of this chapter you should be able to:

- document your code so that it is easy to **maintain**;
- distinguish between **compile-time errors** and **run-time errors**;
- test a program using the strategies of **unit testing** and **integration testing**;
- generate test data using the strategies of **black box testing, white box testing** and **stress testing**;
- document your test results professionally using a test log;
- explain the meaning of a Java program **throwing an exception**;
- format your output to improve the **usability** of your programs.

8.1   Introduction

If you buy a new computer, you will probably want that computer to be of a **high quality**. The features you would expect to find in a computer of high quality would be that it is fast, it has a large storage capacity, it supports the latest graphic and sound features – you may be able to think of others. Similarly, if you buy a piece of software you would want that software to be produced to a high quality. But what does it mean for software to be of a high quality? How can you measure software quality?

There are many desirable features of a piece of software. In this chapter we will concentrate on the following:

- maintainability;
- reliability;
- robustness;
- usability.

The more the software exhibits these features, the greater is the **quality** of the software. Let's look at each of these features in turn.

8.2   Maintainability

The requirements of an application often change over time. **Maintaining** a system refers to the need to *update* an existing system to reflect these changing requirements. Code should be designed in such a way as to make these changes easier rather than harder.

8.2.1   The importance of encapsulation

One of the problems associated with maintaining software systems has been the so-called **ripple effect**. That is, changes to one part of the system having undesirable knock-on effects on the rest of the system, resulting in system errors.

Such effects can often be hard to detect and to trace. As we discussed in chapter 4, programs written in the old structured way can often lead to such ripple effects. The object-oriented principle of *encapsulation*, however, helps ensure that object-oriented code is easier to maintain by reducing such effects: each object should contain within it all the details it needs to operate, and this data should be hidden inside the object so that changes made to it do not affect the rest of the system.

Java is a pure object-oriented language so programs written in Java should be easier to maintain than their structured counterparts. However, the language does not *insist* that you follow the principles of encapsulation when developing your code – that is your responsibility!

In particular, a class could be defined so that its data members are accessible to any other class – thus breaking the principles of encapsulation. Any future changes to such data would require changes to each method that accessed this data directly, resulting once again in the ripple effects you should aim to avoid. The lesson is a simple one – to ensure that your applications are easy to maintain, keep the data attributes of your classes `private`.

8.2.2   Documentation

A complete software system consists of more than just the final program. For example, most applications that you buy will come with some kind of user manual. Additional supporting materials such as these are referred to as the system's **documentation**. A comprehensive system should have documentation supporting *every* stage of software development. The user manual is an example of a piece of documentation that supports software installation and operation.

For a software system to be easy to maintain, the software *design* also needs to be clearly documented. Often, the people responsible for maintaining a software system are not the same people who initially developed the system. Think of the infamous Y2K bug that worried many companies a few years ago. Many of the systems affected were decades old and the identity of the original developers was no longer known. Design documentation helps new developers understand the working of systems that they themselves may not have produced. When developing object-oriented programs, this design documentation should include:

- complete class diagrams;
- clear method definitions (parameter and return types, plus pseudocode when appropriate).

The UML notation that we have been using throughout this book is becoming a common way of expressing these design decisions. The layout of the code itself can help clarify design decisions and make code maintenance easier.

To understand how important in-code documentation like this can be, consider the two classes below: BadReactor and Reactor. Both classes keep track of the temperature within a reactor in exactly the same way except that one has been documented with care, while the other has been documented poorly. If you were asked to maintain this system so that the maximum safe temperature was to be reduced by two degrees, which class would you find easier to understand and modify?

The *BadReactor* class is very poorly documented

```
class BadReactor
{
private int t;
public BadReactor()
{
t = 0;
}
public int getValue (){
return t;
}
public boolean increase(){
boolean b;
if (t < 10)
{t++;
 b = false;
}
else
{
t = 0;
b = true;
}
return b;
}
}
```

The *Reactor* class has been documented with care

```
// controls reactor temperature ensuring it does not go over some maximum
class Reactor
{
        private static final int MAX=10; // set maximum temperature
        private int temperature;

        public Reactor()
        {
            temperature = 0; // set initial level
        }

        public int getTemperature ()
        {   // return current level
            return temperature;
        }


        public boolean increaseTemp()
        {   /* increase temperature if safe,
            drop to zero and raise alarm if not */
            boolean alarm;
            if (temperature < MAX)
            {
                temperature ++;
                alarm = false ;
            }
            else
            {
                temperature = 0;
                alarm = true;
            }
            return alarm;
        }
}
```

When including in-code documentation consider the following:

- comments to make the meaning of your code clear;
- meaningful data names;
- constants in place of fixed literal numbers;
- consistent and clear indentation.

Look at the example programs that we have presented to you and notice how we have tried to stick to these principles throughout this book. In particular, notice the care we have taken with our indentation. We are following two simple rules all the time:

- keep braces lined up under the structure to which they belong;
- indent, by one level, all code that belongs within those braces.

For example, look back at the `increaseTemp` method of the `Reactor` class.

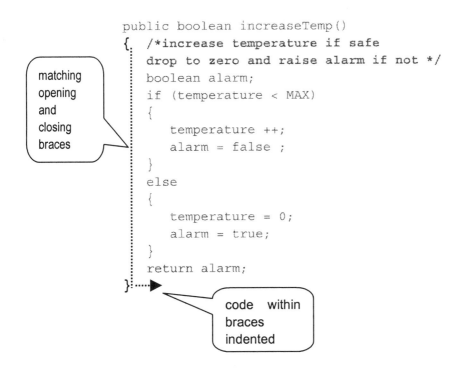

```
public boolean increaseTemp()
{   /*increase temperature if safe
    drop to zero and raise alarm if not */
    boolean alarm;
    if (temperature < MAX)
    {
        temperature ++;
        alarm = false ;
    }
    else
    {
        temperature = 0;
        alarm = true;
    }
    return alarm;
}
```

matching opening and closing braces

code within braces indented

Notice how these rules are applied again with the braces of the inner **if** and **else** statements:

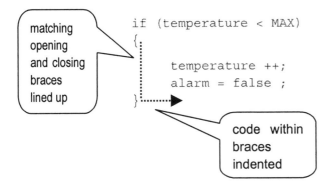

```
if (temperature < MAX)
{
    temperature ++;
    alarm = false ;
}
```

matching opening and closing braces lined up

code within braces indented

Also, if you look back at the `Reactor` class you can see that the careful choice of variable names greatly reduces the need for comments. Always attempt to make the code as self-documenting as possible by choosing meaningful names.

8.3   Reliability

A **reliable** program is one that does what it is supposed to do, in other words what it is *specified* to do. When attempting to build a program, two kinds of errors could occur:

- compile-time errors;
- run-time errors.

As the name implies, **compile-time errors** occur during the process of compilation. Such errors would mean you could not run your program at all as you have not followed the rules of the language to construct a valid program. Examples of these kinds of mistakes include:

- missing semi-colons;
- forgetting to close a bracket;
- being inconsistent with names and/or types;
- attempting to access a variable/object without having first initialized it.

Most Java compilers work very hard in this respect as they trap many errors that many other language compilers do not check for: ensuring that you haven't attempted to access an uninitialized variable being one example. You should become familiar with messages associated with certain kinds of errors, in order to find and fix them quickly. Often, a single mistake can cause the compiler to get confused and produce a long list of errors. Rather than attempting to fix them all, fix the first and then recompile. Look at the program and associated error list in figure 8.1. Although there appear to be many errors, there is in fact just one. Can you spot it?

The only error in the code of figure 8.1 is that the variable `salary`, referenced at many points in the code, was named `Salary` (note a capital 'S') when declared.

```
double Salary; // notice capital letter
salary = EasyIn.getDouble; // will result in compiler error
// more references to 'salary' here causing further compiler errors
```

All these errors can be removed by re-declaring this variable as follows:

```
double salary;
```

If you have no compilation errors then you can begin to think about running your program in order to ensure that it does what it is supposed to do. This process is known as **testing**.

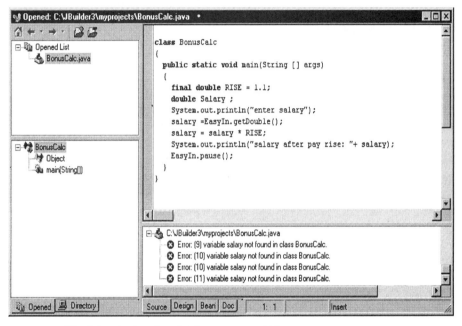

Fig 8.1   A simple mistake may result in many error messages

Testing can never show the *absence* of errors, only the *presence* of them. The aim therefore of any testing strategy is to uncover these errors. A program may not do what it is supposed to do because the original requirements were not precise enough and/or because the programmer has made logical errors in the program. Either way the final program will contain defects. This leads to two areas of testing:

- **validation** (making sure you are building the right product);
- **verification** (making sure you are building the product right).

Validation is a process of ensuring that your final system meets *the user's* requirements. This is an important process as developers often misjudge the original requirements given to them by clients. This may be because the requirements were not expressed clearly to begin with, or the clients were not sure themselves of the exact needs of the final system. Either way, validation will obviously require the interaction of the client. The RAD approach to software development, which we told you about in chapter 1, allows systems to be developed incrementally by means of regular validation.

Verification is a process of ensuring that the code you develop meets *your own* understanding of the user requirements. This will involve running your application in order to trap errors you may have made in program logic. A Java application typically consists of many classes working together. Testing for such errors will start with a process of **unit testing** (testing individual classes) followed by **integration testing** (testing classes that together make up an application).

8.3.1   Unit testing

Let's look at the `Reactor` class as our first example. Before incorporating this class into a larger program you would want to run it in order to test it was working reliably. This class as it stands, however, cannot be run as it has no `main` method in it.

All applications require a class with a `main` method before they can be run. Eventually, when this class is incorporated into a larger program a suitable class with a `main` method will exist, but you'll want to test this class before an entire suite of classes have been developed. One possibility would be to add a `main` method into *this* class.

```
class Reactor
{
 private static final int MAX=10;
 private int temperature;
 // add main method
 public static void main(String[] args)
 {
     // generate Reactor object to test
     Reactor b = new Reactor();
     // testing methods of Reactor object here
 }
 // original methods still here
}
```

Here an object of type `Reactor` is instantiated *within* the `Reactor` class:

```
class Reactor
{
    // some code here
    Reactor b = new Reactor();
    // some more code here
}
```

This object can then be used for testing purposes. While some people do take this approach, we feel it clutters up the original class and mistakes could inadvertently be typed into the original class. For this reason we prefer to take the alternative approach of writing a separate class especially to contain the main method. This new class then acts as the **driver** for the original class. A driver is a special program designed to do nothing except exercise a particular class. If you look back at all our previous examples, this is exactly how we tested individual classes. When testing classes in this way, *every method* of the class should be tested. Program 8.1 is an example of a driver for the Reactor class.

Program 8.1

```
class ReactorTester
{
    // define main method
    public static void main(String[] args)
    {
        char reply;
        Reactor b = new Reactor(); // generate object to test
        do
        {   // test all methods
            System.out.print("current temperature is ");
            System.out.println(b.getTemperature());
            boolean error = b.increaseTemp();
            if (error) // check if increase raised an error
            {
                System.out.println("warning: alarm raised");
            }
            System.out.println("temperature after increase is ");
            System.out.println(b.getTemperature());
            System.out.print("test some more (y/n)? ");
            reply = EasyIn.getChar();
        } while (reply != 'n'); // loop until user quits
    }
}
```

At the moment the methods are tested in strict sequence. The usability of this driver can be improved by, for example, including a menu system to test each method. We shall return to issues that affect the usability of programs later on in this chapter.

Let's continue our look at unit testing by turning our attention to the StudentList class that we asked you to develop in the second practical task of chapter 6. The procedure for testing an individual class requires a bit more thought if that class *relies upon another class* that is yet to be developed. In this case the StudentList class requires the Student class to be available.

```
class StudentList
{
        private Student [] list; // requires access to Student class
        // more attributes and methods of StudentList written here
}
```

If you were developing the StudentList class, you may not have the Student class available to you, either because you had not yet developed it or it was not your responsibility to develop it. It would be impossible, however, to proceed with your class development if you did not know what to expect of the classes you were relying on. The following information on the class you are relying upon is essential before you can start constructing your own class:

- the name of the class;
- the name of the methods;
- the interface (return type and parameter list) of each method.

All this information should already have been recorded in the detailed design documentation for the application you are developing (see figure 8.2).

If you need to unit test a given class that relies upon the development of another class to which you do not have access, you can develop your own **dummy** class in place of the missing class. A dummy class is one that mimics an actual class in order for testing to proceed.

Such a class is often much simpler than the class it is mimicking as it only needs to include enough information to allow the given class you are testing to compile and run effectively.

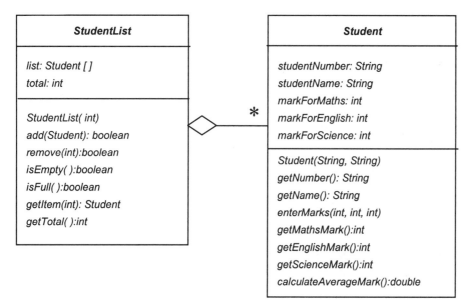

Fig 8.2 Detailed design documentation for the *StudentList* system

In order to allow this StudentList class to compile, an appropriate dummy Student class can be developed as follows:

A dummy *Student* class

```
class Student
{
      // no code in class
}
```

If you look carefully at the StudentList class you will see that the methods of a Student object are never accessed. For this reason, this dummy Student class contains no attributes or methods. If the StudentList class accessed any of the methods of the Student class, associated dummy methods would have to be added into the dummy Student class in order to allow the StudentList class to compile.

For example, consider the situation where there was a findStudentAverage method in the StudentList class as follows:

```
public double findStudentAverage (int i)
{
      return student[i-1].calculateAverageMark( );
}
```

Here, the findStudentAverage method of the Studentlist class is calling a method, calculateAverageMark, of the Student class. But our dummy Student class contains no methods! To get around this problem, the dummy Student class would need to be amended so that an implementation existed for the calculateAverageMark method. This implementation should have an interface that is consistent with that outlined in the design documentation of figure 8.2:

calculateAverageMark():double

So the new dummy Student class could, for example, be implemented as follows:

The amended dummy _Student_ class

```
class Student
{
    // additional dummy method
    public double calculateAverageMark()
    {
        return 50.5;
    }
}
```

The additional dummy method in this case just returns a set mark of 50.5. In the real Student class this may have involved a complicated calculation amongst many individual unit marks.

Note that with this dummy class in place, a driver class with a main function still needs to be written in order to run this application. Any additional Student methods that this tester class requires (such as a constructor) will have to be added into this dummy class in the form of additional dummy methods. This is left as a practical exercise at the end of this chapter.

8.3.2   Integration testing

When the individual classes in a program have been tested they can be integrated and tested together in order to ensure that the interface between classes is working correctly.

In order to test this interface the whole suite of classes needs to be recompiled together. The reason for this is that the interfaces between classes may be inconsistent. If compiler errors occur during integration then check the following:

- all methods that are called have an implementation in the receiving class;

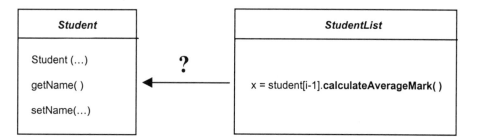

- the names of method calls match **exactly** the names of these methods in the receiving class;

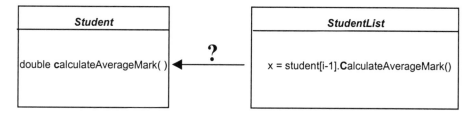

- the parameter list of a method call matches **exactly** the parameter list of these methods in the receiving class;

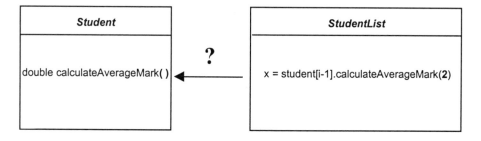

- the expected types of values returned from the method calls match the return types of these methods in the receiving class.

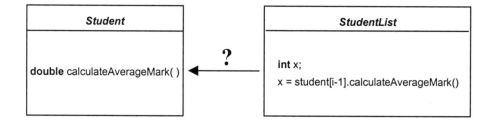

Whether you are carrying out unit testing or integration testing, the choice of test data is crucial in locating defects that may be present in the component. Two common approaches are **black box** and **white box** testing.

8.3.3   Black box testing

Black box testing is an approach to test data generation that treats the component being tested as an opaque box; that is, the details of the code are ignored (see figure 8.3). The specification is used to determine different groups of input values. A group of inputs that all produce the *same output* are regarded as equivalent. In this way inputs can be categorized into **equivalent groups**.

component to test

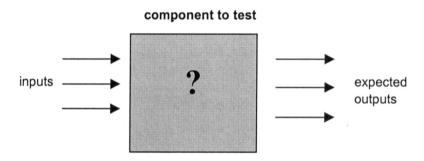

Fig 8.3   The black box approach to testing

For example, consider a method `getGrade`, which accepts a student mark and returns a student grade ('A', 'B', 'C', 'D', 'E' or 'F'). Table 8.1 illustrates how these grades are arrived at.

Table 8.1	Student grades
marks 70 and above	grade 'A'
marks in the 60's	grade 'B'
marks in the 50's	grade 'C'
marks in the 40's	grade 'D'
marks in the 30's	grade 'E'
marks below 30	grade 'F'

Additionally a mark below 0 will produce a "MARK TOO LOW" error message, and a mark over 100 will produce a "MARK TOO HIGH" error message.

Remember that an equivalent group of inputs should all produce the same output. How many equivalent groups can you identify? There are in fact eight equivalent input groups.

1. marks from 70 to 100 are equivalent as they all produce the grade 'A';
2. marks from 60 to 69 are equivalent as they all produce the grade 'B';
3. marks from 50 to 59 are equivalent as they all produce the grade 'C';
4. marks from 40 to 49 are equivalent as they all produce the grade 'D';
5. marks from 30 to 39 are equivalent as they all produce the grade 'E';
6. marks from 0 to 29 are equivalent as they all produce the grade, 'F';
7. marks below 0 are equivalent as they all produce a "MARK TOO LOW" error message;
8. marks above 100 are equivalent as they all produce a "MARK TOO HIGH" error message.

When testing this method you should test *at least one mark* from each equivalent group. Figure 8.4 illustrates one possible set of test data generated in this way.

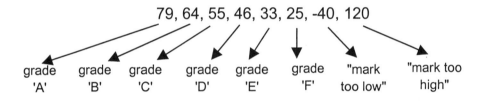

Fig 8.4 Test data generated by examining equivalent groups of input

If a given mark from an equivalence group produces the correct result, you may be tempted to assume that all marks within that group are correct. Remember though that a sample can never *guarantee* that all test cases are correct, they can just *increase your confidence* that the code is correct.

If the code fails to produce the correct result despite having tested a sample from each equivalent group, often the error lies on the boundaries of such equivalent groups. The marks 69, 70 and 71, for example, lie around the boundary between the grade 'A' group of marks and the grade 'B' group of marks.

Therefore, in addition to taking sample test cases from each equivalent group, the boundary values in particular should be tested. In this case the following boundary values should all be tested as well as the sample from each equivalent group identified earlier:

−1, 0, 1, 29, 30, 31,39, 40, 41,49, 50, 51,59, 60, 61, 69, 70, 71, 99, 100, 101

If your test cases include a sample from each equivalent group of inputs and all those values that lie on the boundary of those inputs, you are fairly likely to locate any errors that you may have in your code.

8.3.4   White box testing

White box testing is a test generation strategy that treats a software component like a transparent box into which test designers can peek while designing a test case.

Test designers can take advantage of their knowledge of the component's implementation to design tests that will cover all possible paths of execution through the component (see figure 8.5).You can see in figure 8.5 that a **while** loop is being used, so tests should be generated to allow the **while** loop to be executed:

- zero times;
- once;
- more than once.

Inside the loop there is a series of **if** statements; test cases should be selected so that:

- each **if** condition is executed;
- each **else** condition is executed.

Note that the test cases you use following a black box approach will be the same whatever implementation you have arrived at for your component, but the test cases produced as a result of white box testing may vary from implementation to implementation.

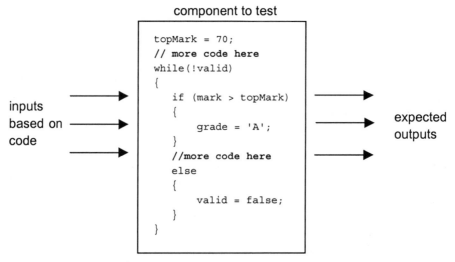

component to test

```
topMark = 70;
// more code here
while (!valid)
{
    if (mark > topMark)
    {
        grade = 'A';
    }
    //more code here
    else
    {
        valid = false;
    }
}
```

inputs based on code

expected outputs

Fig 8.5   The white box approach to testing

8.3.5 The test log

Once a strategy is chosen, the test results should be logged in a **test log**. A test log is a document that records the testing that took place during system development.

Each test case associates an *input* with an *expected output*. The aim of the test is to find a case where the expected output is *not produced*. When such a case is found the reasons for the error have to be identified. A test log needs to record the action associated with entering a given input, the expected result of that action and then the outcome (pass or fail). If the output is not as expected, reasons for this error have to be identified and recorded in the log. Figure 8.6 illustrates a typical test log used to document the testing of the `StudentList` class.

TEST LOG			
Purpose: To test the STUDENTLIST class			
Run Number: 1	**Date: 17th March 2000**		
Action	**Expected Output**	**Pass/ Fail**	**Reason for failure**
Add student ("Ade")	message "student entered"	✓	
set mark to 69	no message expected	✓	
get grade	'B'	✓	
Add student ("Madhu")	message "student entered"	✓	
set mark to 70	no message expected	✓	
get grade	'A'	✗	Displays 'B' instead of 'A'. Due to error in **if** statement
other tests			

Fig 8.6 A test log is used to document the testing process

The test log indicates that an error has been identified when an incorrect grade is displayed. In such a case the reason for the error is investigated and logged. The error has been caused by an incorrect **if** statement as follows:

```
if (mark > topMark)
{
     grade = 'A';
}
```

This will not produce a PASS when the mark is *exactly* 70 (the value of `topMark`). Here is one way to fix the error:

```
if (mark > topMark-1)
{
     grade = 'A';
}
```

Now a mark of 70 would produce an 'A' grade. As soon as an error is encountered the test run is stopped while the error is fixed. When an amendment has been made to your code, **all** the test cases need to be re-executed.

The reason for this is that modifications to your code could cause an error where previously there was no error. For example, if we had used real numbers to store marks, the above modification would produce a grade 'A' for a mark of 69.4 where previously it had accurately displayed this to be a grade 'B' mark.

This form of testing is known as **regression testing**. A new test log is filled in each time a program is run. Figure 8.7 illustrates test run number 2.

You may need a number of test runs before you clear all errors. Your test documentation should include *all* these test runs.

TEST LOG			
Purpose: To test the STUDENTQUEUE class			
Run Number: 2	**Date: 17th March 2000**		
Action	**Expected Output**	**Pass/ Fail**	**Reason for failure**
Add student ("Ade")	message "student entered"	✓	
set mark to 69	no message expected	✓	
get grade	'A'	✓	
set mark to 70	no message expected	✓	
get grade	'B'	✓	
other tests			

Fig 8.7   The testing process may involve many test runs

8.4   Robustness

A program is said to **crash** when it terminates unexpectedly. A **robust** program is one that doesn't crash even if it receives unexpected input values. For instance, if you were playing a computer game that allowed you to move falling blocks left or right using the arrow keys on your keyboard, you wouldn't want that game to suddenly stop if you hit the wrong key!

In chapter 3 we introduced you to the idea of *input validation* to deal with such unexpected values. Generally, whenever a value is received to be processed, it should be checked before processing continues, if an unexpected value could cause the program to crash. This is not only the case when the user enters a value, but also when a method receives a value as a parameter.

As an example, consider a car showroom (cars4U) that employs two sales staff. Each week, the number of cars sold for each employee is recorded and bonus payments are calculated.

A class, SalesStaff, has been developed for this purpose as follows:

The *SalesStaff* class

```
class SalesStaff
{
    private int [] staff; // to hold weekly sales figures for staff
    private static final int MAX = 2; // maximum number of staff
    private double bonus;

    public SalesStaff(double bonusIn) // parameter to set bonus rate
    {
        staff = new int[MAX]; // create array
        for (int i = 0; i<staff.length;i++)
        {
            staff[i] = 0; // set figures to zero
        }
        bonus = bonusIn;
    }


    // method allows a sales figure for a given salesperson to be set
    public void setFigure(int numberIn, int valueIn)
    {   // remember array indices begin at zero
        staff[numberIn-1] = valueIn;
    }
}
```

```
      // method to calculate bonus
      public double getBonus(int numberIn)
      {
            return (staff[numberIn-1]*bonus);
      }


      // method to return the maximum number of sales staff
      public int getMAX()
      {
            return MAX;
      }
}
```

As it stands, this class is not particularly robust. For example, look again at the setFigure method:

```
public void setFigure(int numberIn, int valueIn)
{
      staff[numberIn-1] = valueIn;
}
```

Can you see why this method might cause a program to crash? Well, the reason that this method could cause the program to crash is because it uses the value of one of the parameters, numberIn, to access an element within the hidden array attribute, staff.

```
      public void setFigure(int numberIn, int valueIn)
      {

            staff[numberIn-1] = valueIn;

      }
```

If you look back at the SalesStaff class you will see that this is an array with just two elements indexed, therefore, from 0 to 1. Any attempt to access an element at index 2, for example, would be an error and would cause your program to crash. To illustrate this, program 8.2 is a simple driver written to push the SalesStaff class to its limits.

Program 8.2

```
class PushToLimitSalesStaff
{
    public static void main(String[] args)
    {
        int value;
        double bonus;
        System.out.println("Bonus paid for each car sold ? ");
        bonus = EasyIn.getDouble();
        SalesStaff cars4U = new SalesStaff(bonus); // create object
        // loop to fill up list
        for (int i = 1; i<=3; i++) //counter going up to 3 is an error!
        {
            System.out.println ("enter sales for employee "+ i);
            value = EasyIn.getInt();
            cars4U.setFigure(i, value);
        }
        // display bonuses
        for (int i = 1; i<3; i++) // this time loop counter is ok
        {
            System.out.print("bonus for employee " + i + " = ");
            System.out.println(cars4U.getBonus(i));
        }
        EasyIn.pause("press <Enter> to quit");
    }
}
```

This form of testing, where you push a component to its limits (fill up the array in this case), is referred to as **stress testing**. If you were to run this driver, the program would crash as an attempt is made to enter a third value into an array that can only hold two values (see figure 8.8).

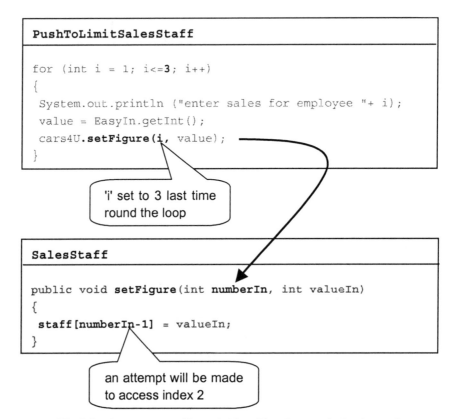

Fig 8.8   A program will crash if an illegal array index is used

When the program crashes it throws out the following error message explaining the reason for the crash:

```
java.lang.ArrayIndexOutOfBoundsException: 2
```

As you can see, the error message is quite descriptive: it's telling you that there is a problem with the *array index*. Also the offending array index (2) is displayed. In Java this type of error is referred to as an **exception** as it is a situation that is out of the norm. The Java system is aware of many exceptional circumstances that can occur during the life of a program and, should such an error occur, the correct exception is reported. This process of reporting an exception is known as **throwing an exception**.

In Java, one way of dealing with an exception when it is thrown is to **catch** it before it causes any damage. However, the details of how you carry this out are a bit too complex for your first semester! For now, you should write your code so that the program does not throw such an exception in the first place. In this case you would need to ensure that an array index is valid before you use it.

This responsibility to check this value could be given to the class in which the method that *supplies* the parameter is contained. While this check may indeed take place, the principle of *encapsulation* requires no assumptions about the calling environment to be made, so it cannot be *assumed* that this parameter has been validated. The setFigure method still has a responsibility to check the value of the parameter, which it could do as follows:

```
public void setFigure(int numberIn, int valueIn)
{    // check index will be valid before accessing array
    if (numberIn <= staff.length)
    {
        staff[numberIn-1] = valueIn;
    }
}
```

Now, the array access is protected inside an **if** statement. This is better as the program will no longer crash when an attempt is made to access array indices greater than 1. However, the caller of this method would have no idea that the given sales figure was not entered. An alternative approach would be to display an error message as follows:

```
public void setFigure(int numberIn, int valueIn)
{
    if(numberIn <= staff.length)
    {
        staff[numberIn-1] = valueIn;
    }
    else // display error message when index is invalid
    {
        System.out.println("error queue is full");
    }
}
```

The problem with this approach is that we have put the error message *in* the setFigure method. However, you cannot predict whether the user of this class would be using a *text screen* for input/output or a *graphics window*, or how the user would wish to report the error – if at all. It should be the *user* of this method that decides on how to *deal with the error*, not the method itself. We can get around this by sending back a **boolean** value indicating success or failure of the method as follows:

```
public boolean setFigure(int numberIn, int valueIn)
{
    if (numberIn <= staff.length)
    {
        staff[numberIn-1] = valueIn;
        return true; // method successful
    }
    else
    {
        return false; // method unsuccessful
    }
}
```

The user of this method is then free to check the value returned and take appropriate action. For example, back in the PushToLimitSalesStaff driver, the following amendment could be made:

```
for (int i = 1; i<=3; i++)
{
    System.out.println ("enter sales for employee "+ i);
    value = EasyIn.getInt();
    // call method and check returned boolean value
    boolean ok = cars4U.setFigure(i, value);
    if (!ok) // unable to set figure successfully
    {
        System.out.println("ERROR:last figure not entered ");
    }
}
```

This loop will no longer cause the setFigure method of SalesStaff to lead to a program crash, even though an attempt is made to access an illegal array index.

8.5   Usability

The **usability** of a program refers to the ease with which users of your application can interact with your program. A program that crashes all the time when receiving unexpected inputs is far from usable, so one way of ensuring that your program is easy to use is to make sure that it is robust. A user manual can also help make your programs easier to follow. The manual forms another important part of the documentation of your system. Such a manual could include:

- details how of how to install your application;
- details of how to use your application once installed;
- a troubleshooting section where common errors that users are likely to make are identified and their solutions given.

Many applications today simply have the first of these in printed form so that the application can be installed. All additional information is then provided within the application in the form of help files. Figure 8.9, for example, illustrates the user documentation built into the JBuilder IDE.

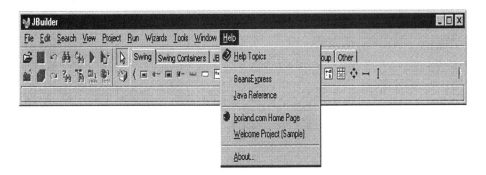

Fig 8.9 An example of built-in user documentation in the form of help files

When designing your programs, you too could think about including user advice in the form of help screens. One way of adding such help files into the types of programs that we have developed so far is to include a HELP option on a menu screen. We refer to the way the user interacts with an application as the **HCI (Human Computer Interaction)** of the program. Menu-based systems offer a much more friendly way of interacting with a user than a simple series of prompts.

As an example, let's go back and look at program 8.1 (the driver for the `Reactor` class). We said at the time that this driver wasn't as user-friendly as it could be. Here is a sample test run of the driver as it was originally written to explain what we mean:

```
current temperature is 0
temperature after increase is 1
test some more (y/n)? y
current temperature is 1
temperature after increase is 2
test some more (y/n)? y
current temperature is 2
temperature after increase is 3
test some more (y/n)? n
```

Not very exciting, is it? Apart from the fact that this interface doesn't *look* very interesting, it's also very rigid. For example, if we wanted to add in some HELP information (to include details of what happens when an attempt is made to increase the reactor temperature above the maximum), where would we add this? Maybe we could include it at the beginning of the program, but then what if the user needs some help later on in the program? Would we have to keep offering help at every stage? By using a menu system, much of this rigidity can be removed. Here is an example of one possible menu interface for the program:

```
*** REACTOR SYSTEM ***


[1] Get current temperature
[2] Increase temperature
[3] HELP
[4] Quit


enter choice [1,2,3,4]: _
```

We've already shown you many examples of such menu-driven programs so you should be able to rewrite program 8.1 yourself to give it such an interface. With this interface the user could now, if he or she chose, increase the temperature *many* times (by repeatedly choosing option 1) and only then decide to get the current temperature (by choosing option 2). Or the user could get the temperature after each increase. The choice is left up to the user – not the program. Also, notice that a HELP option is always available.

Another issue you should think about, when considering the usability of your programs, is the number of actions a user has to carry out in order to achieve a particular task. For example, if the user chooses the 'Quit' option on a menu, adding a further pause in your program and insisting that the user then press the 'Enter' key in order to quit could be quite irritating! As another illustration of this problem let's go back to program 8.2 (the driver for the SalesStaff class). Here is a sample test run, assuming that the alterations discussed in section 8.4 have been made:

```
Bonus paid for each car sold ?
8
enter sales for employee 1
10
enter sales for employee 2
5
enter sales for employee 3
9
ERROR: too many figures
bonus for employee 1 = 80.0
bonus for employee 2 = 40.0
press <Enter> to quit
```

This interface could do with a title and some line spaces; we'll deal with these issues in a while. For now, look at the error message that was raised when an attempt was made to enter details of a third employee:

```
enter sales for employee 3
9
ERROR: too many figures
```

As you can see, the error was raised *after* the sales figure (9) had been entered by the user. This entry of the last sales figure was wasted effort for the user as the figure was never used. The reason the user was asked to enter this figure was that the error was detected only after the figure was sent to the setFigure method:

```
for (int i = 1; i<=3; i++)
{
      System.out.println ("enter sales for employee "+ i);
      // value entered before error checking
      value = EasyIn.getInt();
      // method to set figure called
      boolean ok = cars4U.setFigure(i, value);
      // now error checking is taking place here
      if (!ok)
      {
            System.out.println("ERROR:last figure not entered ");
      }
}
```

The user would probably prefer the error checking to take *place* before he or she enters the sales figure. This can be achieved by checking the maximum number of employees *before* asking the user to enter a sales figure as follows:

```
for (int i = 1; i<=3; i++)
{
    System.out.println ("enter sales for employee "+ i);
    // check if all employee figures entered
    if (i> cars4U.getMAX())
    {
        // produce error message if no more figures to enter
        System.out.println("!!!!!!!!!!!!!!");
        System.out.print(" ERROR:only "+ cars4U.getMAX() +" employees");
        System.out.println("!!!!!!!!!!!!!!");
    }
    // ok to enter more sales figures
    else
    {
        // get the figure
        value = EasyIn.getInt();
        // can now enter the figure without further error checking
        cars4U.setFigure(i, value);
    }
}
```

Now, here is another sample test run of program 8.2 after this amendment has been made:

```
Bonus paid for each car sold ?
8
enter sales for employee 1
10
enter sales for employee 2
5
enter sales for employee 3
!!!!!!!!!!!!
ERROR:only 2 employees
!!!!!!!!!!!!
bonus for employee 1 = 80.0
bonus for employee 2 = 40.0
press <Enter> to quit
```

As you can see, this time, the user did not need to enter a sales figure for a third employee. The error was raised immediately.

8.5.1   Text formatting

Look back at the test runs for the programs discussed earlier in this chapter. To make such output attractive to users, careful use of space can be extremely useful. For example, the line space between the title and the menu options of the `Reactor` class tester makes both the title and the options stand out.

In our example programs so far, we've shown you one way to create such space: just use an empty `println()` command as follows:

```
System.out.println("some output");
System.out.println( ); // creates blank line on screen
System.out.println("more output here");
```

The need to add such space is so common that special formatting characters exist in Java to simplify this task. These characters can be added into strings to include such information as "add a new line", and "create a tab space". These special formatting characters are known as **escape sequences**. An escape sequence always consists of a backslash character '\' followed by a special formatting character. For example, to force a new line the '\n' escape sequence can be embedded into a string. Below we use '\n' escape to achieve the same blank line result above (we have emboldened the escape sequence).

```
System.out.println("some output\n");
System.out.println("more output here");
```

Note that there is no need to include spaces around the escape sequence, in this case it is added directly onto the end of the first message.

In fact, escape sequences can be added anywhere in a string; for example, the following command achieves exactly the same result as the two output statements above by embedding the new line commands in the middle of a single string (again we have emboldened them for you).

```
System.out.println("some output\n\nmore output here");
```

Notice that in this case we needed two new-line commands, one new line to print the string over two lines, and the other line break to create a blank line between the two messages.

Table 8.2 lists a few other useful escape sequences.

Table 8.2	Some useful escape sequences
\t	add a tab space
\"	add a double quote
\'	add a single quote
\\	add a backslash

Careful use of such escape sequences can help in producing output that is clearer and easier to follow.

One other output problem we have come up against, with our sample programs, is the formatting of decimal output. As an illustration of this problem let's go back to program 8.2 (the driver for the `SalesStaff` class). Here is another sample test run, assuming that the alterations discussed in this chapter have been made:

```
Bonus paid for each car sold ?
5.3
enter sales for employee 1
9
enter sales for employee 2
4
enter sales for employee 3
!!!!!!!!!!!
ERROR:only 2 employees
!!!!!!!!!!!
bonus for employee 1 = 47.699999999999996
bonus for employee 2 = 21.2
press <Enter> to quit
```

Look back at the output of the bonus payments. They don't look too pretty, do they?

Typically, monetary values have two digits after the decimal point. The first bonus payment, however, has *sixteen* digits and the second bonus payment only *one*! You can't blame the Java system for this as it has no idea that these numbers represent monetary values, or how we would like such monetary values to be displayed. Don't worry though, Java has a predefined class, DecimalFormat, that you can use to let the program know how you wish to format the display of particular decimal numbers. This class resides in the java.text package so to access it you need to add the following import statement to the top of your program:

```
import java.text.*;
```

Once you have access to this class you can create DecimalFormat objects in your program. These objects can then be used to format decimal numbers for you. As always, you use the **new** operator along with the object constructor to create an object. The DecimalFormat constructor has one parameter, the *format* string. This string instructs the object on how you wish to format a given decimal number. Some of the important elements of such a string are given in table 8.3.

Table 8.3 Special DecimalFormat characters	
Character	**Meaning**
.	insert a decimal point
,	insert a comma
0	display a single digit
#	display a single digit or empty if no digit present

For example, look at the following construction of a DecimalFormat object:

```
DecimalFormat df = new DecimalFormat( "000,000.000");
```

Here the decimal format object, df, that is constructed is being informed on how to format any decimal numbers that may be given to it (see figure 8.10).

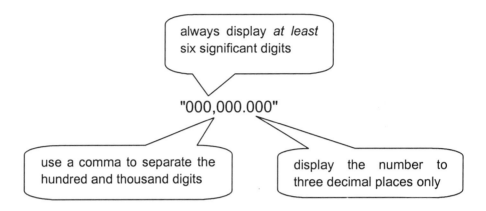

Fig 8.10   A format string used with the *DecimalFormat* class

The format string `"000,000.000"` indicates that the number should be truncated to three decimal places, and a comma should be used between the hundred and thousand columns. Also, the number displayed will always have six significant digits (digits to the left of the decimal point) and three digits after.

At the moment we have just created a `DecimalFormat` object and informed it how to format a given decimal number. We haven't given it any number to format! We do this by using the `format` method of the `DecimalFormat` class. For example:

```
DecimalFormat df = new DecimalFormat( "000,000.000");
double someNumber = 12345.6789;
System.out.println("before\t" + someNumber);
System.out.println("after\t" + df.format(someNumber));
```

Since the `format` method returns the formatted number as a `String`, its returned value can be printed directly to the screen with a `System.out` command (notice also the addition of a tab space with `'\t'`). The instructions above would lead to the following values being displayed:

```
before      12345.6789
after       012,345.679
```

As you can see, not only has the number been truncated to three decimal places, but it has also been rounded up. In this case the format string insisted on having six significant digits so the formatted number has a leading zero added.

Replacing a zero in a format string with a hash (#) would mean that the digit was optional, not compulsory.

For example, look at the following piece of code:

```
DecimalFormat df = new DecimalFormat( "#00,000.000");
double someNumber = 12345.6789;
System.out.println("before\t" + someNumber);
System.out.println("after\t" + df.format(someNumber));
```

This would result in the following output:

```
before      12345.6789
after       12,345.679
```

In case you are wondering, if the decimal number that was to be formatted had *more* than six significant digits, all the extra digits would automatically be displayed. So, only use zeros for digits you insist on displaying, and use hashes for optional formatting.[1]

Bearing all this in mind, how would you format currency values? Well, such values will always have to be given to two decimal places, and they must all have at least one significant digit, so the following format string is required:

```
DecimalFormat df = new DecimalFormat("0.00");
```

Program 8.3 rewrites the PushToLimitSalesStaff driver by including the amendments we discussed in this chapter and improving the text formatting of output.

---

[1] There are several other classes in the java.text package that provide useful formatting methods. The NumberFormat class, for example, contains a getCurrencyInstance method that allows you to format a given real number in the currency format of the local country.

Program 8.3

```java
import java.text.*; // for DecimalFormat
class PushToLimitSalesStaff2
{
    public static void main(String[] args)
    {
      int value;
      double bonus;
      // title added
      System.out.println("\n\t\t*** BONUS CALCULATOR ***\n\n");
      // to set bonus rate
      System.out.print("\t Bonus paid for each car sold ?\t");
      bonus = EasyIn.getDouble();
      SalesStaff cars4U = new SalesStaff(bonus);
      // get figures
      System.out.print("\n\n\t enter sales figures\n\n");
      for (int i = 1; i<=3; i++)
      {
          System.out.print("\t employee "+ i + "\t");

          // only enter data if required
          if (i> cars4U.getMAX())
          {
              System.out.print("ERROR:only "+cars4U.getMAX()
                                                +" employees");
          }
          else
          {
              value = EasyIn.getInt();
              cars4U.setFigure(i, value);
          }
      }
      // display bonuses
      System.out.print("\n\n\t bonus payments\n\n");
      for (int i = 1; i<3; i++) // this time loop counter is ok
      {   // notice the use of DceimalFormat class
          DecimalFormat df = new DecimalFormat( "0.00");
          System.out.print("\t employee " + i + " =\t");
          System.out.println(df.format(cars4U.getBonus(i)));
      }
      EasyIn.pause("\n\n\t press <Enter> to quit");
    }
}
```

Here is a sample test run (we have included an actual screen shot here so that you can fully appreciate the effect of the tab and space formatting).

```
            *** BONUS CALCULATOR ***


    Bonus paid for each car sold ? 5.3


    enter sales figures

    employee 1       9
    employee 2       4
    employee 3       ERROR:only 2 employees

    bonus payments

    employee 1 =     47.70
    employee 2 =     21.20


    press <Enter> to quit
```

Look back at program 8.3 and compare it with this screen shot to see the effect of the various text formatting instructions.

8.5.2   Graphical user interfaces

So far in this book, we haven't talked very much about how to create visual, graphical interfaces of the type illustrated in figure 8.11. Figure 8.11 is the Print screen from Microsoft's *Word for Windows* application. Such interfaces are often referred to as **GUIs (Graphical User Interfaces)**. Most applications that you buy today include such an interface.

Interfaces like this are by far the friendliest and easiest for users to operate. Up until now we haven't looked at how to develop such interfaces because you had to get to know about the basics of software development in Java first. But, now we have covered these basics with you, we think you are ready! In the next chapter we show you not only how to create such interfaces but also how to use them with your existing classes.

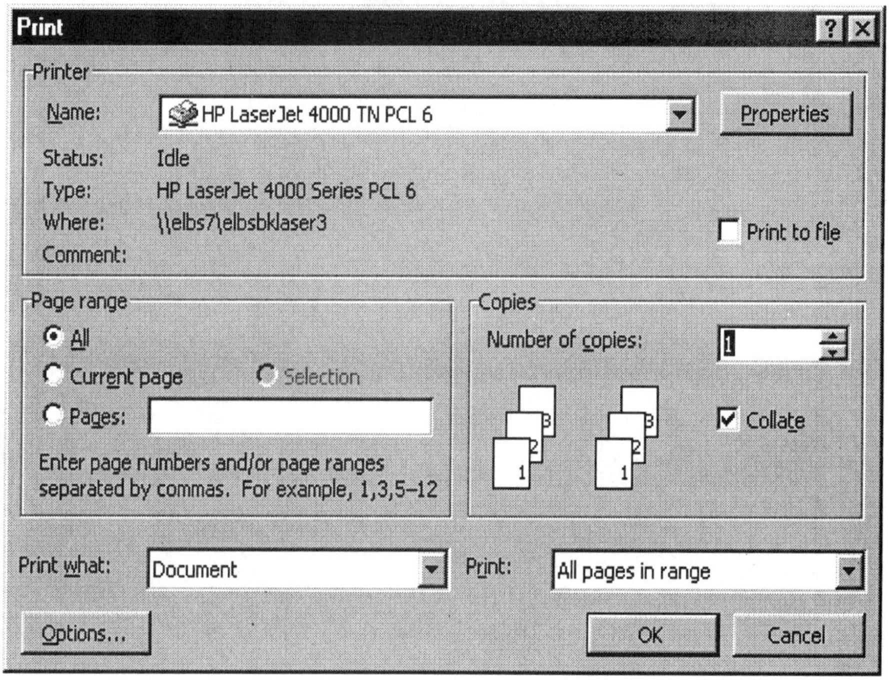

Fig 8.11   A typical GUI interface

Tutorial exercises

1. Identify the documentation required during the following phases of software development:

   - specification/ design;
   - implementation;
   - testing;
   - installation and operation.

2. How does the concept of *encapsulation* contribute to the maintainability of applications?

3. Distinguish between the terms *unit testing, integration testing, black box testing* and *white box testing.*

4. In section 8.2 a dummy `Student` class was developed in order to allow the `StudentList` class to be tested. Now look back at chapter 6 where you developed a `StudentListTester` class. How would the dummy `Student` class need to be amended in order for this tester to work?

5. Look once again at the `SalesStaff` class. Assume that the `getBonus` method has been amended so that sales of five cars or fewer receive the usual bonus, sales of six to 15 cars receive double the usual bonus, and sales of more than 15 cars receive triple the usual bonus. Now:

   a) write a list of suitable sales figures to test, using both *boundary analysis* and *equivalence testing*;
   b) devise a *test log* based upon these test values.

6. Use escape sequences to print out the following strings:

   a) I enjoy reading "Java the first Semester"
   b) I keep important files at C:\MyDocuments\ImportantFiles
   c) please press the 'alt' key

Practical work

1. You have been asked to maintain the Reactor class by providing an additional method: decreaseTemp. This method reduces the reactor temperature by one degree. If an attempt is made to reduce the temperature below zero an alarm is raised but the temperature is maintained at zero. Now:

    a) modify the Reactor class accordingly;
    b) develop a NewReactorTester class that is run from the following menu screen:

    ```
    *** REACTOR TESTER ***

    [1]   Increase temperature

    [2]   Decrease temperature

    [3]   Display current temperature

    [4]   HELP

    [5]   Quit
    ```

    c) develop a suitable test log, with inputs and expected outputs, to test the functionality of the new Reactor class;
    d) run the NewReactorTester class and complete the test log above.

2. Implement the dummy Student class discussed in tutorial question 4 and then combine this class with the StudentList class and the StudentListTester class to check whether testing can proceed.

3. Look back at the SalesStaff class and then:

    a) maintain this system so that the number of employees is increased to ten;
    b) implement the changes to the getBonus method discussed in tutorial question 5;
    c) amend this method so that it cannot throw an ArrayIndexOutOfBounds exception;
    d) rewrite program 8.3 to test whether or not this method still throws the ArrayIndexOutOfBounds exception.

4. Look again at program 2.3 in chapter 2, which calculates and displays the price of a product after sales tax has been added. Amend the program so that:

    a) all currency values are displayed to two decimal places;
    b) line and tab spaces are used to improve the layout of the information displayed.

9 Graphics and event-driven programs

Learning objectives

By the end of this chapter you should be able to:

- explain the structure of the **Abstract Window Toolkit (AWT)**;
- program graphics components to handle mouse-click events;
- add standard AWT components to a frame;
- describe the role of **layout managers**;
- use the `FlowLayout` and `BorderLayout` managers;
- make use of compound containers.

9.1 Introduction

Do you remember the `SmileyFace` class? So far it is the only graphics class we have developed. So now it is time to learn more about graphics programming – and when we have done that we can start to move away from that rather uninteresting text screen we have been using and build attractive windows programs for our input and output.

In order to do this we are going to be using the core Java graphics package, the **Abstract Window Toolkit**, or **AWT** for short. This package provides the graphics tools and components that you need to produce the sort of windows programs that we have all become used to.

So the first thing we are going to do in this chapter is to explore the Abstract Window Toolkit; after that we can go on to develop our first interactive graphical applications.

9.2 The Abstract Window Toolkit

The AWT provides graphics classes that are based on an inheritance structure. This is shown in figure 9.1 – you can see from this diagram that at the top of this hierarchy is a basic `Component` class. This class contains a number of useful methods, which are inherited by the eight subclasses that you see in the diagram. Most of these, like `Button` or `Checkbox`, provide the code for creating and manipulating the basic graphics components that you are used to seeing in windows applications.

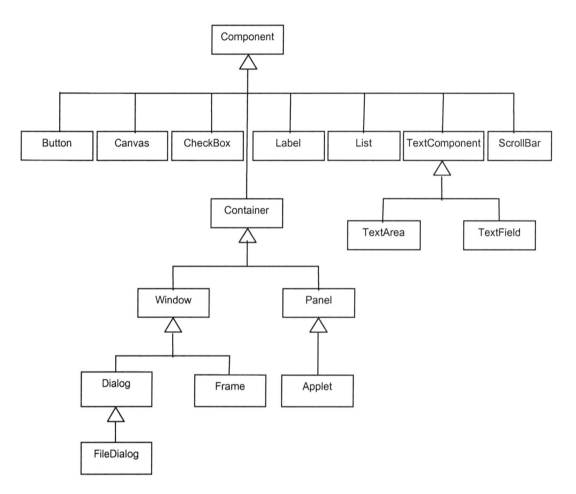

Fig 9.1   The classes of the Abstract Window Toolkit

Notice that two of the classes, Container and TextComponent (which are abstract classes), are further subclassed to provide additional classes. You will explore some of these as you progress through the chapter and develop more and more complex graphical applications. Appendix 1 provides a description of some of the common AWT components and their methods.

Some examples of these common components can be seen in figure 9.2, which shows a Frame containing a Button, a Checkbox and a Scrollbar.

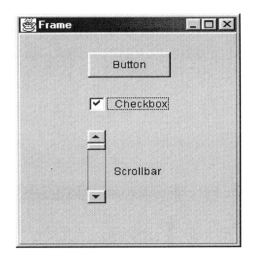

Fig 9.2   A frame containing a button, a checkbox and a scrollbar

9.3   The *SmileyFace* class revisited

Do you remember the `SmileyFace` class that we introduced in chapter 4? When we ran it in a frame it produced a display like the one shown in figure 9.3.

Fig 9.3   The *SmileyFace* class running in a frame

In this chapter we are going to make a few changes to it – but first a reminder of the code:

The *SmileyFace* class

```java
import java.awt.*;
import java.applet.*;

class SmileyFace extends Applet
{
    public void paint(Graphics g)
    {
        g.setColor(Color.red);
        g.drawOval(85,45,75,75);
        g.setColor(Color.blue);
        g.drawOval(100,65,10,10);
        g.drawOval(135,65,10,10);
        g.drawArc(102,85,40,25,-0,-180);
        g.drawString("Smiley Face", 90,155);
    }
}
```

The code for running this class in a frame appears below (program 9.1).

Program 9.1

```java
import java.awt.*;

class RunFace
{
    public static void main(String[] args)
    {
        Frame frame = new Frame();
        SmileyFace face = new SmileyFace();
        frame.setSize(250,200);
        frame.setBackground(Color.yellow);
        frame.add(face);
        frame.setVisible(true);
    }
}
```

9.4   The *EasyFrame* class

Do you remember the slight problem with the above program when it was first introduced in chapter 4? The simple frame doesn't close when we click on the crosshairs in the top right-hand corner! To adapt the frame so that it closes requires a bit of code that is a little too complicated for the first semester.

So rather than trouble you with it at this stage we have provided you with an EasyFrame class which you can download or copy from appendix 2. From now on we will use this frame in our classes and there will be no problems with closing your windows when you are done. The new program for running the SmileyFace class with EasyFrame is now shown in program 9.2.

Program 9.2

```java
import java.awt.*;

class RunFace
{
    public static void main(String[] args)
    {
        EasyFrame frame = new EasyFrame(); // we are now using EasyFrame
        SmileyFace face = new SmileyFace();
        frame.setSize(250,200);
        frame.setBackground(Color.yellow);
        frame.add(face);
        frame.setVisible(true);
    }
}
```

9.5   The *ChangingFace* class

Now we are going to try to change our SmileyFace class into a ChangingFace class that can change its mood so it can be sad as well as happy. The first thing we are going to do is to add a couple of buttons, as shown in figure 9.4.

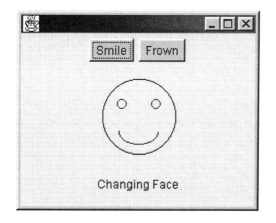

Fig 9.4 The *ChangingFace* class (still smiling)

You can see that we have now changed our caption from "Smiley Face" to "Changing Face" – because when we have finished we will be able to click on the *Frown* button and get the face to look like the one you see in figure 9.5.

Fig 9.5   The *ChangingFace* class (frowning)

We will build the `ChangingFace` class in two stages. The first step is to add the buttons: this is shown below; we have called this class `ChangingFaceStep1`. The new lines, which are all concerned with adding the buttons, have been emboldened.

The *ChangingFaceStep1* class

```
import java.awt.*;
import java.applet.*;
import java.awt.event.*;

class ChangingFaceStep1 extends Applet
{
    private Button happyButton = new Button("Smile");
    private Button sadButton = new Button("Frown");

    public ChangingFaceStep1()
    {
        add(happyButton);
        add(sadButton);
    }

    public void paint(Graphics g)
    {
        g.setColor(Color.red);
        g.drawOval(85,45,75,75);
        g.setColor(Color.blue);
        g.drawOval(100,65,10,10);
        g.drawOval(135,65,10,10);
        g.drawString("Changing Face", 80,155);
        g.drawArc(102,85,40,25,-0,-180);
    }
}
```

Let's take a closer look at these new lines.

Firstly we declare the buttons as attributes of the class, and initialize them at the same time:

```
private Button happyButton = new Button("Smile");
private Button sadButton = new Button("Frown");
```

We are creating new objects of the Button class; this class has a constructor that allows us to create the buttons with the required caption by sending in this caption as a parameter.

Now that we have created the buttons we have to add them to the applet (you should remember from chapter 5 that we defined our class as a subclass of the Applet class to enable us to add it to a frame). We are going to add the buttons at the time an object is created, in other words via the constructor.

```
public ChangingFaceStep1()
{
    add(happyButton);
    add(sadButton);
}
```

We use the add method, which is a method of the Container class and is therefore available to all derived classes such as Applet.

In actual fact these lines are short for:

```
this.add(happyButton);
this.add(sadButton);
```

The keyword **this** is used when a class method refers to the object itself – in this case an object of the ChangingFaceStep1 class; it can often be omitted.

A container, like our ChangingFace applet, has always got a layout policy attached to it – this policy determines the way in which components are added to it. The default policy is called FlowLayout which means that the components are just placed in the order in which they were added. When one row fills up then the next row starts to be filled. There are other layout policies that we can choose, and these are discussed in section 9.10.

If we were to run the class in a frame then we would get the output shown in figure 9.5 – but of course pressing the buttons would not have any effect; we need to write the code to bring about the desired result when the buttons are pressed. This is called **event-handling**.

9.6   Event-handling in Java

The complete ChangingFace class appears below. The code that is to do with the event-handling routines has been emboldened. We will discuss them after you have taken a look at the complete code for the class.

The *ChangingFace* class

```java
import java.awt.*;
import java.applet.*;
import java.awt.event.*;

class ChangingFace extends Applet implements ActionListener
{
    private boolean isHappy;
    private Button happyButton = new Button("Smile");
    private Button sadButton = new Button("Frown");

    public ChangingFace()
    {
        add(happyButton);
        add(sadButton);
        isHappy = true;
        happyButton.addActionListener(this);
        sadButton.addActionListener(this);
    }


    public void paint(Graphics g)
    {

        g.setColor(Color.red);
        g.drawOval(85,45,75,75);
        g.setColor(Color.blue);
        g.drawOval(100,65,10,10);
        g.drawOval(135,65,10,10);
        g.drawString("Changing Face", 80,155);
        if(isHappy == true)
        {
            // draw a smiling mouth
            g.drawArc(102,85,40,25,-0,-180);
        }
        else
        {
            // draw a frowning mouth
            g.drawArc(102,85,40,25,-0,180);
        }
    }
```

```
      // this is where we code the event-handling routines
      public void actionPerformed(ActionEvent e)
      {
         if(e.getSource() == happyButton)
         {
            isHappy = true;
            repaint();
         }
         if(e.getSource() == sadButton)
         {
            isHappy = false;
            repaint();
         }
      }
   }
```

We can now analyse this line by line. The first line of interest is the class header:

```
class ChangingFace extends Applet implements ActionListener
```

Notice how we have appended the words implements ActionListener to our class header. The ActionListener class is a special class called an **interface**; these classes contain abstract methods which, you will remember from chapter 7, means that we are forced to code them. In this case the ActionListener class insists that we code a method called actionPerformed to handle our events. We will see how this is done in a moment.

Before we do that, take a look at this new attribute we have included:

```
private boolean isHappy;
```

You can probably guess how we are going to use this – it will be set to **true** when the *Smile* button is pressed and **false** when the *Frown* button is pressed; the face will then be repainted with the appropriate expression.

Now let's look at our new constructor:

```
public ChangingFace()
{
    add(happyButton);
    add(sadButton);
    isHappy = true;
    happyButton.addActionListener(this);
    sadButton.addActionListener(this);
}
```

After adding the buttons we set isHappy to **true**, so that the face starts off happy.

The next two lines are important. When we use the keyword **implements** with an interface class like ActionListener we achieve an effect very similar to that achieved by inheritance – our class actually becomes *a kind of* ActionListener, just as if it were a subclass of some superclass, created with the keyword **extends**. The buttons, like all subclasses of component, have a method called addActionListener, which receives an object of the ActionListener class as a parameter – and since our class is now a kind of ActionListener we can send it to the addActionListener method of a Button. We do it with the keyword **this**; effectively we are registering *this* applet with the button, which will then wait for an **event** – normally a mouse-click – and then do something to the applet.

The "something" that it does is determined by coding a special routine for that button – this routine is called an **event-handler**.

Before we come to that, however, you need to look at the new bit of the paint method:

```
if(isHappy == true)
{
    g.drawArc(102,85,40,25,0,-180);
}
else
{
    g.drawArc(102,85,40,25,0,180);
}
```

You should remember from chapter 5 how the drawArc method of a Graphic object works. If you look back at this section you will see that by changing the very last parameter from a negative value to a positive value the arc will be drawn clockwise instead of anti-clockwise – this will make the mouth frown instead of smile! So if the isHappy attribute is set to **true** the mouth will smile – if not it will frown!

Now at last we come to our event-handlers:

```
public void actionPerformed(ActionEvent e)
{
    if(e.getSource() == happyButton)
    {
        isHappy = true;
        repaint();
    }
    if(e.getSource() == sadButton)
    {
        isHappy = false;
        repaint();
    }
}
```

We determine what happens when the mouse-button is clicked by coding the actionPerformed method that is required by the ActionListener interface. When the mouse is clicked, this method is automatically sent an object of the class ActionEvent. This class has a method called getSource that returns the name of the object that was clicked on. We use this method in the condition of the **if** statement to find out which button was clicked. You can see that if it was the happyButton that was pressed, isHappy is set to **true** and then a special method – repaint – is called. This causes the paint method to be called again so that the screen is repainted. The sadButton works in the same way, but sets isHappy to **false**. Take one more look at the paint method to remind yourself how this works.

The ChangingFace class can be run in a frame as shown in program 9.3.

Program 9.3

```java
import java.awt.*;

class RunChangingFace
{
    public static void main(String[] args)
    {
        EasyFrame frame = new EasyFrame();
        ChangingFace face = new ChangingFace();
        frame.setSize(250,200);
        frame.setBackground(Color.yellow);
        frame.add(face);
        frame.setVisible(true);
    }
}
```

9.7   An interactive graphics class

The next class – which we have called PushMe – that we are going to develop is the first class that allows the user to input information via a graphics screen. The program isn't all that sophisticated, but it introduces the basic elements that you need to build interactive graphics classes.

This program allows the user to enter some text and then by clicking on a button to see the text that was entered displayed in the graphics window. You can see what it looks like in figure 9.6.

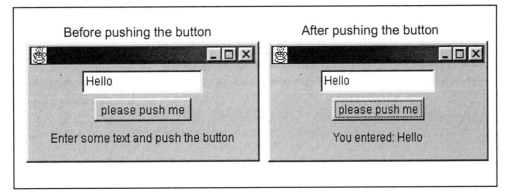

Fig 9.6   The *PushMe* class running in a frame

As usual we will show you the code first and discuss it afterwards:

The *PushMe* class

```java
import java.awt.*;
import java.awt.event.*;
import java.applet.*;

class PushMe extends Applet implements ActionListener
{
    private TextField myTextField = new TextField(15);
    private Button myButton = new Button("please push me");
    private Label myLabel
              = new Label("Enter some text and push the button",1);
    // the constructor (adds the components and the ActionListener)
    public PushMe()
    {
        add(myTextField);
        add(myButton);
        add(myLabel);
        myButton.addActionListener(this);
    }

    // the event-handler
    public void actionPerformed(ActionEvent e)
    {
        if(e.getSource() == myButton)
        {
            String myText;
            myText = myTextField.getText();
            myLabel.setText("You entered: " + myText);
        }
    }
}
```

As you can see, there are three components involved here, and we have declared them all as attributes of the class and initialized them at the same time:

```java
private TextField myTextField = new TextField(15);
private Button myButton = new Button("please push me");
private Label myLabel
                  = new Label("Enter some text and push the button",1);
```

The first of the above three components is a TextField – we have used the fact that it has a constructor that accepts an integer value (in this case 15) that allows you to specify the number length of the text field to be displayed (a TextContainer consists of rows and columns of characters).

Next we declare the button, which, as before, we have initialized with the required caption ("please push me").

Finally we have declared and instantiated a Label. The constructor that we are utilizing here takes two parameters: the text to be displayed and an integer value which determines the alignment of the text – 0 for left, 1 for centre and 2 for right; these can also be entered as Label.LEFT, Label.CENTER and Label.RIGHT.

All of these components also have empty constructors (and others) which you can use if you wish. You can change the properties later using the various methods that exist; for example, the setLabel method of the Button class, the setColumns method of the TextField class or the setText method of the Label class. Some selected methods of these and other components are provided in appendix 1.

Next comes the constructor where we add the buttons to the applet and the ActionListener to the button.

```java
public PushMe()
{
    add(myTextField);
    add(myButton);
    add(myLabel);
    myButton.addActionListener(this);
}
```

Finally we have the event-handling routine:

```java
public void actionPerformed(ActionEvent e)
{
    if(e.getSource() == myButton)
    {
        String myText;
        myText = myTextField.getText();
        myLabel.setText("You entered: " + myText);
    }
}
```

Notice how we are using the `getText` method of the `TextField` class to read the current "value" of the text in `myTextField`, and then using the `setText` method of the `Label` class to "transfer" it to `myLabel`.

Program 9.4 provides the code for running the class in a light grey frame measuring 250 by 120.

Program 9.4

```java
import java.awt.*;

class RunPushMe
{
    public static void main(String[] args)
    {
        EasyFrame frame = new EasyFrame();
        PushMe pushme = new PushMe();
        frame.setSize(250,120);
        frame.setBackground(Color.lightGray);
        frame.add(pushme);
        frame.setVisible(true);
    }
}
```

9.8   A graphical user interface (GUI) for the *Oblong* class

Up till now, when we wanted to write programs that utilize our classes, we have written text-based programs. Now that we know how to write graphics programs we can, if we wish, write graphical user interfaces for our classes. Let's do this for the `Oblong` class we developed in chapter 5. The sort of interface we are talking about is shown in figure 9.7.

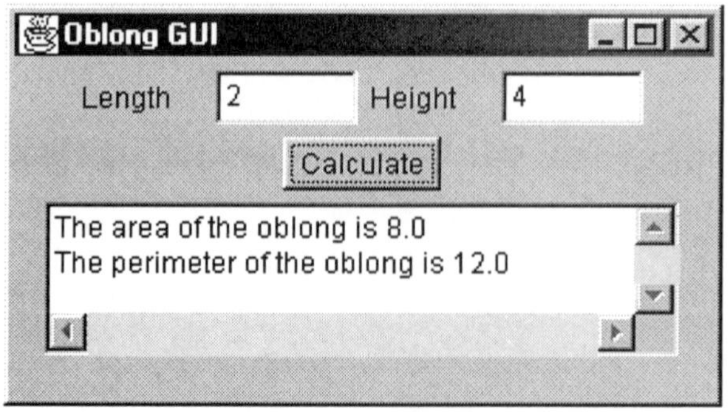

Fig 9.7   A GUI for the *Oblong* class

Here is the code for the GUI:

The graphical user interface for the *Oblong* class

```java
import java.awt.*;
import java.awt.event.*;
import java.applet.*;

class OblongGui extends Applet implements ActionListener
{
    // declare a new oblong with a length and height of zero
    private Oblong oblong = new Oblong(0,0);

    // now declare the graphics components
    private Label lengthLabel = new Label("Length");
    private TextField lengthField = new TextField(5);
    private Label heightLabel = new Label("Height");
    private TextField heightField = new TextField(5);
    private Button calcButton = new Button("Calculate");
    private TextArea displayArea = new TextArea(3,35);

    public OblongGui()
    {
        // add the graphics components
        add(lengthLabel);
        add(lengthField);
        add(heightLabel);
        add(heightField);
        add(calcButton);
        add(displayArea);

        // now add the ActionListener to the calcButton
        calcButton.addActionListener(this);
    }

    /* finally write the code for handling a mouse-click on the
    calcButton */
    public void actionPerformed(ActionEvent e)
    {
        String lengthEntered = lengthField.getText();
        String heightEntered = heightField.getText();
        if(e.getSource() == calcButton)
        {
```

```
                    // make sure the fields aren't blank
                    if(lengthEntered.length() == 0 || heightEntered.length() == 0)
                    {
                        displayArea.setText("Length and height must be entered");
                    }
                    else
                    {
                        // we have to convert the input strings to doubles
                        Double dLength = new Double(lengthEntered);
                        Double dHeight = new Double(heightEntered);
                        oblong.setLength(dLength.doubleValue());
                        oblong.setHeight(dHeight.doubleValue());
                        displayArea.setText("The area of the oblong is "
                                            + oblong.calculateArea()
                                            + "\n"
                                            + "The perimeter of the oblong is "
                                            + oblong.calculatePerimeter());
                    }
                }
            }
        }
```

You can see that the first attribute that we declare is an `Oblong` object, `oblong`, which we initialize as a new `Oblong` with a length and height of zero (since the user hasn't entered anything yet):

```
private Oblong oblong = new Oblong(0,0);
```

After this we declare the graphics components; the only one of these that you have not yet come across is the `textArea`, which is the large text area that you see in figure 9.7, where the area and perimeter of the oblong are displayed. As you can see, it is a useful component for entering and displaying text. We declared it like this:

```
private TextArea displayArea = new TextArea(3,35);
```

You can see that it has a constructor that allows you to fix the size by entering values for the number of rows and columns (in that order, by the way!).

After declaring and initializing the components, we have coded the constructor which is straightforward – it simply adds these components to the applet, and then adds the `ActionListener` to the `calcButton`.

Next we have the event-handling routing for the `calcButton`; this is worth taking a look at:

.

```java
public void actionPerformed(ActionEvent e)
{
    String lengthEntered = lengthField.getText();
    String heightEntered = heightField.getText();
    if(e.getSource() == calcButton)
    {
        // make sure the fields aren't blank
        if(lengthEntered.length() == 0 || heightEntered.length() == 0)
        {
            displayArea.setText("Length and height must be entered");
        }
        else
        {
            oblong.setLength(Integer.parseInt(lengthEntered));
            oblong.setHeight(Integer.parseInt(heightEntered));
            displayArea.setText("The area of the oblong is "
                            + oblong.calculateArea()
                            + "\n" + "The perimeter of the oblong is "
                            + oblong.calculatePerimeter());
        }
    }
}
```

We have declared two local variables, `lengthEntered` and `heightEntered`, to hold the values entered by the user, which we obtain with the `getText` method of `textField`. Then we check that these are not of length zero (that is, that something has been entered). If one of the fields is empty we display an error message. Otherwise we use the `calculateArea` and `calculatePerimeter` methods of `Oblong` to display the area and perimeter of the oblong in the text area. We have used the `setText` method of

`TextArea` to do this; we could also have used the `append` method – the difference is that that this does not clear what was previously written in the area, whereas the `setText` method does.

The program for running the interface in an `EasyFrame` appears in program 9.5 below.

Program 9.5

```
import java.awt.*;

class GuiDriver
{
    public static void main(String[] args)
    {
        EasyFrame frame = new EasyFrame();
        frame.setTitle("Oblong GUI");
        OblongGui gui = new OblongGui();
        frame.setSize(300,170);
        frame.setBackground(Color.lightGray);
        frame.add(gui);
        frame.setVisible(true);
    }
}
```

9.9   A metric converter

We thought that our next example would be a pretty useful one. Most of the world uses the metric system; however, if you are in the United Kingdom like we are, then you will still be only halfway there – sometimes using kilograms and kilometres, sometimes pounds and miles; or buying petrol in litres and then converting into gallons in your mind! And of course if you are in the USA (and you are not a scientist or an engineer) you will still be using the old imperial values for everything. Some might say it's time that the UK and the USA caught up with the rest of the world, but until that happens this little program, which converts back and forth from metric to imperial, is going to be very handy.

We will be building a `MetricConverter` class – program 9.6 provides the code for running our converter in an `EasyFrame` measuring 350 × 255, which we have again coloured light grey.

Program 9.6

```java
import java.awt.*;

class RunConverter
{
    public static void main(String[] args)
    {
        EasyFrame frame = new EasyFrame();
        frame.setTitle("Metric Converter");
        MetricConverter converter = new MetricConverter();
        frame.setSize(350,225);
        frame.setBackground(Color.lightGray);
        frame.add(converter);
        frame.setVisible(true);
    }
}
```

Figure 9.8 shows the result of running this program.

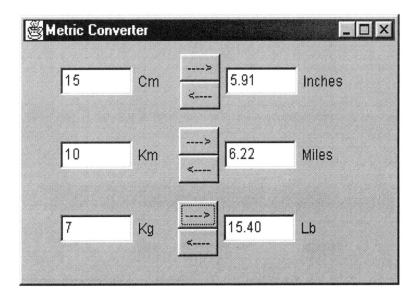

Fig 9.8   The metric converter running in a frame

The `MetricConverter` class is now presented; it looks quite long, but most of it is just more of what you already know. There are, however, two concepts, **layout policies** and **compound containers**, that we need to discuss in some depth, and we do this straight after showing you the code.

The *MetricConverter* class

```java
import java.awt.*;
import java.awt.event.*;
import java.applet.*;
import java.text.*; // required for the DecimalFormat class


class MetricConverter extends Applet implements ActionListener
{
    // we declare the various components as attributes.

    /* first the components for converting back and forth from inches
    to centimetres */

    private TextField cmText = new TextField(6);
    private Label cmLabel = new Label("Cm");
    private Button cmToInchButton = new Button("---->");
    private Button inchToCmButton = new Button("<----");
    private Panel inchCmButtons = new Panel(); // compound container
    private TextField inchText = new TextField(6);
    private Label inchLabel = new Label("Inches");
    private Panel inchCmPanel = new Panel(); // compound container

    /* next the components for converting back and forth from miles
    to kilometres */

    private TextField kmText = new TextField(6);
    private Label kmLabel = new Label("Km");
    private Button kmToMileButton = new Button("---->");
    private Button mileToKmButton = new Button("<----");
    private Panel mileKmButtons = new Panel(); // compound container
    private TextField mileText = new TextField(6);
    private Label mileLabel = new Label("Miles ");
    private Panel mileKmPanel = new Panel(); // compound container

    /* finally the components for converting back and forth from
        pounds to kilograms */
```

```
private TextField kgText = new TextField(6);
private Label kgLabel = new Label("Kg ");
private Button kgToPoundButton = new Button("---->");
private Button poundToKgButton = new Button("<----");
private Panel poundKgButtons = new Panel(); // compound container
private TextField poundText = new TextField(6);
private Label poundLabel = new Label("Lb ");
private Panel poundKgPanel = new Panel(); // compound container

/* the constructor adds the components to the object at the time
   it is created */

public MetricConverter()
{
   inchCmButtons.setLayout(new BorderLayout()); // see section 9.9
   inchCmButtons.add("North",cmToInchButton);
   inchCmButtons.add("South",inchToCmButton);
   inchCmPanel.add(cmText);
   inchCmPanel.add(cmLabel);
   inchCmPanel.add(inchCmButtons);
   inchCmPanel.add(inchText);
   inchCmPanel.add(inchLabel);

   mileKmButtons.setLayout(new BorderLayout()); // see section 9.9
   mileKmButtons.add("North",kmToMileButton);
   mileKmButtons.add("South",mileToKmButton);
   mileKmPanel.add(kmText);
   mileKmPanel.add(kmLabel);
   mileKmPanel.add(mileKmButtons);
   mileKmPanel.add(mileText);
   mileKmPanel.add(mileLabel);
   poundKgButtons.setLayout(new BorderLayout()); // see section 9.9
   poundKgButtons.add("North",kgToPoundButton);
   poundKgButtons.add("South",poundToKgButton);
   poundKgPanel.add(kgText);
   poundKgPanel.add(kgLabel);
   poundKgPanel.add(poundKgButtons);
   poundKgPanel.add(poundText);
   poundKgPanel.add(poundLabel);

   add(inchCmPanel);
   add(mileKmPanel);
   add(poundKgPanel);
```

```
        cmToInchButton.addActionListener(this);
        inchToCmButton.addActionListener(this);
        kmToMileButton.addActionListener(this);
        mileToKmButton.addActionListener(this);
        kgToPoundButton.addActionListener(this);
        poundToKgButton.addActionListener(this);
    }


    // now we code the event-handlers

    public void actionPerformed(ActionEvent e)
    {
        Double D;
        double d;
        String s;
        DecimalFormat df = new DecimalFormat("#####0.0#");
        /* all the following routines could be made simpler by using
        the parseDouble method of the Double class; but you must have
        the latest version of Java */
        if(e.getSource() == cmToInchButton)
        {
            s = new String(cmText.getText());
            D = Double.valueOf(s);
            d = D.doubleValue();
            d = d / 2.54;
            s = df.format(d);
            inchText.setText(s);
        }
        if(e.getSource() == inchToCmButton)
        {
            s = new String(inchText.getText());
            D = Double.valueOf(s);
            d = D.doubleValue();
            d = d * 2.54;
            s = df.format(d);
            cmText.setText(s);
        }
        if(e.getSource() == kmToMileButton)
        {
            s = new String(kmText.getText());
            D = Double.valueOf(s);
            d = D.doubleValue();
            d = d / 1.609;
            s = df.format(d);
```

```
                mileText.setText(s);
        }
        if(e.getSource() == mileToKmButton)
        {
                s = new String(mileText.getText());
                D = Double.valueOf(s);
                d = D.doubleValue();
                d = d * 1.609;
                s = df.format(d);
                kmText.setText(s);
        }
        if(e.getSource() == kgToPoundButton)
        {
                s = new String(kgText.getText());
                D = Double.valueOf(s);
                d = D.doubleValue();
                d = d * 2.2;
                s = df.format(d);
                poundText.setText(s);
        }
        if(e.getSource() == poundToKgButton)
        {
                s = new String(poundText.getText());
                D = Double.valueOf(s);
                d = D.doubleValue();
                d = d / 2.2;
                s = df.format(d);
                kgText.setText(s);
        }
    }
}
```

9.10 Layout policies

We have already described the default layout policy, FlowLayout. But in addition to this policy the AWT package provides a number other classes called **layout managers**. We can create an object of one of these classes and attach it to a container, and thereafter that container will lay out the components it contains according to the policy of that layout manager. The strategy of the only layout manager we have seen so far, FlowLayout, is simply to arrange the components in the order that they were added, starting a new row when necessary. If the window is resized the items move about accordingly, as shown in figure 9.9.

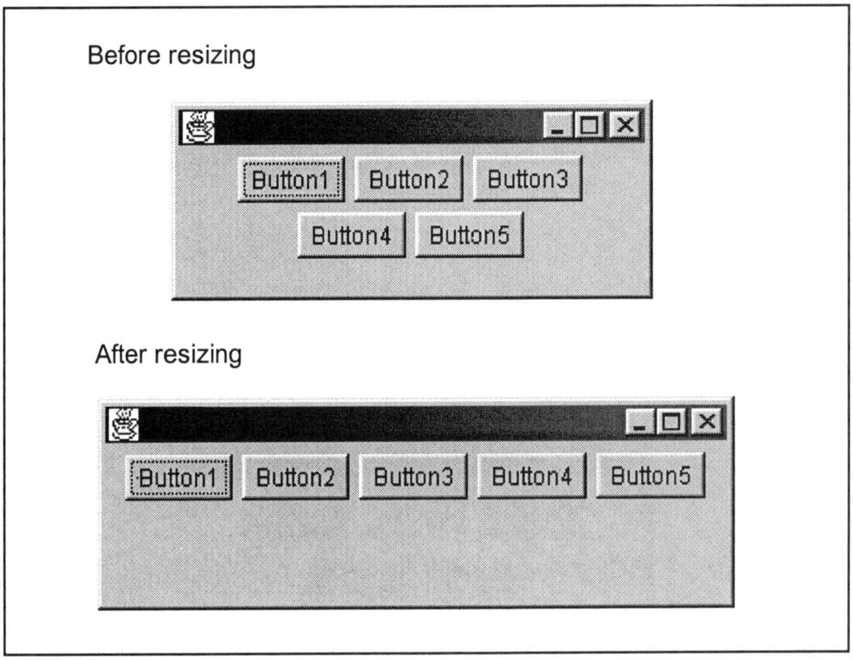

Fig 9.9   The effect of resizing when using the *FlowLayout* Policy

Another commonly used layout manager is BorderLayout. Here the window is divided into five regions called North, South, East, West and Center as shown in figure 9.10.

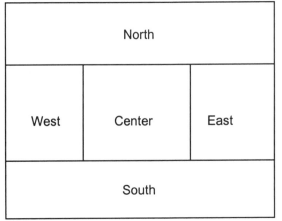

Fig 9.10   The *BorderLayout* Policy

If we use a border layout the components don't get moved around when the window is resized, as you can see from figure 9.11.

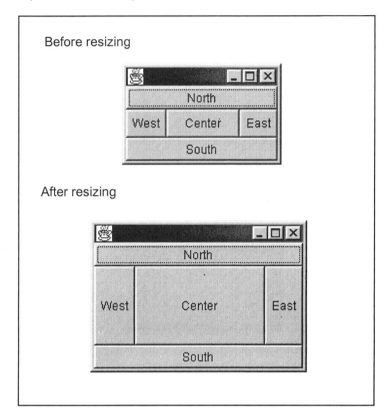

Fig 9.11 The effect of resizing when using the *BorderLayout* Policy

The `MetricConverter` class uses a border layout for some of its components, as explained in the next section. The example below, taken from the `MetricConverter`, shows how components are placed in the different regions.

First, the `setLayout` method is used to add a new `BorderLayout` to a component called `inchCmButtons` (this is in fact a `Panel` as explained in section 9.9):

```
inchCmButtons.setLayout(new BorderLayout());
```

Next we place the `cmToInchButton` in the `North` region:

```
inchCmButtons.add("North", cmToInchButton);
```

There are a number of other layout managers that can be used such as `GridLayout` and `CardLayout`; you can look these up if you like, but we are not going to introduce them to you in this first semester.

9.11 Compound containers

A **compound** container is, as its name suggests, a container that contains other containers. Each container can use a different layout manager. One of the most useful components that we can use when we build graphics programs is a `Panel`. This is a component that we don't actually see, but which can be used to hold other components. We have used panels in the `MetricConverter`. Figure 9.12 shows how each component is named and how we make use of compound containers by constructing the `MetricConverter` by creating three panels named `inchCmPanel`, `mileKmPanel` and `poundKgPanel`. The various components are added to these panels which are then added to the `MetricConverter` itself. In each case one of these components is a panel which contains the two buttons which we press to make the conversions (the ones with the arrows on them); these panels (`inchCmButtons`, `mileKmButtons` and `poundKgButtons`) have a `BorderLayout` policy so that the buttons remain one on top of the other however the window is sized.

Look carefully at figure 9.12 and then look back at the code to see how we build up the components that make up the class.

9.12 GUIs for collections of objects

When we developed the GUI for our `Oblong` class in section 9.8, we connected the GUI to a single instance of an `Oblong` by declaring an `Oblong` object as an attribute of the GUI class; you can use a similar technique for the `Reactor` class in question 3 of the practical examples that follow.

Many real-world examples will of course require you to manipulate more than one object – for example students, employees etc. One way to handle this would be to declare an array of objects as an attribute of the GUI class – you might want to try this out. The disadvantage of this approach, however, is that that you would have to include in the event-handlers all the code for moving through the array (for example to search it or to display items).

Another approach is to use a collection class and to declare an object of this class as an attribute of the GUI class. This is the approach that we have taken in the next two chapters in which we develop a case study that deals with a student hostel.

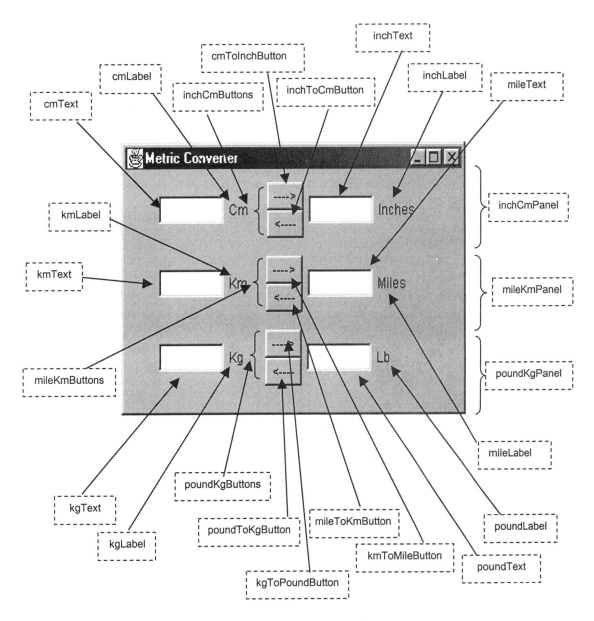

Fig 9.12 The composition of the *MetricConverter* class

Tutorial exercises

1. Explain the difference between the FlowLayout policy and the BorderLayout policy.

2. Consider some changes or additions you could make to the PushMe class. For example, pushing the button could display your text in upper case – or it could say how many letters it contains. Maybe you could add some extra buttons. Think about these changes and sketch out the design and the code.

3. Below is a variation on the ChangingFace class, which now has a neck and three possible moods!

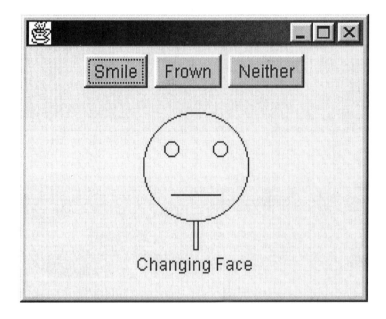

Rewrite the original code to produce this new design.

Hint 1: You will no longer be able to use a **boolean** variable like isHappy, because you need more than two possible values. Can you think of how to deal with this?

Hint 2: There are two useful methods of the Graphics class that you will need:

```
void drawLine (int x1, int y1, int x2, int y2)
```
Draws a line from point (x1, y1) to point (x2, y2).

```
void drawRect (int x, int y, int w, int h)
```
Draws a rectangle of width w and height h with the top left-hand corner at point (x, y).

Practical work

1. Implement the changes you have made to the PushMe class.

2. Add some additional features to the `MetricConverter` – for example Celsius to Fahrenheit or litres to pints.

3. Implement the changes to the `ChangingFace` class that you made in tutorial question 3.

4. Look back at the final version of the `Reactor` class that you wrote in the first practical question of chapter 8. Now you can create a graphical user interface for it, instead of a text menu. A suggested interface is shown below, with an explanation of the different components used.

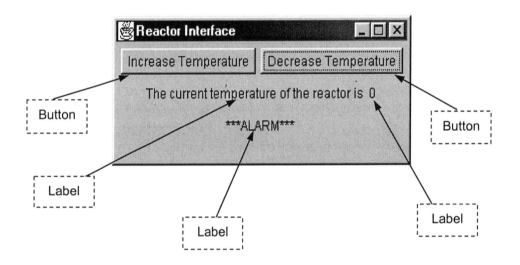

10 Case study – part 1

Learning objectives

By the end of this chapter you should be able to:

- develop a Java implementation from a UML specification;
- use pseudocode to help develop complex algorithms.

10.1 Introduction

In this and the next chapter we are going to develop a case study that will enable you to get an idea of how a real-world system can be developed from scratch; we start with an informal description of the requirements, and then specify the system using UML notation. From there we go on to design our system and implement it in Java. In this chapter we develop the individual classes required, and test them in the way you learnt in chapter 8; in the next chapter we put them together with a graphical user interface and test out our system as a whole.

The system that we are going to develop will keep records of the residents of a student hostel. In order not to cloud your understanding of the system, we have rather over-simplified things, keeping details of individuals to a minimum, and keeping the functionality fairly basic; you will have the opportunity to improve on what we have done in the tutorial and practical work at the end of each chapter.

The case study demonstrates all the important learning points from previous chapters, and allows you to see how these can be brought together to create a working system; in future, as you learn more advanced techniques, the system can be adapted to become more sophisticated and functional.

10.2 The requirements

The local university requires a program to manage one of its student hostels which contains a number of rooms, each of which can be occupied by a single tenant who pays rent on a monthly basis. The program must keep a list of tenants; the information held for each tenant will consist of a name, a room number and a list of all the payments a tenant has made (month and amount). The program must allow the user to add and delete tenants, to display a list of all tenants, to record a payment for a particular tenant, and to display the payment history of a tenant.

10.3 The specification

Figure 10.1 represents the UML specification of the system; the diagram shows **associations** between the two classes, represented in UML by a single line; in this case a single tenant makes a number of payments – a one-to-many relationship. As was explained in chapter 6 when aggregation was discussed, the "many" side of the relationship is indicated by an asterisk. The "one" side is indicated by a 1.

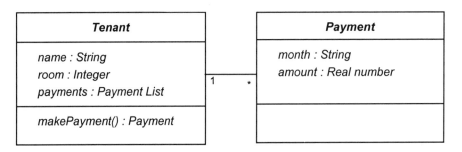

Fig 10.1   The UML specification of the hostel system

10.4 The design

We have made a number of design decisions about how the system will be implemented, and these are listed below:

- instances of the Tenant class and instances of the Payment class will each be held in a separate collection class, PaymentList and TenantList respectively;
- the above collection classes will both inherit common features from the generic ObjectList class that we developed in chapter 7;
- The Hostel class which will hold the TenantList will also act as the graphical interface for the system.

The design of the system is shown in figure 10.2. Note that the standard UML notation of underlining a *class* attribute has been used with the maxNoOfPayments attribute of the Tenant class. The Hostel class itself has not yet been designed and this will be left until the next chapter where we consider the overall system design and testing; for this reason it has been drawn with a dotted line.

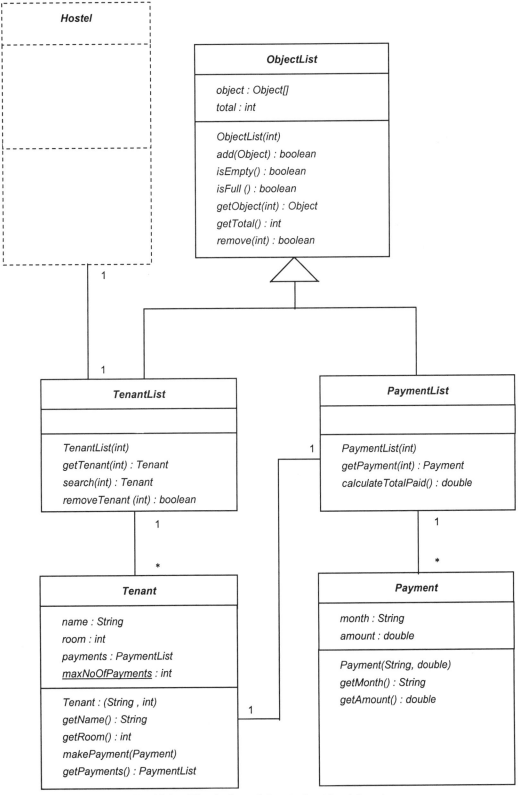

Fig 10.2   The design of the student hostel system

10.5 Implementing the *Payment* class

The code for the Payment class is shown below:

The *Payment* class

```
class Payment
{
    private String month;
    private double amount;

    public Payment(String monthIn, double amountIn)
    {
        month = monthIn;
        amount=amountIn;
    }

    public String getMonth()
    {
        return month;
    }

    public double getAmount()
    {
        return amount;
    }
}
```

As you can see, this class is fairly simple so we won't discuss it any further. A driver to test this class is equally straightforward and we leave it as a practical task at the end of this chapter.

Now let's move on to the more interesting parts of this system. All the remaining classes involve the use of some kind of collection – in each case the type of collection is a list.

This system requires us to develop two kinds of list, a PaymentList and a TenantList. Rather than develop the same code twice we are going to reuse the ObjectList class that we developed in chapter 7, and then use inheritance to add the specific attributes and methods that we need for a PaymentList and a TenantList. If you look back at the UML design in figure 10.2 you can see that after inheriting details from the ObjectList class, there is not a lot of extra work to be done to code the PaymentList class. We present the complete code for this class below, after which we discuss it.

The *PaymentList* class

```
class PaymentList extends ObjectList // inherit from ObjectList
{
    public PaymentList(int sizeIn)
    {   // call ObjectList constructor
        super(sizeIn);
    }


    public Payment getPayment(int indexIn)
    {   // call inherited method and type cast
        return (Payment) getObject(indexIn);
    }


    public double calculateTotalPaid()
    {
        double totalPaid = 0; // initialize totalPaid
        // loop through all payments
        for (int i=1; i<= getTotal();i++)
        {   // add current payment to running total
            totalPaid = totalPaid + getPayment(i).getAmount();
        }
        return totalPaid;
    }
}
```

As you can see, this class requires no additional attributes and, apart from the new constructor, only two additional methods – getPayment and calculateTotalPaid. Let's have a look at each of these methods in turn.

The getPayment method is simply a wrapper for the getObject method from the inherited ObjectList class. If you remember from chapter 7, we said that generic container classes can be used to store items of *any* type, but when returning such items from the container they must be type cast back to the appropriate type. The getPayment method carries out this task of type casting the returned item back to an object of type Payment.

```
return (Payment) getObject(indexIn);
```

The advantage of this is that responsibility for type casting is taken away from the calling method, and given to getPayment itself. An example of the use of this method can be seen in the calculateTotalPaid method.

The calculateTotalPaid method uses a standard **algorithm** for computing sums from a list of items. An **algorithm** is an often-used term in computing texts, and means a set of instructions for achieving a task (such as a recipe). This algorithm can be expressed in pseudocode as follows:

```
SET totalPaid TO 0
LOOP FROM 1st item in list TO last item in list
BEGIN
      SET totalPaid TO totalPaid + amount of current payment
END
return totalPaid
```

As with the remove method we discussed in chapter 6, this algorithm can be implemented in Java with the use of a **for** loop. Notice how the position of the last item in the list is determined by the getTotal method; remember that we do not have access to the total attribute, since this was declared as **private** in the superclass.

```
double totalPaid = 0;
for (int i=1; i<= getTotal();i++)
{
     totalPaid = totalPaid + getPayment(i).getAmount();
}
return totalPaid;
```

The body of the loop takes the amount associated with the current payment and adds it to the running total. As you can see, the getPayment method is used to return the current payment and the getAmount method is used to find out the amount associated with that payment.

getPayment(i).getAmount()

returns current payment

returns amount of a given payment

Before we move on, it is important to test this PaymentList class in order to ensure that it is functioning correctly. Program 10.1 provides a menu-driven interface for this test driver. Notice the careful use of the new line, '\n', and tab, '\t', escape sequences to improve the display of information on the screen.

Program 10.1

```java
class PaymentListTester
{
    public static void main(String[] args)
    {
        char choice;
        int total;
        // declare PaymentList object to test
        PaymentList pl;
        // get size of list
        System.out.print("\nMaximum number of payments? ");
        total = EasyIn.getInt();
        // create PaymentList object to test
        pl = new PaymentList(total);
        // menu
        do
        {
            // display options
            System.out.println("\n[1] Add a payment");
            System.out.println("[2] List all payments");
            System.out.println("[3] Get number of payments made");
            System.out.println("[4] Get total payments made");
            System.out.println("[5] Quit");
            System.out.print("\nEnter a choice [1,2,3,4,5]: ");
            // get choice
            choice = EasyIn.getChar();
            // process choice
            switch(choice)
            {
                case '1': Option1(pl); break;
                case '2': Option2(pl); break;
                case '3': Option3(pl); break;
                case '4': Option4(pl); break;
                case '5': System.out.print("\n\nBYE"); break;
                default: System.out.print("\n1-5 only");
            }
        } while (choice != '5');

    }

    // static worker methods
```

```
      // add payment
      private static void Option1(PaymentList listIn)
      {
          if (!pl.isFull())// only add if list has space
          {
                System.out.print("\nenter month:\t");
                String month = EasyIn.getString();
                System.out.print("enter amount:\t");
                double amount = EasyIn.getDouble();
                listIn.add(new Payment (month, amount));
          }
          else // error message if list is full
          {
                System.out.println("\n!!!SORRY, LIST IS FULL!!!");
          }
      }


      // display payments
      private static void Option2(PaymentList listIn)
      {
          System.out.print("\nMONTH \tAMOUNT\n");// header
          // loop through payments in list
          for (int i =1; i <= listIn.getTotal();i++)
          {
                Payment p = listIn.getPayment(i);
                System.out.print(p.getMonth());
                System.out.println("\t" + p.getAmount());
          }
      }


      // get total number of payments
      private static void Option3(PaymentList listIn)
      {
          System.out.print("\ntotal number payments made: ");
          System.out.println(listIn.getTotal());
      }

      // get total of payments made
      private static void Option4(PaymentList listIn)
      {
          System.out.print("\ntotal sum of payments made: ");
          System.out.println(listIn.calculateTotalPaid());
      }
}
```

To make this driver more readable, menu options have been implemented inside **static** worker methods. There is nothing particularly new here so let's look at a sample test run of this driver program:

```
Maximum number of payments? 2

[1] Add a payment
[2] List all payments
[3] Get number of payments made
[4] Get total payments made
[5] Quit

Enter a choice [1,2,3,4,5]: 1

enter month: Jan
enter amount: 240

[1] Add a payment
[2] List all payments
[3] Get number of payments made
[4] Get total payments made
[5] Quit

Enter a choice [1,2,3,4,5]: 1

enter month: Feb
enter amount: 225

[1] Add a payment
[2] List all payments
[3] Get number of payments made
[4] Get total payments made
[5] Quit

Enter a choice [1,2,3,4,5]: 2

MONTH AMOUNT
Jan 240.0
Feb 225.0

[1] Add a payment
[2] List all payments
[3] Get number of payments made
[4] Get total payments made
[5] Quit
Enter a choice [1,2,3,4,5]: 3
```

```
total number payments made: 2


[1] Add a payment
[2] List all payments
[3] Get number of payments made
[4] Get total payments made
[5] Quit


Enter a choice [1,2,3,4,5]: 4


total sum of payments made: 465.0


[1] Add a payment
[2] List all payments
[3] Get number of payments made
[4] Get total payments made
[5] Quit
Enter a choice [1,2,3,4,5]: 1


!!!SORRY, LIST IS FULL!!!


[1] Add a payment
[2] List all payments
[3] Get number of payments made
[4] Get total payments made
[5] Quit


Enter a choice [1,2,3,4,5]: 5


BYE
```

Although some aspects of the interface could be improved, the PaymentList class appears to be functioning properly. In order to be more confident, more rigorous testing would need to be carried out. For now though, this amount of testing is sufficient so let's move on to the Tenant class.

10.6 Implementing the *Tenant* class

As you can see from the UML diagram of figure 10.2, the Tenant class contains four attributes: name, room, payments, maxNoOfPayments.

The first two of these represent the name and the room of the tenant respectively. The third attribute, payments, is to be implemented as a PaymentList object and the last attribute, maxNoOfPayments, is to be implemented as a **static** class attribute. The maxNoOfPayments attribute will also be implemented as a *constant* as we are assuming that tenants make a *fixed* number of payments in a year (twelve – one for each month). Below is the code for the Tenant class.

The *Tenant* class

```
class Tenant
{
    private String name;
    private int room;
    private PaymentList payments;
    private static final int maxNoOfPayments = 12;

    Tenant(String nameIn, int roomIn)
    {
        name = new String(nameIn);
        room = roomIn;
        payments = new PaymentList(maxNoOfPayments);
    }
    public String getName()
    {
        return name;
    }
    public int getRoom()
    {
        return room;
    }
    public void makePayment(Payment paymentIn)
    { // call PaymentList method
        payments.add(paymentIn);
    }
    public PaymentList getPayments()
    {
        return payments;
    }
}
```

As there is nothing very new in this class, we don't really need to discuss it any further other than to point out that the payments attribute, being of type PaymentList, can respond to any of the PaymentList methods we discussed in section 10.5. The makePayment method illustrates this by calling the add method of PaymentList.

```
public void makePayment (Payment paymentIn)
{     // add method of PaymentList called
      payments.add(paymentIn);
}
```

The implementation of a driver to test this class will be very similar to program 10.1 and is left as a practical exercise at the end of this chapter.

10.7 Implementing the *TenantList* class

The TenantList class, like the PaymentList class of section 10.5, inherits from the generic ObjectList class. As you can see from diagram 10.2, the TenantList class requires no new attributes and, apart from the constructor, has only three new methods:

- getTenant;
- search;
- removeTenant.

The getTenant method behaves in much the same way as the getPayment method of the PaymentList class. That is, it acts as a wrapper for the getObject method of the generic ObjectList class and type casts the returned item back to an object of the correct type, which in this case is an object of type Tenant.

```
public Tenant getTenant (int indexIn)
{     // call inherited method and type cast
      return (Tenant)getObject(indexIn);
}
```

The search method is unique to the TenanList class. Here is a reminder of its interface:

search (int): Tenant

The integer parameter represents the room number of the tenant that this method is searching for. The tenant returned is the tenant living in that particular room; if no tenant is

found in that room then `null` is returned. From this interface we can derive the method
header:

```
public Tenant search (int roomIn)
{
      // code for method goes here
}
```

Searching through a list for a given item is a common activity and many algorithms exist
for this purpose. Here is a fairly standard search algorithm expressed in pseudocode:

```
LOOP FROM first item TO last item
BEGIN
      IF current item = roomIn
      BEGIN
               EXIT loop with current item
      END
END
indicate item not found
```

A **for** loop can be used to implement this algorithm as follows:

```
for(int i=1;i<=getTotal();i++)
{
      // body of loop
}
return null; // no tenant found with given room number
```

The body of the loop can in turn be implemented using a simple **if** statement. The
condition of the selection requires us to check whether the current item is the item we are

looking for. We can do this by checking the room number of the current tenant against the room number we are searching for, roomIn, as follows:

```
if(getTenant(i).getRoom() == roomIn)
{
    // body of if statement
}
```

Finally, the body of the **if** statement requires us to exit the loop with the given tenant. The **return** statement allows us to exit with a value so the following statement would be appropriate:

```
return getTenant(i);
```

Notice that as soon as this **return** statement is executed the loop will terminate and the method will be complete. Finally, let's look at the removeTenant method. The interface for this method is given as follows:

removeTenant(int): boolean

Here the integer parameter represents the room number of the tenant who is to be removed from the list and the **boolean** return value indicates whether or not such a tenant has been removed successfully. From this interface we get the following method header:

```
public boolean removeTenant (int roomIn)
{
    // code for methods goes here
}
```

Most of the work of this method is going to be carried out by the `remove` method of the `ObjectList` class. The job of the `removeTenant` method is to determine which tenant to delete before calling the `remove` method. This once again requires a *search* so we will use the basis of the `search` algorithm we presented earlier to devise an algorithm for this method.

```
LOOP FROM first item TO last item
BEGIN
      IF current item = roomIn
      BEGIN
            remove current item from list
            EXIT from loop and indicate success
      END
END
indicate failure (item not found)
```

Remembering that we will use **boolean** values **true** and **false** to indicate success or failure in this method, we arrive at the following implementation for the body of the `removeTenant` method:

```
for(int i=1;i<=getTotal();i++)
{ // remove tenant with given room number
    if(getTenant(i).getRoom() == roomIn)
    {
        remove(i); // call remove method of ObjectList
        return true; // indicate success
    }
}
return false; // indicate failure
```

The complete code for the `TenantList` class is now presented below.

The *TenantList* class

```
class TenantList extends ObjectList
{
    public TenantList(int sizeIn)
    {   // call ObjectList constructor
        super(sizeIn);
    }


    public Tenant getTenant(int indexIn)
    {   // call inherited method and type cast
        return (Tenant)getObject(indexIn);
    }


    public Tenant search(int roomIn)
    {
        for(int i=1;i<=getTotal();i++)
        {   // find tenant with given room number
            if(getTenant(i).getRoom() == roomIn)
            {
                return getTenant(i);
            }
        }
        return null; // no tenant found with given room number
    }


    public boolean removeTenant(int roomIn)
    {
        for(int i=1;i<=getTotal();i++)
        {   // remove tenant with given room number
            if(getTenant(i).getRoom() == roomIn)
            {
                remove(i);
                return true;
            }
        }
        return false; // no tenant found with given room number
    }
}
```

Program 10.2 is a driver to test the TenantList class. Once again, notice the use of escape sequences to help format output on the screen.

Program 10.2

```
class TenantListTester
{
    public static void main(String[] args)
    {   // declare variables
        char choice;
        int total;
        TenantList tl;
        // get size of list
        System.out.print("\nHow many tenants will there be ? ");
        total = EasyIn.getInt();
        // create list
        tl = new TenantList(total);
        // menu
        do
        {   // display options
            System.out.println("\n[1] Add a tenant");
            System.out.println("[2] List all tenants");
            System.out.println("[3] Add a payment");
            System.out.println("[4] List payments");
            System.out.println("[5] Remove a tenant");
            System.out.println("[6] Quit");
            System.out.print("\nEnter a choice [1,2,3,4,5,6]: ");
            choice = EasyIn.getChar();// get choice
            // process choice
            switch(choice)
            {
                    case '1':Option1(tl); break;
                    case '2':Option2(tl); break;
                    case '3':Option3(tl); break;
                    case '4':Option4(tl); break;
                    case '5':Option5(tl); break;
                    case '6':System.out.print("\n\nBYE"); break;
                    default: System.out.print("\n1-5 only");
            }
        } while (choice != '6');
    }

    private static void Option1(TenantList tl)
    {
        if (!tl.isFull())// only add if list is not full
        {
            System.out.print("\nenter name:\t");
```

```
                    String name = EasyIn.getString();
                    System.out.print("enter room:\t");
                    int room = EasyIn.getInt();
                    tl.add(new Tenant (name, room));
            }
            else // error message if list is full
            {
                    System.out.println("\n!!!SORRY, LIST IS FULL!!! \n");
            }
    }


    private static void Option2(TenantList tl)
    {
            System.out.print("\nNAME \tROOM\n");// header
            // loop through tenants in list
            for (int i =1; i <= tl.getTotal();i++)
            {
                    Tenant t = tl.getTenant(i);
                    System.out.print(t.getName());
                    System.out.println("\t" + t.getRoom());
            }
    }


    private static void Option3(TenantList tl)
    {   // get room number of tenant
            System.out.print("\nenter room number of tenant:\t");
            int room = EasyIn.getInt();
            // find relevant tenant
            Tenant t = tl.search(room);
            if (t != null) // check tenant exists before adding payment
            {
                    System.out.print("\nenter month:\t");
                    String month = EasyIn.getString();
                    System.out.print("enter amount:\t");
                    double amount = EasyIn.getDouble();
                    Payment p = new Payment (month, amount);
                    t.makePayment(p);
            }
            else // no tenant with given room number found
            {
                    System.out.print("\n!!!NO TENANT IN THIS ROOM!!! \n");
            }
    }
```

```java
    private static void Option4(TenantList tl)
    {   // get room number of tenant
        System.out.print("\nenter room number of tenant:\t");
        int room = EasyIn.getInt();
        // find relevant tenant
        Tenant t = tl.search(room);
        if (t != null)// check such a tenant exists before displaying
        {
                PaymentList pl = t.getPayments();
                System.out.print("\nMONTH \tAMOUNT\n");// header
                // loop through payments in list
                for (int i =1; i <= pl.getTotal();i++)
                {
                        Payment p = pl.getPayment(i);
                        System.out.print(p.getMonth());
                        System.out.println("\t" + p.getAmount());
                }
                // display total amount paid
                System.out.print("\nTOTAL PAID:\t");
                System.out.println(pl.calculateTotalPaid());
        }
        else // no tenant with given room number found
        {
                System.out.print("\n!!!NO TENANT IN THIS ROOM!!! \n");
        }
    }


    private static void Option5(TenantList tl)
    {   // get room number of tenant
        System.out.print("\nenter room number of tenant:\t");
        int room = EasyIn.getInt();
        // check tenant exists
        Tenant t = tl.search(room);
        if (t != null)// only remove if tenant exists
        {
                tl.removeTenant(room);
        }
        else // no tenant in given room
        {
                System.out.print("\n!!! NO TENANT IN THIS ROOM!!! \n");
        }
    }
}
```

By now, such a menu system should be familiar to you. We just draw your attention to the validation that we have added to some of these menu options.

Option 1 allows the user to add a tenant to the list. We have ensured that a tenant is only added if the list is currently *not full*.

```
if (!tl.isFull())// only add if list is not full
{
     // code to get tenant details and add
}
else // error message if list is full
{
     System.out.println("\n!!!SORRY, LIST IS FULL!!! \n");
}
```

Notice we haven't carried out any error checking on the rooms at this stage. Responsibility for ensuring that tenants do not occupy the same room has not been given to the TenantList class so should not be tested here. This job will be given to the Hostel class that we will develop in the next chapter.

Option 3 allows the user to record the payment for a tenant in a given room. We have ensured that a tenant actually exists in that room before recording the payment.

```
int room = EasyIn.getInt();
// find relevant tenant
Tenant t = tl.search(room);
// check tenant exists before adding payment
if (t != null)
{
     // code to get and record payment goes here
}
else // no tenant with given room number found
{
     System.out.print("\n!!!NO TENANT IN THIS ROOM!!! \n");
}
```

Options 4 and 5 include similar validation as both require a tenant to exist in a given room before further action can be taken. Below is a sample test run of program 10.2 – examine it closely as we will ask you a question about it in the tutorial section at the end of this chapter.

How many tenants will there be ? 2

[1] Add a tenant

[2] List all tenants

[3] Add a payment

[4] List payments

[5] Remove a tenant

[6] Quit

Enter a choice [1,2,3,4,5,6]: **1**

enter name: **Bart**

enter room: **3**

[1] Add a tenant

[2] List all tenants

[3] Add a payment

[4] List payments

[5] Remove a tenant

[6] Quit

Enter a choice [1,2,3,4,5,6]: **1**

enter name: **Louise**

enter room: **1**

[1] Add a tenant

[2] List all tenants

[3] Add a payment

[4] List payments

[5] Remove a tenant

[6] Quit

Enter a choice [1,2,3,4,5,6]: **2**

NAME ROOM

Bart 3

Louise 1

[1] Add a tenant

[2] List all tenants

[3] Add a payment

[4] List payments

[5] Remove a tenant

[6] Quit

```
Enter a choice [1,2,3,4,5,6]: 1

!!!SORRY, LIST IS FULL!!!

[1] Add a tenant
[2] List all tenants
[3] Add a payment
[4] List payments
[5] Remove a tenant
[6] Quit


Enter a choice [1,2,3,4,5,6]: 3


enter room number of tenant: 5


!!!NO TENANT IN THIS ROOM!!!

[1] Add a tenant
[2] List all tenants
[3] Add a payment
[4] List payments
[5] Remove a tenant
[6] Quit
Enter a choice [1,2,3,4,5,6]: 3


enter room number of tenant: 3


enter month: Jan
enter amount: 240


[1] Add a tenant
[2] List all tenants
[3] Add a payment
[4] List payments
[5] Remove a tenant
[6] Quit


Enter a choice [1,2,3,4,5,6]: 3


enter room number of tenant: 3


enter month: Feb
enter amount: 225
```

```
[1] Add a tenant
[2] List all tenants
[3] Add a payment
[4] List payments
[5] Remove a tenant
[6] Quit

Enter a choice [1,2,3,4,5,6]: 4

enter room number of tenant: 2

!!!NO TENANT IN THIS ROOM!!!


[1] Add a tenant
[2] List all tenants
[3] Add a payment
[4] List payments
[5] Remove a tenant
[6] Quit
Enter a choice [1,2,3,4,5,6]: 4

enter room number of tenant: 3

MONTH AMOUNT
Jan 240.0
Feb 225.0

TOTAL PAID: 465.0


[1] Add a tenant
[2] List all tenants
[3] Add a payment
[4] List payments
[5] Remove a tenant
[6] Quit
Enter a choice [1,2,3,4,5,6]: 5

enter room number of tenant: 7

!!! NO TENANT IN THIS ROOM!!!
```

```
[1]  Add a tenant
[2]  List all tenants
[3]  Add a payment
[4]  List payments
[5]  Remove a tenant
[6]  Quit
Enter a choice [1,2,3,4,5,6]: 5


enter room number of tenant: 3


[1]  Add a tenant
[2]  List all tenants
[3]  Add a payment
[4]  List payments
[5]  Remove a tenant
[6]  Quit


Enter a choice [1,2,3,4,5,6]: 2

NAME ROOM
Louise 1


[1]  Add a tenant
[2]  List all tenants
[3]  Add a payment
[4]  List payments
[5]  Remove a tenant
[6]  Quit
Enter a choice [1,2,3,4,5,6]: 6


BYE
```

Tutorial exercises

1. What advantages did the use of inheritance have in the student hostel case study?

2. What is the meaning of an underlined attribute in a UML diagram and how should such an attribute be implemented in Java?

3. What is the purpose of returning a **null** value from the search method of section 10.7?

4. Here is an alternative algorithm for the search method of section 10.7.

```
SET found TO false
SET position TO 1
WHILE   found = false AND more items to check
BEGIN
        IF current item = roomIn
                SET found TO true
        ELSE
                increment position
        ENDIF
END
IF found = true
        RETURN tenant at current position
ELSE
        RETURN null
ENDIF
```

Develop Java code for this alternative search method.

5. Look back at the sample test run of program 10.2. Complete a test log so that this test run could be repeated with the same inputs and the same expected results.

Practical work

1. Test the Payment class of section 10.5 by implementing a suitable driver class.

2. Amend the driver from practical task 1 above so that instead of the user entering a month directly, another menu is displayed with the 12 months listed as follows:

```
    [1]    January
    [2]    February
    [3]    March
    [4]    April
    [5]    May
    [6]    June
    [7]    July
    [8]    August
    [9]    September
    [10]   October
    [11]   November
    [12]   December

enter month [1 to 12]:
```

3. Test the Tenant class by implementing a suitable driver class.

4. Implement the TenantList class but replace the original search method with that developed in tutorial question 4.

5. Implement and run program 10.2 to test the amended TenantList tester class developed in task 4 above using the test log you created in tutorial question 5.

6. Amend program 10.2 so that all monetary values are displayed to two decimal places. (Hint: Look back at the DecimalFormat class discussed in chapter 8).

11 Case study – part 2

Learning objectives

By the end of this chapter you should be able to:

- use your knowledge of software development to create a small integrated application;
- design and implement an attractive graphical user interface.

11.1 Introduction

All that remains for us to do to complete our case study is to design, implement and test the `Hostel` class which will not only keep track of the tenants but will also act as the graphical user interface for the system.

11.2 Keeping permanent records

In practice, an application such as the Student Hostel System would not be much use if we had no way of keeping permanent records – in other words, of saving a file to disk. However, reading and writing files is not something that we expect you to learn in your first semester, so in order to make it possible to keep a permanent record of your data we have created a special class for you to use; we have called this class `TenantFileHandler`. It has two **static** methods: the first, `saveRecords`, needs to be sent two parameters, an integer value indicating the number of rooms in the hostel, and a `TenantList`, which is a reference to the list to be saved; the second, `readRecords`, requires only a reference to a `TenantList` so that it knows where to store the information that is read from the file.

The class can be downloaded with the rest of the files from this case study (or copied from appendix 2); the `readRecords` method will be called when the application is first loaded (so this method call will therefore be coded into the constructor), and the `saveRecords` method will be called when we finish the application (and will therefore be coded into the event-handler of a "Save and Quit" button). We will also provide the option of exiting without saving, just in case, for any reason, the user should want to abandon any changes.

11.3 Design of the GUI

There will be two aspects to the design of the graphical interface. Firstly we need to design the visual side of things; then we need to design the algorithms for our event-handling routines so that the buttons do the jobs we want them to, like adding or displaying tenants.

Let's start with the visual design. We need to choose which graphics components we are going to use and how to lay them out. One way to do this is to make a preliminary sketch such as the one shown in figure 11.1. We have named our components so that it is obvious what kind of component we are talking about; for example, `roomLabel` is a `Label`, `nameField` is a `Field`, `addButton` is a `Button` and `displayArea` is a `TextArea`.

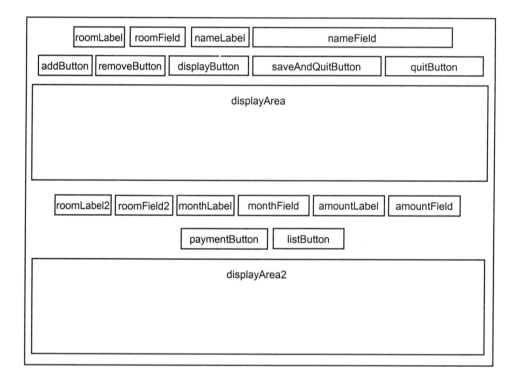

Fig 11.1   Preliminary design of the *Hostel* interface

We are going to use a simple `FlowLayout` policy, so to get our components where we want them we will have to play about with the size of the components and the size of the frame. To help you see what we are aiming at, we have, with figure 11.2, "cheated" and let you look ahead at the end result. This shows the effect of running our `Hostel` interface in a 570 × 500 frame.

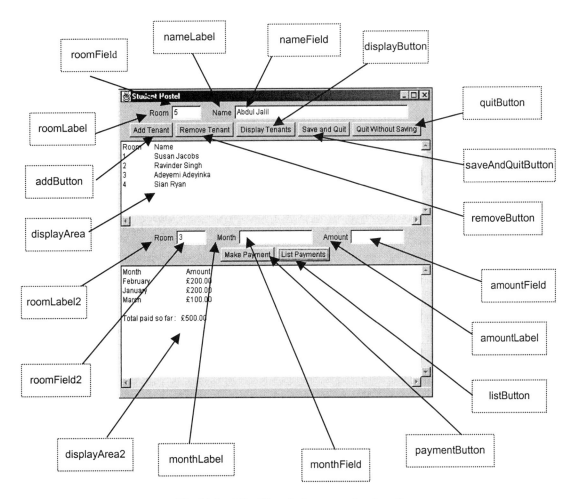

Fig 11.2   The *Hostel* class running in a frame

Now that we know the components we need it is an easy matter to complete the UML class diagram. Each of the components must be declared as an attribute of the class – and, in addition, there are two more attributes that we will need. Firstly we will need to hold information about the number of rooms available in the hostel, so we must declare an attribute of type **int** for this purpose; we have called our attribute noOfRooms. Secondly we must, of course, declare an attribute of type TenantList (which we have called list) to keep track of the tenants in residence.

We are going to need only two methods: a constructor to add the components and read the data from the file, and an actionPerformed method for the event-handling routines.

The class design is shown in figure 11.3.

```
┌─────────────────────────────────────────────┐
│                   Hostel                      │
├─────────────────────────────────────────────┤
│ noOfRooms : int                               │
│ list : TenantList                             │
│ addButton : Button                            │
│ removeButton : Button                         │
│ displayButton : Button                        │
│ saveAndQuitButton : Button                    │
│ quitButton : Button                           │
│ roomLabel : Label ·                           │
│ roomField :TextField                          │
│ nameLabel : Label                             │
│ nameField : TextField                         │
│ displayArea : TextArea                        │
│ displayArea2 : TextArea                       │
│ roomLabel2 : Label                            │
│ roomField2 : TextField                        │
│ monthLabel : Label                            │
│ monthField : TextField                        │
│ amountLabel : Label                           │
│ amountField : TextField                       │
│ paymentButton : Button                        │
│ listButton : Button                           │
├─────────────────────────────────────────────┤
│ Hostel(int)                                   │
│ actionPerformed(ActionEvent)                  │
└─────────────────────────────────────────────┘
```

Fig 11.3   The *Hostel* class

11.4 Designing the event-handlers

As you can see, there are seven buttons that need to be coded so that they respond in the correct way when pressed. Our code for the `actionPerformed` method will therefore take the following form:

```
public void actionPerformed(ActionEvent e)
{
     if(e.getSource() == addButton)
     {
            // code for add button goes here
     }

     if(e.getSource() == displayButton)
     {
            // code for display button goes here
      }

     if(e.getSource() == removeButton)
     {
            // code for remove button goes here
      }

     if(e.getSource() == paymentButton)
     {
            // code for payment button goes here
     }

     if(e.getSource() == listButton)
     {
            // code for list button goes here
     }

     if(e.getSource() == saveAndQuitButton)
     {
            // code for saveAndQuit button goes here
     }
     if(e.getSource() == quitButton)
     {
            // code for quit button goes here
     }
}
```

We have summarized below the task that each button must perform, and then gone on to design our algorithms using pseudocode:

The *addButton*

The purpose of this button is to add a new `Tenant` to the list. The values entered in `roomField` and `nameField` must be validated; first of all, they must not be blank; secondly, the room number must not be greater than the number of rooms available (or less than 1!); finally, the room must not be occupied. If all this is okay, then the new tenant is added (we will make use of the `add` method of `TenantList` to do this) and a message should be displayed in `displayArea`. We can express this in pseudocode as follows:

```
read roomField
read nameField
IF roomField blank OR nameField blank
    display blank field error in displayArea
ELSE IF roomField value <1 OR roomField value >noOfRooms
    display invalid room number error in displayArea
ELSE IF tenant found in room
    display room occupied error in displayArea
ELSE
BEGIN
    add tenant
    blank roomField
    blank nameField
    display message to confirm success in displayArea
END
```

The *displayButton*

Pressing this button will display the full list of tenants (room number and name) in `displayArea`.

If all the rooms are vacant a suitable message should be displayed; otherwise the list of tenants' rooms and names should appear under appropriate headings as can be seen in figure 11.2. This can be expressed in pseudocode as follows:

```
IF list is empty
     display rooms empty error in displayArea
ELSE
BEGIN
     display header in displayArea
     LOOP FROM first item TO last item in list
     BEGIN
             append tenant room and name to displayArea
     END
END
```

The *removeButton*

Clicking on this button will remove the tenant whose room number has been entered in
`roomField`.

As with the `addButton`, the room number entered must be validated; if the number is a
valid one then the tenant is removed from the list (we will make use of the `remove` method
of `TenantList` to do this) and a confirmation message is displayed. The pseudocode for
this event-handler is given as follows:

```
read roomField
IF roomField blank
     display blank field error in displayArea
ELSE IF roomField value < 1 OR roomField value > noOfRooms
     display invalid room number error in displayArea
ELSE IF no tenant found in room
     display room empty error in displayArea
ELSE
BEGIN
     remove tenant from list
     display message to confirm success in displayArea
END
```

The *paymentButton*

This button records payments made by an individual tenant whose room number is entered in roomField2. The values entered in roomField2, monthField and amountField must be validated to ensure that none of the fields is blank, that the room number is a valid one and, if so, that it is currently occupied.

If everything is okay then a new payment record is added to that tenant's list of payments (we will make use of the makePayment method of PaymentList to do this) and a confirmation message is displayed in displayArea2. This design is expressed in pseudocode as follows:

```
read roomField2
read monthField
read amountField
IF roomField2 blank OR monthField blank OR amountField blank
     display fields empty error in displayArea2
ELSE IF roomField2 value<1 OR roomField2 value>noOfRooms
     display invalid room number error in displayArea2
ELSE IF no tenant found in room
     display room empty error in displayArea2
ELSE
BEGIN
     create payment from amountField value and monthField value
     add payment into list
     display message to confirm success in displayArea2
END
```

The *listButton*

Pressing this button causes a list of payments (month and amount) made by the tenant whose room number is entered in roomField2 to be displayed in displayArea2.

After validating the values entered, each record in the tenant's payment list is displayed. Finally, the total amount paid by that tenant is displayed (we will make use of the calculateTotalPaid method of PaymentList to do this). The pseudocode is given as follows:

```
read roomField2
IF roomField2 blank
      display room field empty error in displayArea2
ELSE IF roomField2 value<1 OR roomField2 value>noOfRooms
      display invalid room number error in displayArea2
ELSE IF no tenant found in room
      display room empty error in displayArea2
ELSE
BEGIN
      find tenant in given room
      get payments of tenant
      IF payments = 0
            display no payments error in displayArea2
      ELSE
      BEGIN
            display header in displayArea2
            LOOP FROM first payment TO last payment
            BEGIN
                  append amount and month to displayArea2
            END
            display total paid in displayArea2
            blank monthField
            blank amountField
      END
END
```

The *saveAndQuitButton*

Pressing this button causes all the records to be saved to a file (here we make use of the `saveRecords` method of the `TenantFileHandler` class that we talked about in section 11.2); it then closes the frame, terminating the program.

It contains only two lines of code and we have therefore not written pseudocode for it.

The *quitButton*

Pressing this button terminates the program without saving the changes.

11.5 Implementation

The complete code for the `Hostel` class now appears below. When you come to reading the code, you should notice that we have utilized the `NumberFormat` class (which is to be found in the `java.text` package) to print the amounts in the local currency. Also note the use of the `parseInt` method of the `Integer` class to convert the room values, entered as text, into integer values.

There is very little new in this `Hostel` class apart from some formatting detail, which has been explained by means of comments throughout the code. Study the code carefully and compare it with the pseudocode to make sure you understand it.

The *Hostel* class

```java
import java.awt.*;
import java.awt.event.*;
import java.applet.*;
import java.text.*;


class Hostel extends Applet implements ActionListener
{
    // the attributes
    private int noOfRooms;
    private TenantList list;
    private Button addButton = new Button("Add Tenant");
    private Button displayButton = new Button("Display Tenants");
    private Button removeButton = new Button("Remove Tenant");
    private Label roomLabel = new Label("Room");
    private TextField roomField = new TextField(4);
    private Label nameLabel = new Label("Name");
    private TextField nameField = new TextField(40);
    private Button saveAndQuitButton = new Button("Save and Quit");
    private Button quitButton = new Button("Quit Without Saving");
    private TextArea displayArea = new TextArea(8,75);
    private TextArea displayArea2 = new TextArea(12,75);
    private Label roomLabel2 = new Label("Room");
    private TextField roomField2 = new TextField(4);
    private Label monthLabel = new Label("Month");
    private TextField monthField = new TextField(15);
```

```
private Label amountLabel = new Label("Amount");
private TextField amountField = new TextField(10);
private Button paymentButton = new Button("Make Payment");
private Button listButton = new Button("List Payments");


// the constructor
public Hostel(int numberIn)
{
    noOfRooms = numberIn;
    list = new TenantList(noOfRooms);
    add(roomLabel);
    /* We are using the setAlignment method of the Label class
    to get our text lined up to the right. Possible values of
    the parameter to this method are Label.LEFT,
    Label.CENTER and Label.RIGHT */
    roomLabel.setAlignment(Label.RIGHT);
    add(roomField);
    add(nameLabel);
    nameLabel.setAlignment(Label.RIGHT);
    add(nameField);
    add(addButton);
    add(displayButton);
    add(removeButton);
    add(saveAndQuitButton);
    add(quitButton);
    add(displayArea);
    add(roomLabel2);
    roomLabel2.setAlignment(Label.RIGHT);
    add(roomField2);
    add(monthLabel);
    monthLabel.setAlignment(Label.RIGHT);
    add(monthField);
    add(amountLabel);
    amountLabel.setAlignment(Label.RIGHT);
    add(amountField);
    add(paymentButton);
    add(listButton);
    add(displayArea2);

    // add ActionListeners to the buttons
    addButton.addActionListener(this);
    displayButton.addActionListener(this);
    paymentButton.addActionListener(this);
    listButton.addActionListener(this);
```

```
        removeButton.addActionListener(this);
        listButton.addActionListener(this);
        saveAndQuitButton.addActionListener(this);
        quitButton.addActionListener(this);

        // read the records file from disk
        TenantFileHandler.readRecords(list);
}


// the event-handlers
public void actionPerformed(ActionEvent e)
{
    if(e.getSource() == addButton)
    {
        String roomEntered = roomField.getText();
        String nameEntered = nameField.getText();

        // if room number or name not entered
        if(roomEntered.length()==0 || nameEntered.length()==0)
        {
            displayArea.setText
                        ("Room number and name must be entered");
        }

        // if room number is out of range
        else if(Integer.parseInt(roomEntered)< 1
                || Integer.parseInt(roomEntered)>noOfRooms)
        {
            displayArea.setText("There are only " + noOfRooms
                                            + " rooms");
        }


        // if the room is occupied
        else if(list.search(Integer.parseInt(roomEntered))!= null)
        {
            displayArea.setText("Room number "
                            + Integer.parseInt(roomEntered)
                            + " is occupied");
        }
```

```
        // if everything is okay then add new tenant
        else
        {
            Tenant t = new
                Tenant(nameEntered,Integer.parseInt(roomEntered));
            list.add(t);
            roomField.setText("");
            nameField.setText("");
            displayArea.setText("New tenant in room "
                                        + roomEntered
                                        + " successfully added");
        }
    }


    if(e.getSource() == displayButton)
    {
        int i;
        // if the list is empty
        if(list.isEmpty())
        {
            displayArea.setText("All rooms are empty");
        }


        // if the list is not empty then display the tenants
        else
        {
            // display a heading
            displayArea.setText("Room" + "\t" + "Name" + "\n");

            // display each tenant in turn
            for(i= 1; i <= list.getTotal(); i++)
            {
                displayArea.append(list.getTenant(i).getRoom()
                        + "\t"
                        + list.getTenant(i).getName() + "\n");
            }
        }
    }



    if(e.getSource() == removeButton)
    {
        String roomEntered = roomField.getText();
```

```
        // if the room number is not entered
        if(roomEntered.length()==0)
        {
           displayArea.setText("Room number must be entered");
        }


        // if the room number is out of range
        else if(Integer.parseInt(roomEntered) < 1
                   || Integer.parseInt(roomEntered)>noOfRooms)
        {
           displayArea.setText("Invalid room number");
        }



        // if the room is empty
        else if(list.search(Integer.parseInt(roomEntered)) == null)
        {
           displayArea.setText("Room number " + roomEntered
                                          + " is empty");
        }


        // if everything is okay then remove the tenant
        else
        {
           list.removeTenant(Integer.parseInt(roomEntered));
           displayArea.setText("Tenant removed from room "
                              + Integer.parseInt(roomEntered));
        }
     }


if(e.getSource() == paymentButton)
{
    String roomEntered = roomField2.getText();
    String monthEntered = monthField.getText();
    String amountEntered = amountField.getText();

    // if room number, month or amount not entered
    if(roomEntered.length()==0 || monthEntered.length()==0
                                 || amountEntered.length()==0)
    {
       displayArea2.setText
         ("Room number, month and amount must all be entered");
    }
```

```
                       // if room number out of range
           else if(Integer.parseInt(roomEntered) < 1
                       || Integer.parseInt(roomEntered) > noOfRooms)
           {
              displayArea2.setText("Invalid room number");
           }


           // if room is empty
           else if(list.search(Integer.parseInt(roomEntered)) == null)
           {
              displayArea2.setText("Room number " + roomEntered
                                              + " is empty");
           }

           // if everything is okay then add the new payment
           else
           {
              Payment p = new
              Payment(monthEntered,Double.valueOf(
              amountEntered).doubleValue());
              list.search(Integer.parseInt(roomEntered)).
                                         makePayment(p);
              displayArea2.setText("Payment recorded");
           }
        }

        if(e.getSource() == listButton)
        {
           int i;
           String roomEntered = roomField2.getText();

           // if room number not entered
           if(roomEntered.length()==0)
           {
              displayArea2.setText("Room number must be entered");
           }

           // if room number out of range
           else if(Integer.parseInt(roomEntered) < 1
                       || Integer.parseInt(roomEntered) > noOfRooms)
           {
              displayArea2.setText("Invalid room number");
           }
```

```
                    // if room is empty
                    else if(list.search(Integer.parseInt(roomEntered)) == null)
                    {
                            displayArea2.setText("Room number "
                                            + Integer.parseInt(roomEntered)
                                            + " is empty");
                    }


                    // if everything is okay then list the payments
                    else
                    {
                        Tenant t =
                                list.search(Integer.parseInt(roomEntered));
                        PaymentList p = t.getPayments();
                        if(t.getPayments().getTotal() == 0)
                        {
                            displayArea2.setText
                                            ("No payments made for this tenant");
                        }


                        else
                        {
                            /* The NumberFormat class is similar to the
                               DecimalFormat class that we used previously.
                               The getCurrencyInstance method of this class
                               reads the system values to find out which
                               country we are in, then uses the correct
                               currency symbol */


                            NumberFormat nf =
                            NumberFormat.getCurrencyInstance();
                            String s;


                            // display a heading
                            displayArea2.setText("Month"  + "\t\t"
                                                    + "Amount"
                                                    + "\n");
```

```
                    // display each payment in turn
                     for(i = 1; i <= p.getTotal(); i++)
                     {
                         s = nf.format(p.getPayment(i).getAmount());
                         displayArea2.append(""
                                          + p.getPayment(i).getMonth()
                                          + "\t\t"
                                          + s
                                          + "\n");
                     }
                     displayArea2.append("\n" + "Total paid so far : "
                                      + nf.format(p.calculateTotalPaid()));
                     monthField.setText("");
                     amountField.setText("");
                 }
             }
         }

         if(e.getSource() == saveAndQuitButton)
         {
             // save the records to file
             TenantFileHandler.saveRecords(noOfRooms,list);
             // terminate the program
             System.exit(0);
         }

         if(e.getSource() == quitButton)
         {
             // terminate the program without saving the records
             System.exit(0);
         }
     }
 }
```

The code needed to run the `Hostel` class appears below as program 11.1. This program creates a hostel with five rooms; in the tutorial questions you will be given the opportunity to adapt this program so that the number of rooms can be entered by the user.

Notice that we are not using the `EasyFrame` class here, as we do not want the cross-hairs to work; the user should always exit by choosing either the "Save and Quit" button or the "Quit without Saving" button.

```
Program 11.1

    import java.awt.*;

    class RunHostel
    {
        public static void main(String[] args)
        {
            Frame frame = new Frame();
            frame.setTitle("Student Hostel");
            // assume only 5 rooms available
            Hostel property = new Hostel(5);
            frame.setSize(550,500);
            frame.setBackground(Color.lightGray);
            frame.add(property);
            frame.setVisible(true);
        }
    }
```

Before concluding this case study we shall consider how to test the application to ensure that it conforms to the original specification.

11.6 Testing the system

If you look back at the Hostel class you can see that much of the event-handling code is related to the validation of data entered from the graphical interface. Much of the testing for such a system will, therefore, be geared around ensuring such validation is effective. This is a form of *white box* testing as we are looking at the implementation to determine this validation; it is not made explicit in the specification.

Amongst the types of validation we need to test is the display of suitable error messages when input text fields are left blank, or when inappropriate data has been entered into these text fields. Of course, as well as input validation, we also need to test the basic functionality of the system. The specification can be used to determine suitable test data in this case and so a form of *black box* testing may also be appropriate.

Figure 11.4 is one possible test log that may be developed for the purpose of testing the Hostel class. As we will be running this program in the UK, we have defined the expected currency output to be displayed with a pound symbol (£); obviously you should replace this currency symbol with that of your own country.

We include a few sample screen shots produced from running program 11.1 against this test log in figures 11.5–11.8. We will leave the complete task of running program 11.1 against the test log as a practical exercise at the end of this chapter.

TEST LOG

Purpose: To test the HOSTEL class

Run Number:	Date:		
Action	**Expected Output**	**Pass/ Fail**	**Reason for Failure**
Display tenants	"Empty list" message		
Add tenant: Patel, Room Number blank	"Blank field" message		
Add tenant: blank, Room Number 1	"Blank field" message		
Add tenant: Patel, Room Number 1	Confirmation message		
Add tenant: Jones, Room Number 6	Error message: There are only 5 rooms		
Add tenant: Jones, Room Number 1	Error Message: Room 1 is occupied		
Add tenant: Jones, Room Number 2	Confirmation Message		
Display tenants	ROOM NAME 1 Patel 2 Jones		
List payments, Room Number 1	"Empty list" message		
Make payment: Room blank, Month January, Amount 100	"Blank field" message		
Make Payment: Room 1, Month blank, Amount 100	"Blank field" message		
Make payment: Room 1, Month January, Amount blank	"Blank field" message		
Make payment: Room 1, Month January, Amount 100	Confirmation message		
Make payment: Room 1, Month February, Amount 200	Confirmation message		
List payments: Room Number blank	"Blank field" message		
List payments, Room Number 1	MONTH AMOUNT January £100 February £200 Total paid so far £300		
List payments: Room Number 2	"Empty list" message		
List payments: Room Number 5	"Room Empty" message		
Remove tenant: Room Number blank	"Blank field" message		
Remove tenant: Room Number 1	Confirmation Message		
Display tenants	2 Jones		
List payments: Room Number 1	"Room Empty" message		

Fig 11.4   A test log to ensure the reliability of the *Hostel* class

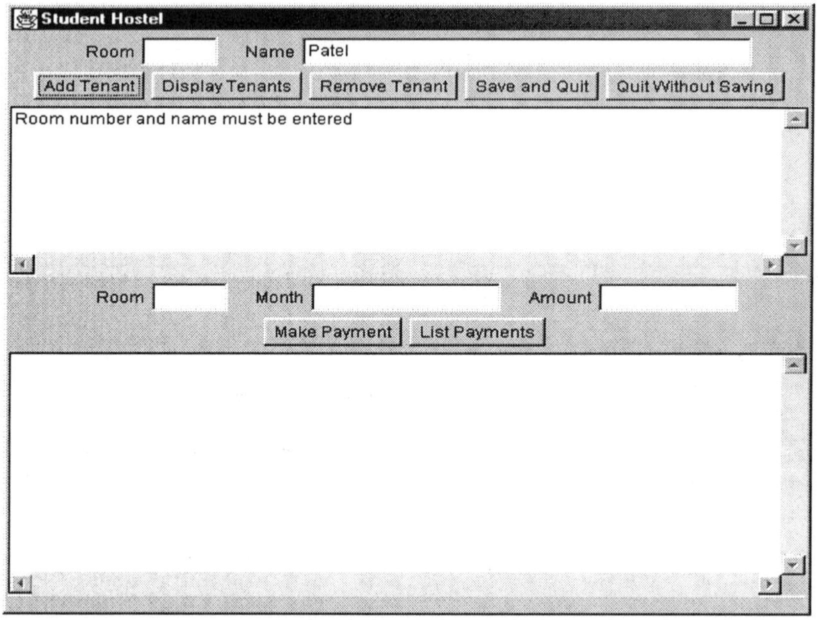

Fig 11.5   Error messages are produced in the _displayArea_. In this case an attempt is made to add a tenant without filling in the _roomField_

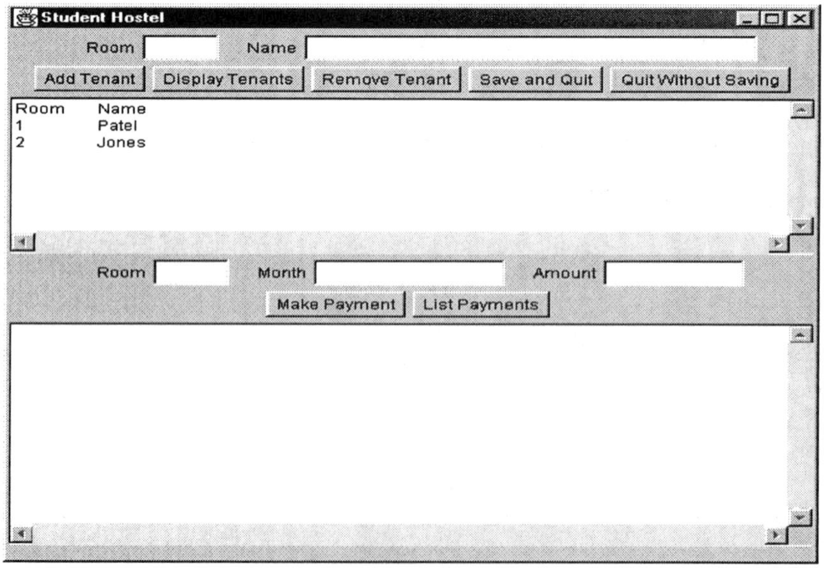

Fig 11.6   The _displayArea_ is also used to display a list of tenants entered

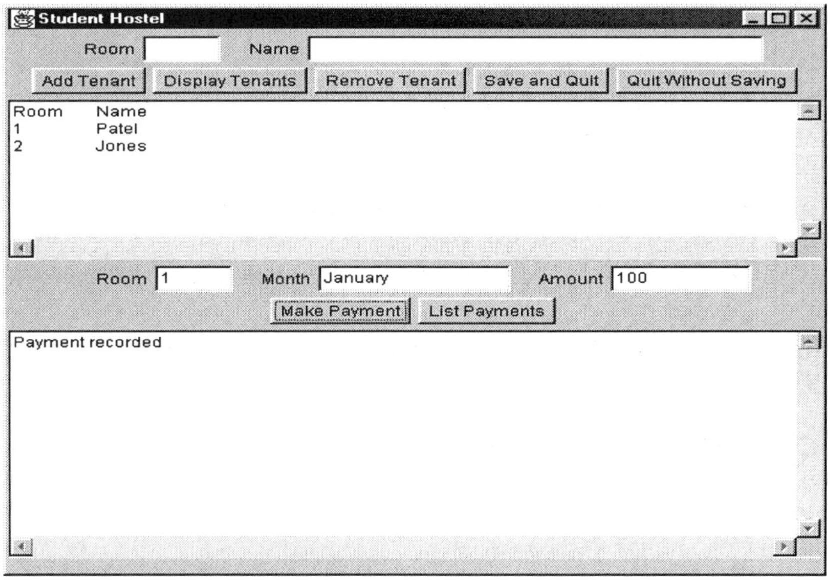

Figure 11.7   A payment is recorded for the tenant in room 1

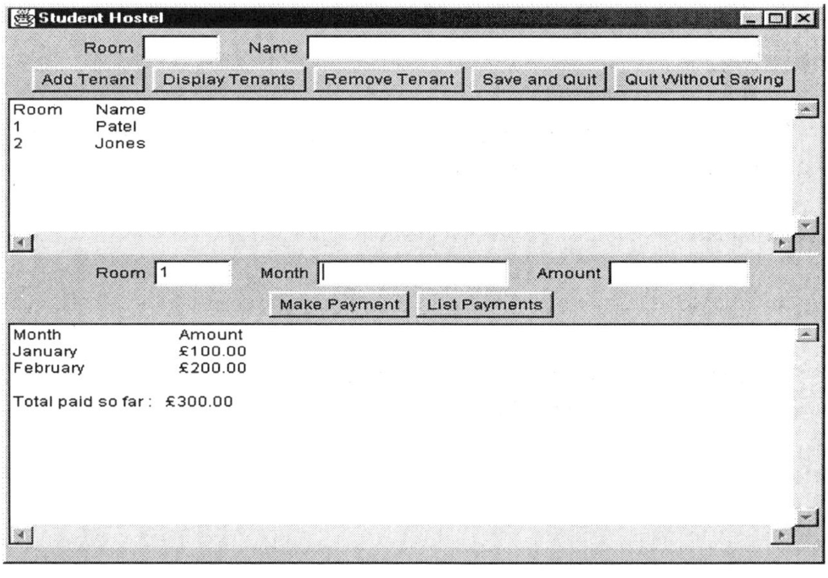

Fig 11.8   Details of payments are displayed in *displayArea2* when the *ListPayments* button is pressed

Tutorial exercises

1. Consider the addition of a search button that displays the details (name and room number) of a tenant in a room entered in the roomField text box. The details are to be displayed in the displayArea.

    a) What would be a suitable name for this visual component?
    b) Develop pseudocode for the event-handler of this button.
    c) Modify the test log in figure 11.4 to include the testing of this event-handler.

2. Look at the test data given in the test log of figure 11.4. Pick out three test cases that are

    a) examples of black box testing;
    b) examples of white box testing.

    In each case, justify your answers above.

3. Rewrite program 11.1 so that instead of fixing the number of rooms to 5, the user is asked how many rooms the hostel is to have.

4. Make a list of any shortcomings of the Student Hostel system, and think of ways in which the system could be enhanced and improved.

Practical work

You will need to download the entire suite of classes that make up the student hostel system from our website (or copy them from this chapter).

1. Run program 11.1 against the test log given in figure 11.4.

2. Modify the Hostel class by adding the search button as defined in tutorial question 1.

3. Re-run program 11.1 with the modified Hostel class against the modified test log developed in tutorial question 1 (c).

12 Programming for the World Wide Web

Learning objectives

By the end of this chapter you should be able to:

- explain the difference between an **application** and an **applet**;
- write the HTML code needed to load an applet into a browser;
- pass parameters to an applet from an HTML file;
- explain the purpose of the `init`, `start`, `stop` and `destroy` methods;
- implement the `MouseListener` and the `MouseMotionListener` interfaces.

12.1   Introduction

As you have seen throughout this book, a Java program is made up of a number of classes; so far in this book we have made our classes runnable by providing a `main` method; a program that contains a class with a `main` method is called an **application**. The `main` method provides the overall means of controlling the program.

In the case of the graphical applications that we have developed, the other principal function of the `main` method, in addition to providing the overall control, was to create a frame in which to run the program. In each case we needed to add our class to the frame and we therefore made our classes extensions of the Java AWT component `applet` – because an `applet` can be added to a frame. But, as we explained in the first chapter, there is something much more interesting and important about an applet. An applet (a little application) can run in a browser such as Internet Explorer or Netscape. Control of the applet then becomes the responsibility of the browser and there is no need for a `main` method – if there were a `main` method in the class, it would simply be ignored when the applet runs.

You will have observed that in this book, apart from the earlier very simple text-based programs, we have organized things in such a way that the `main` method is never included in the functional class, but instead is placed in a separate "driver" or "tester" class. Other textbooks you come across will often "mix up" the `main` method in the class itself – but for three reasons we don't like this approach. Firstly, it can be a very confusing way of doing things for somebody who is just starting to program. Secondly, we believe that our approach is more in the spirit of object-oriented development, because it makes classes more autonomous and able to be easily "plugged in" to any system. Finally, and most relevant to this chapter, is the fact that, as you will soon see, our graphics classes can be run as applets with very little change.

12.2   Running an applet in a browser

In order to run an applet in a browser (or in one of the applet viewers provided with most Java IDEs), we need to include an instruction in a web page that tells the browser to load the applet and run it. Web pages are written in a special language known as **Hypertext Markup Language (HTML)**. HTML code is interpreted by browsers such as Netscape and Internet Explorer to produce the formatted text and graphics that we are used to seeing.

We are not going to go into any detail here about how to write HTML; we will talk only about the commands you need in order to get your applets running. Commands in HTML are called **tags** and are enclosed in angle brackets. The tag that we are interested in here is the one that tells the browser to load and run a Java class. This uses the key word **applet**, as we shall see in a moment.

Cast your mind back to the ChangingFace class from chapter 9. We are going to make two small changes. Firstly, we are going replace the constructor with a special method called init (short for *initialize*). The code that we originally had in the constructor will now be placed in this special init method. We will explain more about this in the next section. Secondly, we are going to declare the class as **public** so that it is accessible from outside any package.

The ChangingFaceApplet class is shown below:

The *ChangingFaceApplet* class

```java
import java.awt.*;
import java.applet.*;
import java.awt.event.*;


// the class is declared as public

public class ChangingFaceApplet extends Applet implements ActionListener
{
    private boolean isHappy;
    private Button happyButton = new Button("Smile");
    private Button sadButton = new Button("Frown");


    // the constructor is replaced with an init method

    public void init()
    {
        add(happyButton);
```

```
            add(sadButton);
            isHappy = true;
            happyButton.addActionListener(this);
            sadButton.addActionListener(this);
        }

    public void paint(Graphics g)
    {
            g.setColor(Color.red);
            g.drawOval(85,45,75,75);
            g.setColor(Color.blue);
            g.drawOval(100,65,10,10);
            g.drawOval(135,65,10,10);
            g.drawString("Changing Face", 80,155);
            if(isHappy == true)
            {
                    g.drawArc(102,85,40,25,0,-180);
            }
            else
            {
                    g.drawArc(102,85,40,25,0,180);
            }
    }

    public void actionPerformed(ActionEvent e)
    {
        if(e.getSource() == happyButton)
        {
                isHappy = true;
                repaint();
        }
        if(e.getSource() == sadButton)
        {
                isHappy = false;
                repaint();
        }
    }
}
}
```

We have provided below the bare minimum HTML code that will load and run this class in a browser; it doesn't add any headings, or attempt to produce a pretty web page – those of you who know HTML will be able to add those features if you wish:

```
<HTML>
<APPLET CODE = "ChangingFaceApplet.class" WIDTH = 250 HEIGHT = 175 >
</APPLET>
</HTML>
```

As some of you might know, HTML tags often have an opening and a closing version, the latter starting with a forward slash (/). The relevant text is contained within these tags. So in our example the HTML tags tell the browser that the text contained represents an HTML page. The text within the APPLET tags provides the information about the applet that needs to be loaded; this is done with special words (called *attributes* just to confuse us!) which are part of the tag. In this case we provide the name of the class (with the CODE attribute) and the dimensions of the applet window (with the attributes WIDTH and HEIGHT).

Figure 12.1 shows the ChangingFace class running in a browser.

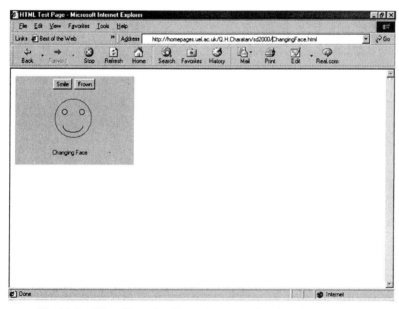

Fig 12.1   The *ChangingFace* class running in a browser

Of course it is necessary to have the correct file (in this case `ChangingFaceApplet.class`) in the same directory as the HTML file; alternatively it is possible to make absolute references to directories in the HTML code, but you should look at books on HTML in order to find out more about this. Do notice, however, that it is the compiled byte code that you need (that is, the file with the `.class` extension), and not the Java source code.

12.3   Guidelines for creating applets

When creating applets as opposed to applications there are a few differences that you need to be aware of. These are explained below.

1. Firstly, as we have stated above, you should place any initialization routines, such as setting initial values, in an `init` method rather than in a constructor. As we explain in section 12.5, this method is a special method and is called each time the applet is loaded or reloaded by the browser.

2. Do not include any `main` method, as any code in the `main` method is ignored by the browser.

3. Make sure that any input and output goes through the AWT interface – the user will not normally see the text console when using a browser.

4. Do not include any buttons or other controls that attempt to terminate the program – applets terminate when the page is closed in the browser.

5. Always declare your class as **public**.

12.4   Passing parameters from an HTML file

Cast your mind back to chapter 9 again. Remember the `OblongGUI` class we developed? First, we are going to modify this so that it can be run as an applet – once again, the way we have designed it means that there is no `main` method to worry about, so we don't have to do very much to it. All we have to do, in fact, is to make our class **public** and to change the constructor to an `init` method. Here is the new class:

The *OblongApplet* class

```java
import java.awt.*;
import java.awt.event.*;
import java.applet.*;


// make sure the class is declared public
public class OblongApplet extends Applet implements ActionListener
{
    // declare a new oblong with a length and height of zero
    private Oblong oblong = new Oblong(0,0);

    // now declare the graphics components
    private Label lengthLabel = new Label("Length");
    private TextField lengthField = new TextField(5);
    private Label heightLabel = new Label("Height");
    private TextField heightField = new TextField(5);
    private Button calcButton = new Button("Calculate");
    private TextArea displayArea = new TextArea(3,35);

    //replace the constructor with an init method
    public void init()
    {
        add(lengthLabel);
        add(lengthField);
        add(heightLabel);
        add(heightField);
        add(calcButton);
        add(displayArea);
        calcButton.addActionListener(this);
    }

    public void actionPerformed(ActionEvent e)
    {
        //as before
    }
}
```

The following HTML code is just sufficient to load and run the applet in a 300 × 150 window:

```
<HTML>
 <APPLET CODE = "OblongApplet.class"
 WIDTH = "300"
 HEIGHT= "150" >
 </APPLET>
</HTML>
```

The result of running the applet is shown in figure 12.2; this time, for a change, we are showing it running in an applet viewer provided with one of the common Java IDEs.

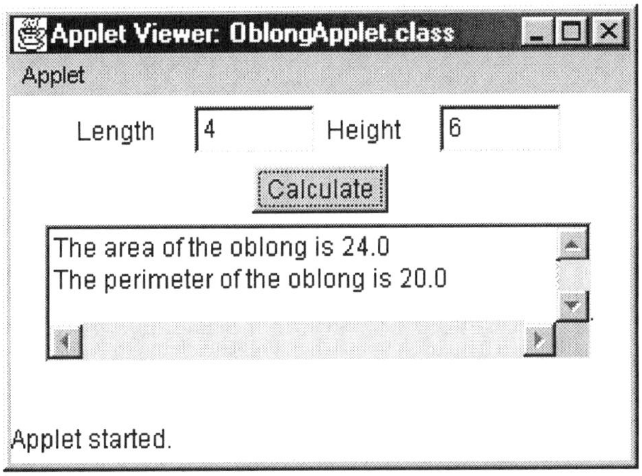

Fig 12.2   The *Oblong* applet running in an applet viewer

In previous programs you have seen how parameters are passed to class methods from other classes. Now, it is also possible to pass values from an HTML file to a class. Consider the following HTML code which loads and runs a class that we have called `ParameterizedOblongApplet`:

```
<HTML>
 <APPLET CODE = "ParameterizedOblongApplet.class"
      WIDTH = "300"
      HEIGHT="150" >
 <PARAM NAME = displayAreaLength VALUE = "5">
 <PARAM NAME = displayAreaHeight VALUE = "28">
 </APPLET>
</HTML>
```

You can see that we have used the PARAM tag and the associated NAME and VALUE parameters to name and give values to two variables which will be passed to the applet; notice that they must be defined as `Strings`. We are going to use these values to set the size of the TextArea that we use to display the area and perimeter of the oblong. The changes that we have made in our applet in order to get it to use these parameters are shown below in bold and are explained afterwards.

The *ParameterizedOblongApplet* class

```java
import java.awt.*;
import java.awt.event.*;
import java.applet.*;

public class ParameterizedOblongApplet extends Applet
                                        implements ActionListener
{
    // declare a new oblong with a length and height of zero
    private Oblong oblong = new Oblong(0,0);

    // now declare the graphics components
    private Label lengthLabel = new Label("Length");
    private TextField lengthField = new TextField(5);
    private Label heightLabel = new Label("Height");
    private TextField heightField = new TextField(5);
    private Button calcButton = new Button("Calculate");
    private TextArea displayArea;

    public void init()
    {
        displayArea = new TextArea(
                    Integer.parseInt(getParameter("displayAreaLength")),
                    Integer.parseInt(getParameter("displayAreaHeight"))
                                );
        add(lengthLabel);
        add(lengthField);
        add(heightLabel);
        add(heightField);
        add(calcButton);
        add(displayArea);
        calcButton.addActionListener(this);
    }
    public void actionPerformed(ActionEvent e)
    {
        //as before
    }
}
```

As you can see, we have used the `getParameter` method of the `Applet` class (which returns a `String`) to read a value from the HTML file. However, we cannot do this at the same time as we declare the attributes, so the code has now been placed in the `init` method; notice that now when we declare the `TextArea` variable, `displayArea`, we do not initialize it; this is now done in the `init` method as follows:

```
displayArea =
        new TextArea(Integer.parseInt(getParameter("displayAreaLength")),
                        Integer.parseInt(getParameter("displayAreaHeight")));
```

With the values as stated in the HTML code above (5 and 28) we get the output shown in figure 12.3. You can see that because the length of the `TextArea` has been reduced the components have moved around – that is because we have used the default `FlowLayout` manager.

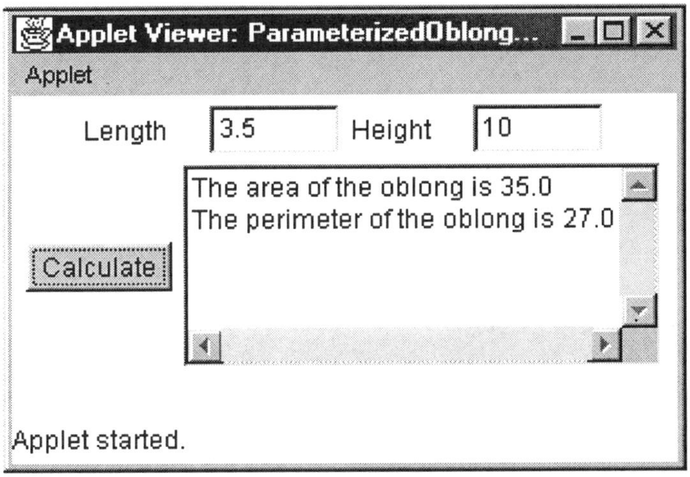

Fig 12.3   The *ParamaterizedOblongApplet*

12.5   Special applet methods

In addition to the `init` method there are three other special applet methods that you can code if you wish; `start`, `stop` and `destroy`. Together with the `paint` method these are automatically called in a special order which is explained in Table 12.1 below.

Table 12.1 The special applet methods (working with the `paint` method)	
Method	**Invocation**
`init`	Invoked the first time the applet is loaded (or reloaded) by a browser
`start`	Invoked after `init` when the applet is first loaded (or reloaded) and then invoked each time the applet is made visible again by returning to the page
`paint`	Invoked immediately after `start`
`stop`	Invoked when the applet is hidden (by pointing the browser at a different page)
`destroy`	Invoked after `stop` when the applet is abandoned (by closing the browser)

12.6   The *RedCircle* applet

The next applet is one that you can use to amuse your friends. Figure 12.4 shows how it looks when it runs in a browser. We have called it – rather unimaginatively – the `RedCircle` applet; a red circle always moves away from the cursor so you can never click on it, despite being told to do so! And if in desperation you start to click the mouse, the words "Keep Trying" flash onto the screen!

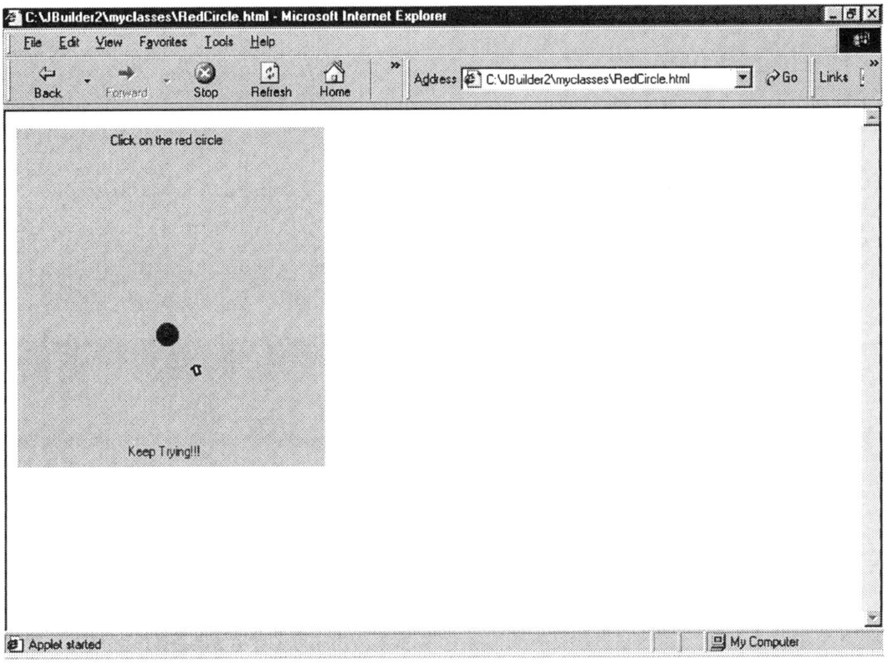

Fig 12.4 The *RedCircle* applet running in a browser

As well as being a bit of fun it also introduces something new, namely the way to program a response to different mouse events like moving and dragging as well as just clicking; this will involve using two new interface classes instead of the single `ActionListener` interface that we have used before.

Here is the code for the applet:

The *RedCircle* applet

```
import java.awt.*;
import java.applet.*;
import java.awt.event.*;


public class RedCircle extends Applet
                        implements MouseMotionListener, MouseListener
{
    private int xPos;
    private int yPos;
    private int winWidth;
    private int winHeight;
    boolean mouseDown = false;
```

```
// the init method
public void init()
{
    addMouseMotionListener(this);
    addMouseListener(this);
    /* get the width and height of the applet window from the
    HTML file */
    winWidth = Integer.parseInt(getParameter("windowWidth"));
    winHeight = Integer.parseInt(getParameter("windowHeight"));
}


// the start method
public void start()
{
    xPos = winWidth/2 - 20;
    yPos = winHeight/2 - 20;
}


// the paint method
public void paint(Graphics g)
{
    g.drawString("Click on the red circle",85,15);
    g.setColor(Color.red);
    g.fillOval(xPos,yPos,20,20);
    if(mouseDown)
    {
        g.drawString("Keep Trying!!!", winWidth/2 - 40,
        winHeight - 10);
    }
}


/* The next two methods define what happens when the mouse is
moved or dragged. They are part of the MouseMotionListener
interface. The red circle always stays 50 pixels above and
50 pixels to the left of the cursor*/

public void mouseMoved(MouseEvent e)
{
    xPos = e.getX() - 50;
    yPos = e.getY() - 50;
    repaint();
}
```

```
     public void mouseDragged(MouseEvent e)
     {
          xPos = e.getX() - 50;
          yPos = e.getY() - 50;
          repaint();
     }


     /* The next two methods define what happens when the mouse
     button is pressed or released. They are part of the
     MouseListener interface*/

     public void mousePressed(MouseEvent e)
     {
          mouseDown = true;
          repaint();
     }

     public void mouseReleased(MouseEvent e)
     {
          mouseDown = false;
          repaint();
     }


     /* The MouseListener interface also insists that we implement
     the next three methods. We are not actually going to use them
     here, so we have just left them blank */

     public void mouseClicked(MouseEvent e)
     {
     }

     public void mouseEntered(MouseEvent e)
     {
     }

     public void mouseExited(MouseEvent e)
     {
     }
}
```

You can see that here we are implementing *two* interface classes, MouseListener and MouseMotionListener; notice that the syntax is to separate them by a comma.

```
public class RedCircle extends Applet implements
MouseMotionListener, MouseListener
```

Both of these interface classes will of course have abstract methods which we then have to implement. The first one, MouseMotionListener, has two such methods, MouseMoved and MouseDragged. The second, MouseListener, has five, MousePressed, MouseReleased, MouseClicked, MouseEntered and MouseExited. The last three of these are not used in this applet so we have just left them blank. You may be interested to know their purpose, however, so you can use them in future programs; MouseClicked is invoked when the mouse is clicked on a component, MouseEntered is invoked when the cursor enters a component and MouseExited is invoked when the cursor leaves a component.

The declaration of the attributes is shown below; the first two integer attributes xPos and yPos will be used to keep track of the position of the red circle. The next two attributes, winWidth and winHeight, will be used to hold the width and the height of the applet window as determined by the HTML code. The other attribute, mouseDown, is a **boolean** variable and will be set to **true** while the left-hand button of the mouse is depressed, and **false** once it is released; it is therefore initialized as **false**.

```
private int xPos;
private int yPos;
private int winWidth;
private int winHeight;
boolean mouseDown = false;
```

Next we have the init method:

```
public void init()
{
    addMouseMotionListener(this);
    addMouseListener(this);
    winWidth = Integer.parseInt(getParameter("windowWidth"));
    winHeight = Integer.parseInt(getParameter("windowHeight"));
}
```

Remember that this method is invoked when the applet is loaded (or reloaded) into the browser; its purpose, as you can see, is firstly to add the two listeners to the applet itself; remember that writing the method names without attaching them to an object is actually attaching them to **this** object, and is short for:

```
this.addMouseMotionListener(this);
this.addMouseListener(this);
```

Its other purpose is to read the dimensions of the applet window from the HTML file with the getParameter method, and assign them to winWidth and winHeight.

Now we define a start method:

```
public void start()
{
    xPos = Integer.parseInt(getParameter("windowWidth"))/2 - 20;
    yPos = Integer.parseInt(getParameter("windowWidth"))/2 - 20;
}
```

Remember that this is the method that gets called every time the applet becomes visible; so it will be called after the `init` method when the applet is first loaded and then again each time we return from viewing another page. The idea is to get the circle to appear in the centre of the window each time the applet becomes visible. So we get the width and the height of the window from the HTML file using the `getParameter` method; we convert these to integers and then halve them to find the central point of the window; to get the centre of the circle dead in the middle we subtract 20 (the radius of the circle) from the width and the height – remind yourself of the `drawOval` method in chapter 9 to understand why we have done this.

After the `start` method has finished doing its job, the `paint` method is called, and this is the one that we have coded next:

```
public void paint(Graphics g)
{
    g.drawString("Click on the red circle",85,15);
    g.setColor(Color.red);
    g.fillOval(xPos,yPos,20,20);
    if(mouseDown)
    {
        g.drawString("Keep Trying!!!",winWidth/2 - 40, winHeight - 10);
    }
}
```

After drawing the initial string that tells the user to click on the circle, we set the colour to red, and then draw the circle, this time using `fillOval` instead of `drawOval` to get a solid circle. The circle is drawn at position (xPos, yPos). Remember, this method not only gets called after the `start` method but also every time the program encounters a `repaint` command, and as we shall see in a moment this happens every time the mouse moves; and each time the screen gets repainted xPos and yPos will have changed. After the circle is drawn, the status of the mouse-button is tested by checking the value of mouseDown; as we said earlier, this attribute is going to be set to **true** if the left mouse-button is down, and **false** if not. If it is **true** the words "Keep Trying!!!" are drawn on the screen. We have tried to organize things so that this is drawn centred near the bottom of the window; you can see that we have used the dimensions of the applet window to do this – we have set the x-coordinate to be half the window width minus 40. The value of 40 is what we have estimated to be half the number of pixels taken up by the phrase "Keep Trying!!!". There are actually more accurate ways of doing this using font metrics, but we want to keep things simple at the moment, so we just had a go to see what it looks like, then tried again till we got it right! Similarly we have set the y-coordinate to be 10 pixels higher than the bottom of the window, and, as you can see from figure 12.4, this looks pretty good.

Now we come to the event-handling routines. This time, as we have mentioned, we are not using the `ActionListener` interface but are using two new interface classes, `MouseMotionListener` and `MouseListener`. The first method we implement, `mouseMoved`, is one of the two abstract methods of `MouseMotionListener`:

```
public void mouseMoved(MouseEvent e)
{
    xPos = e.getX() - 50;
    yPos = e.getY() - 50;
    repaint();
}
```

This method is continually invoked while the mouse is moving; each time it is invoked `xPos` and `yPos` are assigned new values. The value assigned to each of them is always the value of the current coordinate of the cursor minus 50. After every assignment the window is repainted; thus, as the cursor moves, the circle moves too – always staying just northwest of it. Notice that the method is automatically sent an object of the `MouseEvent` class and that we use the `getX` and `getY` methods of the `this` class to obtain the current coordinates of the cursor.

The other method of the `MouseMotionListener` interface, `mouseDragged`, determines what happens when the mouse is moved with the button held down (dragged). We have coded it in exactly the same way, so that dragging the mouse has the same effect as above.

The next two methods are declared in the `MouseListener` class and determine what happens when the mouse-button is pressed and released. You can see that we have defined them so that when the button is pressed, the `mouseDown` attribute is set to **true** and the window is repainted; when the button is released it is set to **false**, and the window is repainted once again.

```
public void mousePressed(MouseEvent e)
{
    mouseDown = true;
    repaint();
}


public void mouseReleased(MouseEvent e)
{
    mouseDown = false;
    repaint();
}
```

The `MouseListener` interface also insists that we implement the `mouseClicked`, `mouseEntered` and `mouseExited` methods. We are not actually going to use these here, so as you can see from the code we have just left them blank.

Now that we have completed the code, we just need to write the HTML code to load it into a browser. The code below runs the applet in a 280 × 300 window:

```
<HTML>
 <APPLET CODE = "RedCircle.class" WIDTH = "280" HEIGHT="300">
 <PARAM NAME = "windowWidth" VALUE = "280">
 <PARAM NAME = "windowHeight" VALUE = "300">
 </APPLET>
</HTML>
```

12.7   What next?

Congratulations – you have now completed your first semester in programming; we hope you have enjoyed it. Many of you will be going on to at least one more semester of software development and programming – so what lies ahead?

Well, you have probably realized that there are still a few gaps in your knowledge and that some of the stuff that you have learnt can be developed further to give you the power to write multi-functional programs. Think, for example, about the case study we developed in the last two chapters; you will need to write the code that stores the information permanently on a disk; also, the user interface could be made to look a bit more attractive; and it would be helpful if our collection classes didn't make us decide in advance how many records we are allowed to have, so something a bit better than simple arrays would be useful.

And there is lots more; the many standard Java packages provide classes for networking, linking to databases and much more; there is more to learn about inheritance and interface classes, and about dealing with errors and exceptions; and you need to know how to write programs that can perform a number of tasks at the same time.

Does all this sound exciting? We think so – and we hope that you enjoy your next semester as much as we have enjoyed helping you through this one. So goodbye for now and good luck!

Tutorial exercises

1. Explain the purpose of the following applet methods:

   - `init`;
   - `start`;
   - `stop`;
   - `destroy`.

2. Look at the `MetricConverter` class that we developed in chapter 9. What changes would you need to make to this class in order to run it as an applet?

3. Identify some improvements that could be made to the `RedCircle` applet.

Practical work

1. Implement some of the applets from this chapter (`ChangingFace`, `OblongGUI`, `ParameterizedOblongApplet` and `RedCircle`); write the appropriate HTML code and load it into a browser. If you have your own website, upload the HTML page and the class so you can run it remotely.

2. Apply the changes to the `MetricConverter` class that you identified in tutorial question 2.

3. Implement the improvements to the `RedCircle` applet that you identified in tutorial question 3.

Appendix 1
Selected AWT component methods

<table>
<tr><td colspan="2" align="center">Component
An abstract class</td></tr>
<tr><td align="center">Method</td><td align="center">Description</td></tr>
<tr><td><code>String getName()</code></td><td>Returns the name of the Component.</td></tr>
<tr><td><code>void setVisible(boolean)</code></td><td>Shows or hides the Component depending on the value of the input parameter.</td></tr>
<tr><td><code>boolean isVisible()</code></td><td>Returns true if the Component is visible, otherwise returns false.</td></tr>
<tr><td><code>void setForeground(Color)</code></td><td>Sets the foreground colour of the Component to the value of the input parameter.</td></tr>
<tr><td><code>void setBackground(Color)</code></td><td>Sets the background colour of the Component to the value of the input parameter.</td></tr>
<tr><td><code>void setSize(int, int)</code></td><td>Sets the width of the Component to the value of the first parameter and the height to that of the second.</td></tr>
<tr><td><code>void paint(Graphics)</code></td><td>Paints the Component; called when the Component first becomes visible.</td></tr>
<tr><td><code>void repaint()</code></td><td>Repaints the Component.</td></tr>
<tr><td><code>void addMouseListener(MouseListener)</code></td><td>Accepts a MouseListener as a parameter and adds this to the Component.</td></tr>
<tr><td><code>void addMouseMotionListener(MouseMotionListener)</code></td><td>Accepts a MouseMotionListener as a parameter and adds this to the Component.</td></tr>
</table>

<table>
<tr><td colspan="2" align="center">Button
Inherits all the methods of Component</td></tr>
<tr><td align="center">Method</td><td align="center">Description</td></tr>
<tr><td><code>Button()</code></td><td>Constructs a Button with no label.</td></tr>
<tr><td><code>Button(String)</code></td><td>Constructs a Button with a label specified by the input parameter.</td></tr>
<tr><td><code>void setLabel(String)</code></td><td>Sets the Button's label to the value of the input parameter.</td></tr>
<tr><td><code>String getLabel(void)</code></td><td>Returns the Button's label.</td></tr>
<tr><td><code>void addActionListener(ActionListener)</code></td><td>Accepts an ActionListener as a parameter and adds this to the Button.</td></tr>
</table>

Label	
Inherits all the methods of Component	
Method	**Description**
Label()	Constructs a Label with no text.
Label(String)	Constructs a Label with the text specified by the input parameter.
Label(String, int)	Constructs a Label with the text specified by the first input parameter, and aligned as specified by the second parameter which can be entered as Label.LEFT, Label.CENTER or Label.RIGHT, or as 0, 1 or 2.
void setAlignment(int)	Sets the alignment of the Label to the value specified by the input parameter.
void setText(String)	Sets the Label's text to the value of the input parameter.
String getText()	Returns the Label's text.

TextComponent	
An abstract class; inherits all the methods of Component	
Method	**Description**
void setText(String)	Sets the text presented in this component to that specified by the input parameter.
String getText(void)	Returns the text presented by this component.

TextField	
Inherits all the methods of TextComponent (and Component)	
Method	**Description**
TextField()	Constructs an empty TextField.
TextField(int)	Constructs an empty TextField with the number of columns specified by the input parameter.
TextField(String)	Constructs a TextField with the text specified by the input parameter.
TextField(String, int)	Constructs a TextField with the text specified by the first parameter, with the number of columns specified by the second parameter.
void setColumns(int)	Sets the number of columns to the value specified by the input parameter.
void setEchoChar(char)	Sets the echo character as specified by the input parameter (useful when user input should not be echoed to the screen, for example when entering a password).
void addActionListener(ActionListener)	Accepts an ActionListener as a parameter and adds this to the TextField.

TextArea
Inherits all the methods of `TextComponent` *(and* `Component`*)*

Method	Description
`TextArea()`	Constructs an empty `TextArea`.
`TextArea(int, int)`	Constructs an empty `TextArea` with the number of rows and columns specified by the input parameters.
`TextArea(String)`	Constructs a `TextArea` with the text specified by the input parameter.
`TextArea(String, int, int)`	Constructs a `TextArea` with the text specified by the first parameter and with the number of rows and columns specified by the second and third parameters respectively.
`void insert(String, int)`	Inserts the text specified by the first parameter at the position specified by the second parameter.
`void append(String)`	Appends the text specified by the first parameter (compare with the inherited `setText` method which erases all the old text).
`void setColumns(int)`	Sets the number of columns to the value specified by the input parameter.

Container
An abstract class: inherits all the methods of `Component`

Method	Description
`void add(Component)`	Adds the specified component to the `Container`.
`void setLayout(LayoutManager)`	Sets the `LayoutManager` to that specified by the input parameter.

Window
Inherits all the methods of `Container` *(and* `Component`*)*

Method	Description
`void show()`	Shows the `Window` and brings it to the front.
`void dispose()`	Disposes of the `Window` and releases any resources used.

Frame
Inherits all the methods of `Window` *(and* `Container` *and* `Component`*)*

Method	Description
`Frame()`	Constructs a new `Frame` which is initially invisible.
`Frame(String)`	Constructs a new initially invisible `Frame` with the title specified by the input parameter.
`void setTitle(String)`	Sets the text title to that specified by the input parameter.
`void setResizable(boolean)`	Determines whether or not the `Frame` is resizable, depending on the value of the input parameter.

Panel	
Inherits all the methods of `Container` *(and* `Component`*)*	
Method	**Description**
`Panel()`	Constructs a new `Panel` with the default `FlowLayout` manager.
`Panel(LayoutManager)`	Constructs a new `Panel` with the layout manager specified by the input parameter.

Applet	
Inherits all the methods of `Panel` *(and* `Container` *and* `Component`*)*	
Method	**Description**
`Applet()`	Constructs a new `Applet`.
`void resize(int, int)`	Resizes the applet, assigning a width and height specified be the first and second parameters respectively.
`void init()`	Invoked the first time the applet is loaded (or reloaded) by a browser. The implementation provided does nothing; a subclass of `Applet` must provide the code as required.
`void start()`	Invoked after `init` when the applet is first loaded (or reloaded) and then invoked each time the applet is made visible again by returning to the page. The implementation provided does nothing; a subclass of `Applet` must provide the code as required.
`void stop()`	Invoked when the applet is hidden (by pointing the browser at a different page). The implementation provided does nothing; a subclass of `Applet` must provide the code as required.
`void destroy()`	Invoked after `stop` when the applet is abandoned (by closing the browser). The implementation provided does nothing; a subclass of `Applet` must provide the code as required.

Appendix 2
Utility classes

The *EasyIn* class

```java
// EasyIn.java

import java.io.*;

public abstract class EasyIn
{
  static String s = new String();
  static byte[] b = new byte[512];
  static int bytesRead = 0;

  public static String getString()
  {
    boolean ok = false;
    while(!ok)
    {
      try
      {
        bytesRead = System.in.read(b);
        s = new String(b,0,bytesRead-1);
        s=s.trim();
        ok = true;
      }
      catch(IOException e)
      {
        System.out.println(e.getMessage());
      }
    }
    return s;
  }

  public static int getInt()
  {
    int i = 0;
    boolean ok = false;
    while(!ok)
    {
      try
      {
```

```java
                bytesRead = System.in.read(b);
                s = new String(b,0,bytesRead-1);
                i = Integer.parseInt(s.trim());
                ok = true;
            }
            catch(NumberFormatException e)
            {
                System.out.println("Make sure you enter an integer");
            }
            catch(IOException e)
            {
                System.out.println(e.getMessage());
            }
        }
        return i;
    }


    public static byte getByte()
    {
        byte i = 0;
        boolean ok = false;
        while(!ok)
        {
            try
            {
                bytesRead = System.in.read(b);
                s = new String(b,0,bytesRead-1);
                i = Byte.parseByte(s.trim());
                ok = true;
            }
            catch(NumberFormatException e)
            {
                System.out.println("Make sure you enter a byte");
            }
            catch(IOException e)
            {
                System.out.println(e.getMessage());
            }
        }
        return i;
    }


    public static short getShort()
    {
```

```
        short i = 0;
    boolean ok = false;
    while(!ok)
    {
        try
        {
            bytesRead = System.in.read(b);
            s = new String(b,0,bytesRead-1);
            i = Short.parseShort(s.trim());
            ok = true;
        }
        catch(NumberFormatException e)
        {
            System.out.println("Make sure you enter a short integer");
        }
        catch(IOException e)
        {
            System.out.println(e.getMessage());
        }
    }
    return i;
}


public static long getLong()
{
    long l = 0;
    boolean ok = false;
    while(!ok)
    {
        try
        {
            bytesRead = System.in.read(b);
            s = new String(b,0,bytesRead-1);
            l = Long.parseLong(s.trim());
            ok = true;
        }
        catch(NumberFormatException e)
        {
            System.out.println("Make surre you enter a long integer");
        }

        catch(IOException e)
        {
```

```java
                System.out.println(e.getMessage());
        }
    }
    return 1;
}


public static double getDouble()
{
    double d = 0;
    boolean ok = false;
    while(!ok)
    {
        try
        {
            bytesRead = System.in.read(b);
            s = new String(b,0,bytesRead-1);
            d = (Double.valueOf(s.trim())).doubleValue();
            ok = true;
        }
        catch(NumberFormatException e)
        {
            System.out.println("Make sure you enter a decimal number");
        }
        catch(IOException e)
        {
            System.out.println(e.getMessage());
        }
    }
    return d;
}

public static float getFloat()
{
    float f = 0;
    boolean ok = false;
    while(!ok)
    {
        try
        {
            bytesRead = System.in.read(b);
            s = new String(b,0,bytesRead-1);
            f = (Float.valueOf(s.trim())).floatValue();
            ok = true;
```

```
        }
        catch(NumberFormatException e)
        {
            System.out.println("Make sure you enter a decimal number");
        }
        catch(IOException e)
        {
            System.out.println(e.getMessage());
        }
    }
    return f;
}


public static char getChar()
{
    char c = ' ';
    boolean ok = false;
    while(!ok)
    {
        try
        {
            bytesRead = System.in.read(b);
            s = new String(b,0,bytesRead-1);
            if(s.trim().length()!=1)
            {
                System.out.println("Make sure you enter a single character");
            }
            else
            {
                c = s.trim().charAt(0);
                ok = true;
            }
        }
        catch(IOException e)
        {
            System.out.println(e.getMessage());
        }
    }
    return c;
}



public static void pause()
{
```

```java
        boolean ok = false;
        while(!ok)
        {
            try
            {
                System.in.read(b);
                ok = true;
            }
            catch(IOException e)
            {
                System.out.println(e.getMessage());
            }
        }
    }

    public static void pause(String messageIn)
    {
        boolean ok = false;
        while(!ok)
        {
            try
            {
                System.out.print(messageIn);
                System.in.read(b);
                ok = true;
            }
            catch(IOException e)
            {
                System.out.println(e.getMessage());
            }
        }
    }
}
```

The *EasyFrame* class

```java
// EasyFrame.java
import java.awt.*;
import java.awt.event.*;

public class EasyFrame extends Frame implements WindowListener
{
    public EasyFrame()
    {
        addWindowListener(this);
    }

    public EasyFrame(String msg)
    {
        super(msg);
        addWindowListener(this);
    }

    public void windowClosing(WindowEvent e)
    {
        dispose();
    }

    public void windowDeactivated(WindowEvent e)
    {
    }
    public void windowActivated(WindowEvent e)
    {
    }
    public void windowDeiconified(WindowEvent e)
    {
    }
    public void windowIconified(WindowEvent e)
    {
    }
    public void windowClosed(WindowEvent e)
    {
        System.exit(0);
    }
    public void windowOpened(WindowEvent e)
    {
    }
}
```

The *TenantFileHandler* class

```java
import java.io.*;

class TenantFileHandler
{
   public static void saveRecords(int noOfRoomsIn, TenantList listIn)
   {
     try
     {
        FileOutputStream ostream = new FileOutputStream("Tenants.txt");
        PrintWriter pw = new PrintWriter(ostream);
        pw.println(listIn.getTotal());
        for(int i=1; i <= noOfRoomsIn; i++)
        {
           if(listIn.getTenant(i) != null)
           {
              pw.println(listIn.getTenant(i).getRoom());
              pw.println("\"" + listIn.getTenant(i).getName() + "\"");
              pw.println(listIn.getTenant(i).getPayments().getTotal());
              for(int j = 1;
                     j<= listIn.getTenant(i).getPayments().getTotal(); j++)
              {
                pw.println("\""
                + listIn.getTenant(i).getPayments().getPayment(j).getMonth()
                + "\"");
                pw.println(listIn.getTenant(i).getPayments().
                                              getPayment(j).getAmount());
              }
           }
        }
        pw.flush();
        ostream.close();
     }
     catch(IOException ioe)
     {
        System.out.println("Error writing file");
     }
   }

   public static void readRecords(TenantList listIn)
   {
     try
     {
```

```java
        FileInputStream istream = new FileInputStream("Tenants.txt");
        InputStreamReader ir = new InputStreamReader(istream);
        BufferedReader br = new BufferedReader(ir);
        StreamTokenizer st = new StreamTokenizer(br);
        int tempRoom = 0;
        String tempName = new String("");
        String tempMonth = new String("");
        double tempAmount = 0 ;
        Tenant tempTenant = null;
        Payment tempPayment =  null;
        int tot = 0;
        int totpay = 0;

        st.nextToken();
        tot = (int) st.nval;
        for(int j = 1; j<=tot; j++)
        {
            st.nextToken();
            tempRoom = (int) st.nval;
            st.nextToken();
            tempName = st.sval;
            tempTenant = new Tenant(tempName,tempRoom);
            st.nextToken();
            totpay = (int) st.nval;
            for(int k = 1; k <= totpay; k++)
            {
                st.nextToken();
                tempMonth = st.sval;
                st.nextToken();
                tempAmount = st.nval;
                tempPayment = new Payment(tempMonth, tempAmount);
                tempTenant.makePayment(tempPayment);
            }
            listIn.add(tempTenant);
        }
    }
    catch(IOException ioe)
    {
        System.out.println("No records found");
    }
    }
}
```

Index

abstract , 178 - 184
    class, 178
    method, 180
Abstract Windowing Toolkit, 233-235
ActionListener, 242
actual parameter, 97
addActionListener, 243, 333
addMouseListener, 327, 333
addMouseMotionListener, 327, 333
aggregation, 148
    UML notation, 148
algorithm, 270
analysis, 2
applet, 6, 13
    methods, 322
    parameters 317, 321
    running in an applet viewer, 314, 319
    running in a browser, 314-317
Applet, 239-240
application, 7, 313
application software, 2
arcs (drawing), 109
arithmetic operators, 24-26
arguments, 97
array, 124-135
    access, 127-132
    ArrayIndexOutOfBounds, 129
    creation, 125-127
    declaration, 126
    index, 127
    initializing, 127
    length attribute, 130
    of objects, 149
    passing as a parameter, 132-135
assembler, 4
assembly language, 4
assignment, 21-23
association, 266
    UML notation, 266
attribute, 74, 93
AWT, *see* Abstract Windowing Toolkit

base class, 164
black box testing, 208-210
  see also robustness, testing
boolean, 18

boolean condition, 41
boolean operators, 62
BorderLayout, 258
boundary analysis, 209
    see also robustness, testing
break, 53
browser, 6, 314
Button, 233, 234, 333
byte code, 7

cast, *see* type cast
catching an exception, 216
char, 18
Class, 10, 74
    abstract, 178
    Applet, 239-240
    Arithmetic, 67
    BadReactor, 197
    BankAccount, 103
    BankAccountTester, 88
    BankAccountTester2, 112
    Calculate, 37
    ChangingFace, 241
    ChangingFaceApplet, 314
    DisplayResult, 45-46
    DisplayResult2, 47
    DisplayResult3, 63
    DisplayStars, 59
    EasyFrame, 237, 343
    EasyIn, 9, 337-342
    Employee, 166
    ExtendedOblong, 173
    ExtendedOblongTester, 175
    final, 184-185
    FindCost, 28
    FindCost2, 30
    FindCost3, 32
    Frame, 90
    FullTimeEmployee, 181
    Graphics, 107
    Hello, 9
    Hello2, 13
    Hello3, 13
    Hello4, 14
    Hello5, 15
    Hostel, 300-307

IntegerStack, 139-141
IntegerStackTester, 141-143
MetricConverter, 254-257
ObjectList, 185-187
ObjectListTester, 188-189
ObjectListTester2, 190-192
Oblong, 95-96
OblongApplet, 318
OblongGui, 249-250
OblongTester, 78
ParamaterizedOblongApplet, 120
ParameterTest, 115
PartTimeEmployee, 182
PartTimeEmpTester, 170
Payment, 268
PaymentList, 269
PaymentListTester, 271-272
PushMe, 246
PushToLimitsSalesStaff, 215
PushToLimitsSalesStaff2, 228
Reactor, 198
ReactorTester, 203
RedCircle, 323-325
RollerCoaster, 44
RunChangingFace, 245
RunCircle, 132
RunConverter, 233
RunFace, 89
RunHostel, 308
RunParameterTest, 115
RunParameterTest2, 116
RunPushMe, 248
RunStatusTester, 184
SalesStaff, 213-214
SmileyFace, 106
StatusTester, 183
String, 83-86
StringList, 150-151
StringListTester, 155-158
StringTest, 86
StringToDouble, 118
StringToInteger, 117
Student, 74
TemperatureReadings, 131
TemperatureReadings2, 135
Tenant, 275
TenantList, 280
TenantListTester, 281-283

ThreeDOblong, 177
ThreeDOblongTester, 178
Timetable, 51
TimetableWithLoop, 65
TimetableWithSwitch, 52

collection classes, 136-160
    generic, 185-192
comment, 14-15
compareTo, 85
comparison operators, 49
compiler, 4
compiler vs. interpreter, 6
compile-time error, 200
Component, 233, 333
compound containers, 254
concat, 85
constants, 24
constructor, 77
        default, 98-99
Container, 234, 240, 335

data type, 18-19
DecimalFormat, 225-229
declaration, 19-21
default, 53
design, 2, 94, 102
    see also pseudocode, UML
destroy, 322, 336
documentation, 196-200
    see also comments, indentation
double, 18
Double, 117, 118
do while, 64-66
drawArc, 108-109
drawOval, 107-108
drawString, 109
driver, 203
    see also robustness, testing
dummy class, 204-206
    see also robustness, testing

encapsulation, 75-76
endsWith, 85
equals, 85
equivalence classes, 208-210
escape sequences, 223-224
event-handling, 240-245

exception, 216
expression, 25
extends, 168

final, 24, 184-185
float, 18
FlowLayout, 257-258
for loop, 54-59
formal parameters, 97
Frame, 90
functions, 72

generic collection classes, 189-192
   pros and cons, 192
getLabel, 333
getName, 333
getText, 334
graphical user interface (GUI), 229-230

high-level languages, 4
Hyper Text Markup Language, 314
   tag, 314

if statement, 40-44
if...else statement, 45-50
   nested, 50
implementation, 2
implements, 242
indentation, 198-199
information-hiding, 71
inheritance, 163-170
   UML notation, 164
init, 314, 317, 322
input validation, 60-61
instantiation, 81
int, 18
Integer, 117
integration testing, 206-208
interface, 242, 243
   ActionListener, 242
   MouseListener, 325-326
import, 89-90
iteration, 53-66

Java interpreter, 7
Java Virtual Machine, 6

Label, 247, 334

layout manager, 257-260
   BorderLayout, 258
   FlowLayout, 257-258
length (array attribute), 130
length (String method), 85
linking, 5
list, 136
loader, 5
logical operators, 62
long, 18

machine code, 4
main method, 11-12
maintainability, 196-200
message passing, 75-76
method, 74, 93
   addActionListener, 243, 333
   addMouseListener, 327, 333
   addMouseMotionListener, 327, 333
   compareTo, 85
   concat, 85
   destroy, 322, 336
   drawArc, 108-109
   drawOval, 107-108
   drawString, 109
   endsWith, 85
   equals, 85
   final, 184-185
   getLabel, 333
   getName, 333
   getText, 334
   init, 314, 317, 322
   length, 85
   overriding, 176-178
   paint, 107, 243, 244, 322, 333
   parseInt, 117
   repaint, 244, 328, 333
   setAlignment, 301
   setBackground, 333
   setColor, 107
   setColumns, 334
   setEchoChar, 334
   setForeground, 333
   setLabel, 333
   setLayout, 259
   setResizable, 335
   setSize, 333
   setTitle, 335

setText, 334
setVisible, 333
start, 322
startsWith, 85
stop, 322
substring, 85
super, 169, 174
toLowerCase, 85
toUpperCase, 85
MouseEvent, 329
MouseListener, 325-326

new, 80-81
null, 81

object, 73-74
   creation, 81
   sending messages to, 75-76
Object, 185
object code, 4
object-orientation, 71-74
overloading, 26, 84

package, 90
paint, 107, 243, 244, 322, 333
Panel, 260, 336
parameter, 97
   actual, 97
   applet, 317-321
   array, 132-135
   formal, 97
parseInt, 117
polymorphism, 99, 176-178
private, 96
procedures, 72
programmimg languages, 4
protected, 168
prototypes, 3
pseudocode, 34
   see also design
public, 97

quality of software, 195
queue, 136

rapid application development (RAD), 3
real number, 18
regression testing, 212

repaint, 244, 328, 333
return, 99-100
ripple effect, 196
robustness, 213-218
run-time error, 200
   see also robustness, testing

scalar types, 18
scope, 134
searching, 277
selection, 39-53
set, 135
setAlignment, 301
setBackground, 333
setColor, 107
setColumns, 334
setEchoChar, 333
setForeground, 333
setLabel, 333
setLayout, 259
setResizable, 335
setSize, 333
setText, 334
setTitle, 335
setVisible, 333
sequence, 39
short, 18
software, 2
   quality, 195
specification, 2
stack, 136
start, 322
startsWith, 85
statement
   break, 53
   do while, 64-66
   for, 54-59
   if, 40-44
   if else, 45-50
   return, 99-100
   switch, 50-53
   while, 60-63
static, 110-114
   attribute, 110-113
   method, 113-114
stop, 322
String, 83-86
   methods, 85

structured approach, 72
subclass, 164
`substring`, 85
`super`, 169, 174
superclass, 164
syntax error, 4
system software, 2
`switch`, 50-53

testing, 201-212
    driver, 203
    dummy class, 204-206
    integration testing, 206-208
    stress testing, 215-216
    test log, 211-212
    unit testing, 202-206
`text`, 225
`TextArea`, 335
text formatting, 223-229
third generation languages, 4
`this`, 240
`toLowerCase`, 85
`toUpperCase`, 85
type cast, 26, 173, 174-175

Unified Modelling Language (UML), 10
    aggregation, 148
    association, 266
    class notation, 10-11
    inheritance notation, 164
    see also design
unicode, 18
UNIX   *see* system software
usability, 219-222

validation, 201
    see also input validation
variable, 19
    assigning, 21-23
    declaring, 19-21
    naming, 19
    scope, 134
verification, 201

waterfall model, 2-3
Windows98 *see* systems software
`while`, 60-63
World Wide Web, 6
wrapper classes, 117-119